FIONA STOCKER

Saddleback Wife

Slow Food in Tasmania

First published by Scarlet Robin Books 2023

Copyright © 2023 by Fiona Stocker

All rights reserved. No part of this publication may be reproduced, stored or transmitted in any form or by any means, electronic, mechanical, photocopying, recording, scanning, or otherwise without written permission from the publisher. It is illegal to copy this book, post it to a website, or distribute it by any other means without permission.

Fiona Stocker asserts the moral right to be identified as the author of this work.

Some names, places and identifying details have been changed to protect the privacy of individuals.

Front cover 'snapshot' images by Jacob Collings and Lusy Productions, Fiona Stocker, Dermot McElduff Photography and r e impact photography. Images used throughout the book are by Fiona and Oliver Stocker.

First edition

ISBN: 978-0-6453606-3-9

This book was professionally typeset on Reedsy. Find out more at reedsy.com

For Matt

Acknowledgment of Country

The author wishes to acknowledge the Traditional Owners of the lands upon which this story is set, and to pay respect to the Elders past, present and emerging as the original and rightful custodians.

Contents

Prologue	iii
Rare Breed	1
Farm Romance	12
Country Cuisine	22
'In Pig'	29
Piglets	39
Farming	52
Pork	67
Sausages	73
Licensed to Feed	81
Evandale	88
Some Like It Hot	95
To Market	104
Big Time	115
Events	128
Smokers	138
Pig Lady	146
Providores	152
Dinner	162
Co-Pilot Bob	171
Supply and Demand	180
Welfare	199
On the Menu	210
Diversification	225

Vale Bella	239
Closure	250
Eleven Days	262
Politics	270
End Game	278
For the Love of Pigs	297
Small Farm Dream	309
Acknowledgements	315
Sources and Further Reading	317
About the Author	319
Also by Fiona Stocker	320

Prologue

Typically, we had lost Oliver.

While the children and I were in a long wooden shed at the Chudleigh Agricultural Show, peering at the fluffed-up, prize-winning bantams, my husband had given us the slip. This was not a deliberate act on his part. It's just that the whereabouts of his children, and his wife, escapes his attention when his mind is drawn to more important matters such as livestock.

It's common to drive through Chudleigh without seeing a soul or passing another vehicle, unless there's a coach parked outside the honey shop. Every bit as bucolic and picture-perfect as its name suggests, the small township perches on the fertile plains below the Western Tiers of Tasmania. These escarpments rise from nowhere, blue and rocky and austere, forming the edge of the island's central plateau. The land below is a patchwork of farms and paddocks, criss-crossed by streams of crystal-clear water and single-track roads lined with hawthorn. It's a landscape which combines wilderness with two hundred years of ruthless occupation by colonial settlers and somehow manages a beguiling charm, less so if your ancestors were among the Aboriginal people forced from the places they had lived for forty thousand years.

But Chudleigh's agricultural show brings people in the know from far and wide. A smaller affair than many shows, we'd been told it was worth the drive along narrow lanes which appeared to go nowhere but into the mountains. There was an old-fashioned feel about the day. An arena for pony club competitions was cordoned off with straw bales on which members of the local community sat, chatting with neighbours and applauding the young riders. Next to the arena, spread out in rumpled, colourful fashion over the town's sports oval was a collection of stalls and marquees. These were mostly food vendors keeping people fuelled up with barbecued sausages, vendors of farm tools and machinery, and the occasional politician attempting to ingratiate him or herself from behind a pull-up banner.

Outside the bantam shed, we found Oliver in a cordoned-off area that was half grass, half dust, and scoured by sharp breezes from the mountains. He was deep in conversation with a woman sporting a white lab-coat and a ten-gallon hat, an intriguing combination which she carried off surprisingly well. Tucked under one arm, she held a small, black and white piglet which squirmed vigorously. Before her stood a wooden crate filled with straw, and scuffling about in it were two more black piglets with white stripes around their shoulders.

'You can bring on the gilts by feeding them whey, if you happen to have a cow,' she was saying to Oliver, who was giving her his rapt attention, leaning in to hear as her words were whipped away by the wind. 'But we use a commercial pig feed that has leftover bits from the chocolate factory in it. They like that.' This woman and her partner, Oliver told me later, were the biggest breeders of Wessex Saddleback pigs in Tasmania. Little did I know then how much her ideas of whey-fed gilts and chocolaty pig-feed would figure in our future.

Their conversation had all the signs of being a long, drawn-out affair, so the children and I headed off to see the vintage tractors. On our way, we watched a miniature Thomas-the-Tank-Engine pass by, crushing a fluorescent-pink hippo from side-show alley into the mud with its miniature wheels. It seemed a cruel fate for such an innocent, if erroneously-coloured creature.

'Ew, now he is all dirty!' Daisy remarked, clutching my hand. 'Will his mum clean him?'

'Yes, he's probably machine-washable.'

'Can he go in the bath, Mummy?' Kit chipped in.

'He might make the bath water a bit muddy.'

'Mummy, can we go for a ride in the train?' asked Daisy.

'Want a sausage, Mummy.' Kit had turned his mind to more important matters.

And so I turned my attention to the kind of decision millions of adult women confront daily: how to decide between the entertainment value of the miniature train versus the sustenance of the sausage. Would the sustenance repeat on us as we trundled over the bumpy paddocks? The hungry toddler won the day and we headed off to find a sausage sizzle, never far away at an outdoor event in Australia.

Oliver had, of late, been preoccupied with the subject of pigs and I could sense the build-up to a change in our circumstances on the tiny five-acre plot we occupied. Television lifestyle shows have a lot to answer for. They're responsible for many of the unexpected turns our married life has taken, and we've sourced many of our most experimental ideas from them. It was after reading an article about Tasmania in a Sunday newspaper that I decided we should move there. A couple of years later, we finally did so, largely on the strength of that article and a two-week tour of the island in a camper-van.

Where Oliver's interest in pigs was concerned, the English broadcaster Hugh Fearnley-Whittingstall was squarely to blame. We had become devotees of his *River Cottage* television series, which documented his move from London to country-living in Devonshire, and mirrored so much of our own move to Tasmania. We began to refer simply to 'Hugh', as if he were a friend who might call round for a cup of tea and a slice of beetroot brownie. The episodes about the Bristol families who kept pigs were especially enjoyable. Their joy and pride in the pigs was infectious, and the segments in which they learned the traditional art of butchering were unexpectedly riveting. I could tell the idea of keeping livestock appealed to Oliver, and the idea of making English-style sausages appealed even more.

Having a husband who could grow things which I could cook had considerable appeal for me. Inspired by *River Cottage* and egged on by Oliver, I began to cook more pork, buying pieces of belly and making succulent rolls stuffed with apricots, herbs and breadcrumbs.

The Wessex Saddleback pigs featured in *River Cottage*, we learned, were the pig most favoured by small-holders. Good-natured and great respecters of electric fencing, they were easy to keep in. They also produced tender, succulent pork of unmistakable flavour and character. As we sat on our sofa one evening, watching Hugh preparing a straw-filled birthing shed for his sows, Oliver turned to me. 'We could keep those pigs in our bush block, you know,' he said.

I could have sworn I saw a light bulb flickering over his head. Thus a new chapter of our life began with an idea we got from the telly.

Before you could say 'Gloucestershire Old Spots', Oliver was talking non-stop about his new objects of desire. One morning I was barely awake when he turned to me and said, 'I can't decide between Wessex Saddlebacks and Berkshires. What do you think?'

I had no idea, but it certainly made a change from 'Are you making tea?' or 'Do you fancy a quick one before the kids wake up?'

Oliver went on intelligence-gathering missions which revealed more reasons for keeping pigs. They could be used to polish off most of your household food waste, being capable of eating pretty much anything.

'They'll get rid of a dead body for you, as long as you cut it up,' he told me. It seemed beyond our requirements.

Pigs could be used to replace expensive farm machinery, it seemed. They could turn over a block of land that was invaded by weeds or unwanted plants such as blackberry, rooting them out in a matter of weeks or even days. They would consume vast quantities of unwanted windfall fruit from orchards, and would delight in sorting through and eating much of the waste from your vegetable garden.

If you had pigs and could cope with the idea of sending them to slaughter, you also had pork. And the meat from Wessex Saddlebacks was quite different to the pork you found on supermarket shelves, we were told. That came from three breeds, the Landrace, the Duroc and the Large White. All three breeds had been refined over the decades to grow fast and produce as much pork per animal as feasible. These three breeds were the source of ninety percent of the pork found on supermarket shelves and in most high-street butchers' cabinets.

But Wessex Saddleback pork, a darker and more flavoursome meat, had been listed in the Slow Food Movement's Ark of Taste. This was a worldwide list of foods of exceptional flavour and nutritional value which were in danger of disappearing unless we made the effort to preserve them. The breed was highly acclaimed and had won prizes as the 'best bacon'.

The cohort who did not praise the Wessex Saddleback to the high heavens was serious business owners. Saddlebacks are not grown commercially by those who want to run a successful business, and if your aim is to support yourself with an income stream, Saddlebacks are not the pig for you. They take twice as long to grow as pigs in commercial farms, and they're small, so you don't get as much pork from them. Australian writer and broadcaster Matthew Evans writes that Wessex Saddlebacks are known as 'commercial suicide'. But I didn't read his book until it was several years too late.

We had come to love our life on five acres since moving to Tasmania. I loved to open the back door of my house first thing in the morning, look out across the paddocks and inhale the unmistakable piercing scent of eucalyptus trees in the early warmth of a new day. Kookaburras would racket from the towering swamp gums and crows caw to each other. In the late afternoons, if I went out to the vegetable garden, I'd find Oliver bent over the garden beds in the same way his parents had bent over theirs, pulling out weeds and giving the broccoli, corn, tomatoes and asparagus the space they needed to grow. Those foods from the garden I brought inside, and they formed the basis for the meals on our family's table. We loved providing for ourselves, and the sense of a life lived slowly, simply and well.

With the prospect of our own pork becoming a reality, the country wife in me came to the fore with her apron securely tied. I had been watching *French Leave,* a television series made by the English chef John Burton-Race, who moved his family to France for a year. His evident passion for the food traditions there was palpable: crusty bread from wood-fired ovens, orchard-grown peaches cooked in syrup and eaten at a rickety table under a tree on a summer's afternoon. In one episode, he visited a village and helped with the annual slaughter of a pig, which was then processed by the villagers and made into charcuterie and meat products for a year-round larder. The woman in charge led Burton-Race into a barn, lit by shafts of light from high windows, dust motes glinting in the air. In the tangible hush and stillness of the barn's interior, she lifted the lid of a wooden chest containing hams. They had been buried in salt for a fortnight and then bedded down in ash for two years. She peeled off a wafer-thin slice with a paring knife and offered it to Burton-Race. As he held it up, the light shone through the pale pink meat with its skirt of creamy fat. He ate it with relish and begged another. The flavour of those slivers of ham, made in time-honoured tradition, using ash from the hearth and the knowledge of that woman's ancestors, no doubt reflected every nuance of the knowledge and integrity which went into the making of it.

'That's what I want our life in Tasmania to be like,' I told Oliver when he found me watching the program for the umpteenth time. Now it seemed there was a chance it could come to pass. I was picturing a leg of ham in our pantry, cured and smoked in a timber hut, and slivers of it on a platter on our table.

Books about pigs and pork began to appear on our shelves. Oliver lay alongside me at night with *The Illustrated Guide to Pigs - how to choose them, how to keep them*, held up to the light. As he mulled over the contents, he occasionally interrupted my Virginia Woolf to pepper me with snippets of information. Waves of porcine intelligence passed between us. Besides growing his own knowledge, this was his way of ensuring I'd be fit for the role of co-partner. Looking at him propped up on the pillows with his reading specs on, I predicted silently that I'd soon be firmly roped in, and find myself holding the legs of some little piglet while he slipped a rubber band over its testicles.

He talked about pigs so persistently that sometimes I had to tune him out. One morning, I was packing lunch-boxes and thinking about getting the children and their associated paraphernalia into the car for school and childcare. 'I can't think about Gloucester bloody Old Spots right now,' I told him. Seeing his hurt expression, I relented slightly. I had a morning full of my own work to do, making a website for the local community centre. 'Make an appointment to see me later,' I suggested.

When I returned from the school run, he was still there at the breakfast bar with a book propped up before him and a steaming mug of tea to aid his thoughts. 'Is now a good time to talk about which breed we should get?' he asked.

What else could I do but join in? In an unexpected turn of events I was apparently about to become one half of a rare-breed pig-farming enterprise. It wasn't what I thought would happen when I took my arts degree, or said 'for better or worse'. As it turned out, keeping pigs on five acres and making sausages from the pork is neither a sensible nor financially viable way to earn a living. So at least 'for richer, for poorer' was accurate.

Rare Breed

When I wasn't writing about our pursuit of pigs on the blog I wrote about our farm life, I wondered about my own role in our new potential enterprise. I never expected to be a pig farmer or a pig farmer's wife. Yet here I was, running a sort of kitchen consultancy. I had counselled Oliver in his cabinet-making business, and now I was counselling him in pig-husbandry. I knew little about either, but I did know something about small businesses, having run my own in London. I knew two heads were better than one, since we stood a better chance of having all bases covered. It became evident that having a couple of pigs could soon morph into breeding and setting up a small business to sell pork.

Slowly, a curious imbalance came into view. As Oliver researched how to keep pigs, he came to know more about them than he did about children. On that topic, he had never read any books and scoffed at the idea of doing so.

'You don't need to read books to be a parent,' he insisted.
'It's just a way of picking up clues,' I said.
'You don't need clues. It's instinctive.'
'You mean it's any old codswallop you make up on the spot?'
'Exactly.'

Where his parenting methods consisted of ad hoc responses, his proposed keeping of pigs was carefully considered. I tried to even up the balance by removing *Practical Pig Keeping* from his bedside table and replacing it with *Raising Boys* and *Playful Parenting*, but those titles remained untouched. When he muttered darkly and twitched in his sleep, I knew he was dreaming not about wrestling playfully on the living room floor with his children, but of wrangling his first Saddleback slips from the back of the ute into a pen full of straw.

The way things were going, there were no guarantees that we might ever have pigs to farm. Despite myself, I began lying awake at night wondering if there was a sow somewhere in the fertile dark of the Tasmanian night, farrowing piglets that could one day be ours. There was strange satisfaction in knowing we were in this together, and it came to pervade both our lives. When Oliver laid aside his copy of *Living With Pigs* at night and I felt the brush of his skin against mine, I wondered if he was thinking about how a Saddleback sow had fourteen nipples instead of just two.

There were just nine registered pedigree herds of Wessex Saddleback pig in Australia. Originally from the New Forest area of England, it was a foraging breed suited to living on woodland pasture. 'They'd be perfect for keeping in our bush block,' Oliver enthused, as if this were a perfectly normal thing to suggest.

Saddlebacks had been imported to Australia and New Zealand in the early 20th century, and were still to be found there in small numbers. Oliver became assiduous in tracking them down. He telephoned or emailed everyone in pigs across Tasmania, and one woman on the Australian mainland too.

Predictably, given the small numbers, they were difficult to get hold of. One friend in particular enjoyed pointing out the nature of the problem.

'Ah, they really are a *rare breed* pig, aren't they - it's all in the name!' he quipped whenever we saw him.

'I think I'm going to say something to him if he says that again,' Oliver complained.

'Like what?'

'Like get stuffed.'

Oliver was determined to find registered bloodstock to launch his empire. Registered pigs came with papers documenting their ancestry, and were the purest of the pure, the Royal family of pigs. His insistence on the best made it hard to find stock to start our own herd. Farmers wanted to keep hold of their best animals for themselves.

Oliver grumbled but could understand their reasoning. 'It's simple economics,' he said. No farmer would sell him a piglet for a modest sum when they could grow it to full size and get a much better price for the pork. 'And why would they sell their pigs to me when I'm starting up an operation that might compete with theirs?'

For a time it looked as if our best bet was an Englishman called George, who had two gilts that he was keen to breed from. He'd purchased them from mainland Australia, and brought them to Tasmania in crates on the passenger ferry.

The terminology of the porcine world was still new to me. 'What's a gilt?' I asked Oliver.

'It's a young female that hasn't been bred from yet.'

'Why not just call it a sow?'

'That's different. A sow is a female that has had piglets.'

'That's a bit technical. You don't get different names for

women before and after we've had children.'

'I can think of a few,' Oliver said.

Farmer George's problem was that his sows couldn't get pregnant. George kept his livestock on a rocky, sloping block of ground. Every time the boar visited from another farm to try and impregnate George's sows, he would mount them enthusiastically but lose his balance on the sloping ground and fall off. This left both the boar and George unsatisfied and the girls remained gilts rather than becoming sows.

'He wants me to agist them here, and have the boar visit here too,' said Oliver over breakfast one morning. 'We'll keep them here while they have their piglets, and then he'll leave us a couple of slips in payment.'

I tried to listen carefully and understand this porcine wheeling and dealing.

'What are slips?' I asked.

'They're piglets which have been weaned from the sow.'

'I thought those were weaners?'

'No, they come later. It's not that complicated. What's wrong with you?'

Oliver was troubled by the idea of having other people's pigs on our property. Pig farmers from discussion forums on the internet discouraged hosting pigs from other farms, for biosecurity reasons. There was danger of them bringing bacteria and other microbial life to our farm on their trotters, which could stay in the soil and spread disease to our pigs. If we ever got any.

In the end, the matter was resolved for us. George didn't have the right paperwork for his gilts and couldn't get it from the breeder, who had stopped returning calls. Without their documents, George's gilts were no better than garden-variety porkers, and were worth next to nothing. And without a boar, he had no prospects of a herd. It was the death knell for his pig-keeping ambitions, and his ability to help Oliver.

George finally admitted defeat in a phone call which Oliver took in the car one Sunday afternoon as we coasted home after a Sunday outing and Devonshire tea. In desperation, he offered to sell his gilts to Oliver at a knock-down price. Oliver turned them down, believing he needed properly registered pigs. George's muffled voice could be heard close to tears on the other end of the line.

'What will he do with them?' I asked once Oliver was off the phone.

'He said he'll probably have to shoot them and eat them,' Oliver replied, his voice full of sorrow. 'He says he's sick of the whole affair and he's just going to give up.'

We travelled the rest of the way home in silence. It seemed there was a dark side to rare breed pig farming.

A couple of months later, the farmer George had purchased his unregistered gilts from was featured in the pages of a glossy lifestyle magazine. In the article, he waxed lyrical about bringing the Wessex Saddleback breed to farms across Australia.

I showed the magazine to Oliver. 'That's unbelievable,' he spluttered, gazing at the multi-page spread. We pictured George in his lonely shack on its sloping ground, throwing darts at the torn out pages and burping softly from too many pork sausages.

Perhaps it was vain hope, but we refused to give up on the idea of one day being the proud owners of a tiny, thriving pig farm. We went back to what we were good at: watching telly, and possibly we should have left it at that. People who knew we were looking for pigs continued to ask with eager anticipation, 'When are you getting your pigs?' After months of looking, it became a wearisome 'Have you got any pigs yet?'

It was clear that most people thought it was an elaborate ruse.

Finally the day came. Oliver secured two gilts from a farm in the north coast hinterland. It was owned by Heidi, the woman with the ten-gallon hat who Oliver had met at Chudleigh, and her partner Jeff. Both had been raised on farms in Tasmania, with cows providing milk for the house, and pigs being raised on the whey and household waste. They'd both had modern-day careers in broadcasting and teaching, but were drawn back to the land and the way of life they knew from childhood. Pooling their resources, they had purchased land and a house together at Mount Roland, in the low-lying ranges behind the northwest coast. With rich soils and lush pastures it was perfect for a small farming enterprise. Soon Heidi and Jeff were selling their pork at a farmers' market in the northern city of Launceston, and branching out into rare breed cattle and ducks, all kept in the outdoors, free range and roaming around according to their natural instincts.

Oliver had been keeping in touch with Heidi and knew that she and Jeff had their own boar. They'd purchased him from an organic pig farm on the mainland, and we had seen him on display at a Sustainable Living fair.

'Skinny little thing, isn't he?' Oliver remarked as we all gazed down at the little boar, who was then only a couple of months old. He snuffled around his pen unaware of the great tasks ahead of him. On his bony little shoulders rested the responsibility of expanding the breeding herd of the couple's farm, and possibly of Tasmania. Heidi nodded her agreement.

'They were all skinny like that, not great big fat things like ours.'

The couple seemed open to the idea of selling some stock to us, and suddenly this brought the prospect of starting our own small herd closer. They knew we intended to start a smaller version of their own farm, but since they had over one hundred acres and we had just five, our ambitions were smaller and we weren't a threat to their well-established business. Plus, with the resurgence of interest in rare breed pigs and pork, we hoped there would be enough consumer demand to support both farms.

On a breezy day in June, Oliver and Daisy drove to the rolling green hinterland where Mount Roland Farm was situated. A few hours later, they returned with a small wooden crate on the back of the ute. Inside it were two very quiet and apparently contented little gilts, two months old and snuggled in a bed of straw. We peered over the rim of the crate, the children clambering into the ute to get a better look. Rosie and Bella, named by Daisy on the return journey, looked back at us placidly. Both were black with a white stripe around their shoulders and down their front legs, the signature markings of the Wessex Saddleback pig.

Welcome Bella and Rosie

We hadn't intended to name our pigs, as we all knew this was farming stock for the purpose of raising more stock for the table. Neither of us liked the tradition that some people favoured of calling their pigs 'Cassoulet' and 'Sausage'. But with Daisy in the frame, these two ended up with names. It seemed natural: as our breeding stock, they could be with us for years.

Oliver eased one of them out of the crate and carried her, squealing and wriggling, to the pen he had prepared.

'Can I carry the other one?' cried Daisy.

'I don't think you'd manage it,' Oliver replied, glancing over his shoulder with a grin. 'They weigh a ton already and they're really strong!' He carried the second gilt to the pen and put her down gently on the ground outside their shed.

The pigs' living quarters had been the object of his ministrations for the past couple of weeks. He had spent hours every day outside with his ear protectors firmly clamped to his head, sawing, digging and hammering. He dug foundations and put poles in as corner supports. These he connected with studwork and then clad the whole thing with tin. A sloping tin roof meant the rain would run off. Around the inside walls at a low height was a length of timber which created a safety channel for piglets. They could scurry along the walls in relative safety while the bar prevented their mother from lying on them. This sometimes happened in pigsties, we'd heard. The far corner was cordoned off with another timber bar, and over this was a heat lamp with a cosy bed of straw beneath it.

Puzzled by the amount of time he'd spent building this dwelling, I came to have a look at it. These pigs had got more benefit from Oliver's cabinet-making skills than we'd had in our own house.

'Are you putting a spa bath in the other corner?' I asked.

'They won't need that, there'll be a wallow outside,' he replied, without missing a beat.

It turned out to be worth all the trouble. After dinner on Rosie and Bella's first night on the farm, we picked our way with torches across the bush block to see how they were settling in. Quietly we peered over the fence and into the doorway. They were huddled together at the back of shed, and we could hear them snorting softly to one another.

'Move over, you're taking up all the straw!'

'Your trotters are freezing, keep them to yourself!'

Daisy and Kit giggled at the sweet sounds they were making.

'That's just what you sound like when you're asleep,' I whispered to them. It made us all happy to think of these two small creatures in the warmth of their new home, sleeping soundly, safe and content in each other's company.

We saw it as the start of a long and happy association. We'd keep them in comfort in exchange for the livestock they would produce, a food supply for us and for our eventual customers, and an income. It was a new venture for us, this keeping of live things for commerce, but having learned from Heidi and one or two others like her, we had automatically adopted what we saw as good farming practice. We would ensure they were kept in conditions which suited them - free range and able to enjoy outdoor life, rooting around in the bush. It would be a while before we tasted the fruit of our labours, and none of us had really thought about eating the prodigy of Rosie and Bella. Only Oliver had given any thought to the idea that we might one day find ourselves eating Rosie and Bella themselves, but he kept that thought to himself for now.

The excitement of being new pig farmers invigorated us daily. Rosie and Bella were full of character and the children and I loved going over to the pens to visit them with Oliver. We went into their pens while they were still small so that they became used to us and quite tame, taking vegetable scraps from the kitchen, and edible green waste from the garden as treats. Often they would nibble playfully at the toes of our gumboots once they'd eaten whatever we'd brought. Eventually this became less playful and we had to nudge them away with the toe of that boot, before they sank their teeth into it to see how it tasted. Oliver often rubbed their bellies with a stick, whereupon they would collapse to the ground, stretch out and close their eyes in bliss.

'Who'd have known you'd be a pig whisperer?' I called to him, finding him giving Rosie a vigorous massage one day.

'You want to be careful she doesn't get the wrong idea about you,' I added, watching Rosie grunt with contentment and swing from side to side in bliss as Oliver rubbed his gloved hands back and forth across her bristly back.

'What are you doing later?' he called back. 'You could be in luck if she's not in the mood for more.'

Farm Romance

Living in the country was a vital and immediate way of introducing your kids to the facts of life, it turned out. Heading home on the school run on Flowery Gully Road one afternoon, we flashed past a cow in a field. Out of the corner of my eye, I saw it straining and moving its hips from side to side and knew instinctively what was going on. Just visible on the grass behind it lay a furry black heap.

Anybody who's given birth or watched an episode of *Call the Midwife* would recognise that uncomfortable manoeuvring. 'That cow's just given birth!' I exclaimed to my startled children.

We went back for a look. In the farm's driveway, a girl of around six who had just got off the school bus was peering into the paddock through a scrubby hedge. 'Your cow's just had a calf!' I told her, needlessly. Even after a few years of living where we did, it was unprecedented to see a cow giving birth on the school run. The girl looked back at me as if I were a little deranged, and nodded solemnly.

'What's that red thing hanging from its bottom?' asked Daisy. I looked, and realised there'd be some interesting explaining to do.

'That's the afterbirth,' I replied matter-of-factly. 'It's full of food for the calf that comes from its mum.' I had prepared for this. Animals in the paddocks around us experienced all of life's big events in full view, and I had anticipated having to answer questions about life, death and everything in between. I believed in being gentle but frank and not fudging the details. If Daisy and Kit were ready to ask, they were ready for a simple and honest answer.

'Why is dat calf wet?' Kit threw in.

'It lives in a big balloon full of water inside its mum, like a big watery cushion.'

'Where diss calf come from?' his curiosity continued unabated.

'Well, it's just been born,' I replied. I was playing for time now, trying to figure out how much he might guess at, and what gaps I'd have to fill in.

'How?' In the rear view mirror I could see his puzzled expression. Clearly more help was needed.

'It's come out of her fanny,' I said, hoping that would be specific enough for him. He knew about fannies, as he had baths with his sister, and had an indifferent acceptance of them. How he would make the leap to a fanny which could deliver a calf, I wasn't quite sure.

Lucky for me, the mother cow was watching us and seemed intent on doing nothing until we left. I took the opportunity to move off. We carried on home and had icy poles for afternoon tea.

Oliver had informed me that the feed-to-weight conversion rate of pigs was the best of all livestock. When translated, this meant they grew fast. It wasn't long before Rosie and Bella had grown to a size and maturity that meant they could be mated, and begin their lives as breeding sows.

A couple of months after they arrived on the farm, Jeff arrived with a trailer hitched to the back of his ute, keen to see how the girls were doing. He had agreed to take them back to Mount Roland for a fateful meeting with his boar. We walked across the bush paddock and came across Rosie and Bella sunning themselves, lying against the corrugated tin of their shed. It was a warm, sheltered spot and they spooned together, their generous flanks side by side in the afternoon light, tails relaxed and draped down over their backsides.

As soon as they heard our voices, they leapt up and began cavorting around at the fence line, eager to see what food treats we might have brought. Our first pigs, they were spoilt rotten with vegetable peelings and overgrown plants. We liked to pat them as they ate, and often rubbed behind their ears as they snoozed on spring afternoons. They had become quite tame. The flip side to this was that you had to watch your step at feeding time. They were bold as well as tame, and were now the size of a large family dog but heavier and stronger. If you didn't pour their feed into the trough quickly, they'd biff you roughly on the legs with their heads. We had soon realised this wasn't done in a playful way, but was their way of dominating another creature over food, in this case, us.

'Ooh, that's a good pig,' said Jeff, stopping to watch as Bella tore into a cucumber. He gazed at her jiggling flanks, and watched as the kids fed her a couple of apples as dessert. 'I think they might be getting a bit spoilt, though,' he added.

We looked at the two sows, using their snouts to sort through the kitchen waste dumped into their food buckets.

'Bella's bigger because she gets to the food first,' said Oliver.

'That's why I give them separate food bowls.' We had noticed that if the girls ate from the same bowl, Bella biffed Rosie away repeatedly and got the lion's share of the feed. Such was her determination, Bella had grown to be bigger than Rosie, becoming the dominant sow. Oliver now put their feed into two bowls and once they had their snouts in them and were feeding contentedly, he gently kicked the bowls further apart as they ate. That way, Bella stayed focussed on her own feed, and didn't bother Rosie so much.

'So, they're both cycling, are they?' asked Jeff.

'What does cycling mean, Mummy?' Daisy piped up.

'It's a thing that lady pigs do when they're old enough to have babies,' I replied. It was better to be accurate, in case she thought we were training them in circus tricks. Jeff's going to take Rosie and Bella for a holiday at his farm so they can meet a boar, and make some piglets.'

I could sense the danger of the children continuing this conversation and requiring an explanation of the mechanics of what would happen between Rosie, Bella and the boar. Mark must have anticipated the same. 'Best get these two loaded on the trailer,' he said suddenly. 'Shall I back it up all the way to this gate?'

This was the moment Oliver had been dreading. Pigs are naturally suspicious of trailers, or any other vehicle they're not used to. He'd heard you could put a bucket over their head and back them up the ramp onto a trailer, but imagined this led to a lot of thrashing about and squealing.

Thankfully, it didn't come to that. The girls sauntered up the ramp, their noses in the air following the scent of a bucket of windfall apples from a nearby orchard. It was almost as if they knew they were heading off for a rural romance.

As Jeff's ute pulled out and turned its nose towards the northwest, we stood by the gate and waved, as much to the girls as to him. We'd miss them while they were gone. We'd got used to visiting in the afternoons, throwing apples and watching them trot after them, cracking them open with one squeeze of their jaws. But we hoped that when they returned in a couple of months' time, they'd be 'in pig', ready to put their collective twenty-eight nipples to good use.

'I hope they've got enough shelter there,' Oliver moaned after they'd left. 'The paddocks at Mount Roland are a bit exposed, and they're not used to being fed just once a day, either,' he fretted. It was as if he'd sent his own children to their first summer camp. I couldn't help wondering what he'd be like when Jeff rang to say they'd lost their virginity.

While Rose and Bella were off the farm, Oliver went into nesting mode. After mornings spent cabinet-making for clients, he used the afternoons to build a second shed in the bush block. Once again, he made it incredibly sturdy and the work was arduous. He'd come in for a cup of tea sweating, exhausted and covered in dust and pollen from the bush.

With the shed complete, he set about creating a second pen around it, using more electric fencing tape, connected by star pickets hammered into the ground. Having pens next to each other meant the girls could enjoy each other's company, but be kept separate. This was essential for birthing, he told me.

'There's more chance of them lying on a piglet if they're housed together.' I pictured the scene, with two sows and a host of little piglets inside one of the small sheds. It did seem likely that someone would get squashed.

'It gets worse,' Oliver continued. 'They'll eat each other's piglets if they get the chance.'

'What do they do that for?' I asked, agog. While Oliver had worked in a piggery in Suffolk during his teenage years, making him somewhat used to animal habits, farming life was still new to me.

'It's just nature's way,' he replied. 'I think it usually happens if there's a runt or a piglet that's stillborn.' It was hard to imagine Rosie and Bella behaving like this. We fell into a ruminative silence together, staring at the new shed and contemplating this pig-eat-pig world. As we learned more over the years, it turned out that sows eating piglets is a sign of acute stress. It was something we never even came close to seeing on our farm.

Some weeks after their departure, Jeff phoned to say that Rosie and Bella had taken turns in being put in a shed with the boar, and had not 'cycled' again. He was pretty sure he'd seen the boar mating with each of them. Short of calling out a vet with a mobile ultrasound machine, we could assume they were 'in pig' and they could now return home. For their gestation period of three months, three weeks and three days, they could enjoy being waited on hand and foot by Oliver, before giving birth.

The prospect of piglets seemed hugely exciting. Kit had shared the story of Rosie and Bella's visit to Mount Roland during 'Show and Tell' at the childcare centre. I was astonished and touched that our new pig-keeping venture had lodged so firmly in his mind and become a feature of his young life. I was also a little concerned as to what he might have said. The woman from the childcare centre set my mind at rest. 'He just told us your pigs had gone on a play-date!'

When you're four and seven years old, the prospect of

pregnant pigs giving birth practically in your back garden, is far more exciting than anything *Play School* has to offer. Daisy and Kit's young imaginations were running riot, which resulted in further question-and-answer sessions. These severely tested my ability to think on the run. In the car on the way to school and childcare one day, we had not yet reached the end of our road when Kit opened the conversation.

'Mummy? Will the piglets be borned?'

I wasn't quite sure what he was asking, but sensed he would elaborate if encouraged. 'Yes darling, the piglets will be born.'

'Now, Mummy?'

'Well no, darling, first they have to grow inside Rosie and Bella's tummies. And *then* they will be born.' I was hoping that explained it for him.

Daisy chipped in at this point. She was due to accompany Oliver to Mount Roland to pick the girls up. 'And we have to drive slowly on the way back, or the piglets will just die,' she said. It seemed an alarming pragmatism for one so young.

'That's right, we have to be careful and not shake them up.' A journey of any sort during a sow's pregnancy had the associated risk of miscarriage, if the sow became distressed. Given that ours knew the trailer and our farm, we hoped any distress would be kept to a minimum.

'Mummy?' It was Kit again.

'Yes?'

'Will the piglets pop out them mummy's tummy?'

'Yes, they will.' It seemed best to be frank, even if this explanation fudged the anatomical detail a bit.

'Like I popped out?'

'Yes darling, like you popped out of my tummy.' I chuckled a little at the memory, my own labours safely years behind me.

'Was it a big massive pop, Mummy?'

'Well it certainly made my eyes water.'

'Like diss massive, Mummy?' I glanced briefly into the rear view mirror, and could just see Kit holding his arms wide, as if demonstrating the size of a fish catch.

'That looks about right.'

'Mummy?' It was Daisy this time. I made some inner adjustment to allow for three years more life experience, and wondered what line of questioning she would take.

'Yes?'

'Will Jessie's tummy be big?' This was a slight change of tack. Jessie was not a Wessex Saddleback sow, but a cousin in England who was also pregnant, although as far as we knew she hadn't been sent away to be serviced.

'Yes, Jessie's tummy will get big.' I was beginning to sense that they had both identified gaps in their knowledge, and would be ruthless in filling them.

'Is it big now?'

'No, it's not very big yet.'

'How big is it?'

'It's just a bit bigger than normal at the moment,' I said. How far along was Jessie was in her pregnancy, I wondered, and did accuracy matter in this conversation?

'Mummy?' continued Daisy, as if to catch my attention again, in case I'd drifted off since we'd last spoken, five seconds earlier.

'Yes?'

'Babies grow in a man's tummy as well.' This was stated as fact.

'No, darling. Babies don't grow in a man's tummy. A man

has a different job.' I knew the minute I said the words that it was a mistake to bring this up.

'What is dat job, Mummy?' A whole other anatomical area for discussion opened up before us. I launched in.

'A man has a little seed inside him and that's what the baby grows from.'

There was a pause.

'Mummy?'

I braced myself. 'Yes?'

'Where is the little seed, Mummy?'

There was a sense of inevitability about this conversation, I reflected. I had set myself up as being the parent most likely to explain things. I had only myself to blame now.

'It's in his willy,' I said, abandoning all hope. Stifled sniggering came from the back of the car.

'Mummy?'

'Yes?'

'How a baby get in a mummy's tummy?'

I'd have to see this through to the end now. There was no escape. 'A man puts it in there with his willy,' I said.

'How, Mummy?'

I took a deep breath. 'A man puts his willy inside the mummy.' I left the specifics out in the hope that it wouldn't be noticed. Daisy knew the anatomy but I wasn't sure she could handle the configurations.

There was a brief silence, like the one that falls when troops are reloading in battle.

'Mummy?'

'What?'

'What happens if the baby grows in the man's tummy?' For god's sake, I thought, where did they get such ideas from? It was clear that I'd have to explain every tiny detail or they'd get it horrifically wrong.

'That can't happen,' I said. 'A baby can't grow in a man's tummy. He hasn't got the equipment.'

'What if it just did by accident?'

Like in *Alien*, I thought?

'It can't, because the man's little seed has to go into the mummy's tummy and meet up with an egg that the mummy has inside her, and together they make a baby. And that can only happen inside the mummy's tummy.' Please god, I thought, let that give them enough to think about in order for us to make it to the school gates.

There was silence. Relieved, I thought perhaps that had clarified things, hopefully without scarring them psychologically.

'Mummy?'

I gripped the steering wheel, my knuckles white. 'Yes?'

'What we doing tomorrow?'

Country Cuisine

If you have pigs, you potentially have pork, and now that we were bona fide pig-farmers, it seemed necessary to prepare for what was to come.

Ironically, we weren't in the habit of eating pork frequently. I had occasionally purchased chops described as 'moisture infused'. But after being rubbed with herb butter and cooked under the grill, they emerged as a pale husk, and were strangely tasteless.

We had been told that pork from Wessex Saddlebacks was different, and Jeff had kindly given us a pork shoulder from his own farm to try. Oliver had taken charge and cooked it for a long time on a low heat, as per instructions. It emerged smaller and with a shield of dark crispy crackling around it. Carefully, he wrapped it in foil and let it rest, while he polished off a bread sauce and tipped roast potatoes into a serving bowl alongside a mountain of broccoli and carrots. Oliver loves a roast dinner, and occasionally loses count of the numbers in our family or over-estimates how much we can eat. Daisy and Kit were still young enough to be suspicious of anything new that was served to them, and it was hit and miss as to what would be deemed edible.

'All the more leftovers for us,' Oliver grinned, ceremoniously dishing up the dark, tender meat onto our plates. It shredded into tender, steaming fibres when pulled apart with knife and fork, and had a rich, meaty aroma.

'My mouth is watering just looking at it,' said Oliver, grabbing his cutlery and poring over his plate. I dabbed bread sauce onto a bite-sized morsel, and we tentatively tried our first forkfuls of Wessex Saddleback pork. It was as moist and unctuous, and as the juices coated my tongue, the taste filled my mouth, unbelievably rich and savoury and like no other meat I'd had before.

'That is sensational,' I said between mouthfuls.

Oliver, normally a little more circumspect about most things, chewed slowly, his cutlery poised mid-air ready to dig in again. He glanced up at me, his face creased with pleasure. 'It's bloody delicious, isn't it? Tastes like meat would have done years ago.'

Looking at the joint of meat, now shredded into succulent pieces on a serving dish, I could well imagine this pork being served in earlier times, at a long table in some feasting hall, having come from the hunting fields of England and been cooked over an open fire. It was food from long ago, before food became stuff you got from packets or tins.

'Aw, dat is yummy,' said Kit, picking up a strip of crackling with his fingers and gnawing on it. Beside him, Daisy picked delicately at her plate.

'Do you like it, Daisy?' I asked her.

'It's very nice, but I don't like much meat,' she demurred. At nine years of age, Daisy was becoming selective about her consumption of meat. I suspected she had put two and two together about the pigs on our farm, and the pork we might eat, and was having trouble with that idea.

Even so, it was an almost unanimous vote of approval.

Newly fed and motivated, we began to anticipate having more of this delicious pork in the near future, when the pigs born on our farm were the right size to send to slaughter. This was a whole new aspect of farm life to get our heads around.

One or two friends had asked me how we would be able to eat animals we had raised on the farm. I found I didn't really think about how we'd be eating Rosie and Bella's offspring. I simply shut the idea off in my head so the source of the meat remained anonymous.

After that first roast, we developed a taste for more. Taking my lead from Hugh's *River Cottage* and his butcher Ray's teachings on how to cook a small, inexpensive roast, I purchased some pork belly from a local butcher. It wasn't Wessex Saddleback, and was paler than Jeff's roast, but I knew it was sourced from a local farm - the one right round the corner from us. Oliver had visited it when he was researching pigs, and liked the owner. The sheds were clean as a whistle, he said, and the pigs all looked content. We came to think about this more closely in the ensuing years, when the debate over sow stalls raged in the media, and yet bacon continued to roll off the shelves at a price and rate that only an industrialised sector could deliver.

Pork belly was the cut that appealed most to me. It was cheap, but when stuffed with apricots and onions, rolled, trussed and cooked in a hot oven, it produced a Sunday roast that was tasty and succulent. It emerged from the oven wrapped in crackling and with caramelised crusts at either end. I found it hard not to peel these off and scoff them while standing in the kitchen, long before we'd got to the table.

One afternoon, I was preparing a piece of pork belly for roasting. We were having friends over for lunch and I'd purchased a long length of belly. As I turned it over on the kitchen bench-top, I noticed there were five nipples studding the skin, and stopped to consider the young pig that this meat had come from.

Having listened to Oliver talking endlessly about pigs, I had learned a thing or two. I knew the nipple count on a gilt was an indicator of how many piglets she might have, and how good a breeding sow she might be. Since I was used to handling pork in the kitchen, and to hearing details about the pigs as live farm animals from Oliver, I had no problem in connecting the two.

'Look, she had five nipples,' I remarked. Oliver was behind me in the kitchen, making a cup of tea. I moved the bowl of apricot stuffing out of the way and stretched the belly out, skin-side upwards on the kitchen benchtop. 'That's ten if you count both sides, and there's belly missing at the far end so it could have been twelve altogether. She'd have been a pretty good sow, wouldn't she?'

I turned to face Oliver. He was leaning against the kitchen sink looking a little faint.

'It makes me feel a bit funny seeing you handle it like that,' he said. I looked back at the pork belly and its nipples. This had been a small female pig, which had never had piglets. You could tell that because the teats were undeveloped, the nipples just small protrusions on a flat skin. But by the time it was in my kitchen, I saw it as something to be rolled up with apricots and onions, which would go into my oven pale and insipid, and come out a sizzling caramel brown, a delicious feast for my table.

'I can't help thinking you're going to find it easier than me when it comes to sending ours off to be done,' Oliver added.

I thought about that for a moment; it seemed rather a callous judgment. 'Perhaps it's because I handle meat all the time and I'm used to thinking of it as something we eat,' I said.

'Whereas I'm used to feeding the pigs and seeing them in the paddocks. I still think of them as animals.'

This was the result of our division of labour. Oliver fed and tended the livestock and thought of them as creatures, alive and kicking and lovable. I handled the meat we bought from the shops or were given by friends who'd been hunting or fishing. Perhaps to protect my own sanity, I didn't reflect on the creatures our food had once been. It would be interesting to see how each of us felt when the livestock was our own, and that's what was on the plate.

* * *

Pork Roast with Crackling and Gravy

INGREDIENTS
  Pork roast with skin
  For stuffing: onion, apricots, thyme, parsley, salt and pepper
  String
  Olive or other oil

Caraway seeds (optional)

IN ADVANCE

The skin of your roast should be scored. If this hasn't been done, the best tool is a sharp craft knife. Always score away from your hand.

Rub salt liberally over the skin of the roast and place in the refrigerator for at least two hours. Overnight is fine.

PREPARATION

Preheat the oven to 140°

Remove roast from fridge and blot moisture and salt off using paper towel.

Open the roast out and lay flat.

Slice the onion and chop apricots, add thyme, parsley and seasoning.

Lay stuffing ingredients along roast, roll up and secure with string.

Oil the skin of the roast with the oil of your choice. Olive oil is fine.

Sprinkle caraway seeds liberally on the roast.

COOKING

Prepare an oven tray by laying baking paper in the base.

Prop a wire tray across the top of the tray and place the roast on this.

Cook the roast for one to three hours depending on size. Do not overcook as you will burn the juices in the bottom of the pan.

For the last half hour, turn the oven up to 240°. This is the hot blasting that will make the skin crackle. Keep an eye on it and when you think it's ready, open the oven and tap it with a knife. If it's hard, it's done.

Remove from oven and rest with a glass of Pinot Gris (you). The roast should rest too, for half an hour.

GRAVY

Remove the baking paper and any residue that is too scorched or burnt.

Spoon off excess fat.

Put oven tray on the hob over a low heat.

Add a couple of teaspoons of flour and stir into the meat juices, pressing out lumps.

Gather all the caramelized bits from the roast into the mix.

Gradually add liquids of your choice: stock, white wine, cider.

Keep stirring and adding liquid until it is well combined, tasty and the consistency you like.

Sieve if preferred, or keep the tasty bits.

FOR THE TABLE

Slice or pull apart the roast. It should be messy and succulent.

Remove the crackling and slice it.

Serve with gravy, roast or mashed potatoes, cauliflower or parsnip puree, and greens.

WINE

Pork is an incredibly versatile meat and can be enjoyed with many wines including crisp Pinot Gris or Riesling, a Rose, a soft Merlot or Pinot Noir, or even a sparkling Shiraz.

'In Pig'

When Rosie and Bella returned, Oliver put them back into their original pen with its small hut and straw pre-moulded by them - all the familiar comforts and smells of home. It seemed kinder to allow them each other's company until they were closer to their due dates, when he would separate them.

The two girls resumed their daily routine of naps in the sun punctuated by snuffling and rooting amongst the undergrowth in their large pen. Mealtimes were spent with snouts in the trough, vacuuming up the commercial feed Oliver had begun buying for them. It contained mineral supplements specifically designed to help pigs grow, important now they were pregnant. What we fed the pigs would become a source of constant concern to Oliver, both for their health and welfare, and for its cost. Pig feed is based on grains, usually including wheat. When war breaks out on the other side of the world in a country which exports one third of the global supply of wheat, or when there is a drought affecting the USA's wheat crop, that puts the price up.

We began sourcing windfall apples from local orchards as a treat for Rosie and Bella, as hand-feeding pigs is a good way to tame them. Daisy and Kit often came out to the pens at feeding time to throw apples from buckets. Rosie and Bella trotted after them, heads down and ears flapping, bellies rolling from side to side as they expanded in size.

Oliver kept a close eye on the girls and developed an obsessive need for reassurance that they were indeed pregnant. First he kept a keen eye on their teats. Were they getting bigger? He seemed convinced that you could tell a Saddleback was pregnant from her nipples.

'They leak milk when they're getting close to their due date,' he told me. 'Yours did that, didn't they?'

'Not until after I'd had the baby and needed to produce milk,' I replied, wondering at the taken aback at the comparison of my own bosoms to Rosie and Bella's. Still, the same logic could be applied.

'I thought they might be producing milk already,' Oliver persisted.

'Why would they, when they're weeks away from having any piglets to feed?'

Had I known better, I would have thought twice before making myself out to be such an authority on the signs of pregnancy or imminent birth. Oliver began to barrage me with talk about the check-ups he conducted on a daily basis. He'd begun feeding them vegetable waste from the kitchens of a nearby Greek restaurant. We stopped this practice soon afterwards, as kitchen waste counts as swill, and it's illegal to feed this to pigs, for good reason: the passing of bacterial matter from any meat waste can cause disease, and swill-feeding was the cause of the catastrophic outbreak of Foot and Mouth Disease in the United Kingdom in 2001. But before we went into commercial production, and while Rosie and Bella were ripping into vegetables with a balsamic reduction,

Oliver was examining their nipples and now also checking out their back ends, returning to the house to report on his findings.

'Bella looks like she's recycling,' he announced grimly one morning.

'What does that mean? She's separating her paper from her plastics?' I still wasn't up to speed on all the technical terms and was a little tetchy from the barrage of anatomical detail.

'No, it means her bum is swollen as if she's coming back on heat.' This was bad news for Oliver. If Bella was coming on heat again, she could not be pregnant, and her rogering at Mount Roland would be all for nothing.

'Can't you just give it some time?' I asked. In desperation I thought back to my own early days of pregnancy. 'Women can sometimes feel as if they're about to have a period even though they're pregnant. It's just your body sticking to its normal routine.' This was something a doctor had told me when I was first pregnant with Daisy. I knew it was better to try and put Oliver's mind at rest or he would worry heedlessly, and out loud, until the matter was resolved one way or another.

'I thought I might ring Jeff,' he said, still ruminating.

'And ask him what? They're not due to give birth for ages. I think you might be looking for signs too early.'

'I thought maybe the boar hasn't performed.'

'He seems to have done the trick with Rosie.' When I'd last been over at the pens, Rosie was waddling about looking for all the world like a small but pregnant sow. 'Perhaps it's just that Bella's a bigger pig. That could be why she's not showing?' I added.

Bella had become the dominant, larger sow, always at the trough first, biffing Rosie away with a swing of her huge head.

It was easy to imagine a litter of tiny piglets huddled deep inside her without showing through her flanks. It also seemed wise to prevent Oliver from calling Jeff and accusing his boar of shooting blanks.

Nothing could put Oliver's mind at rest. He continued to examine the girls' private parts and check their udders. The due dates calculated from their time with the boar were one week apart, and as their time approached, Oliver's agony increased. He was beside himself for every day that passed without obvious signs of imminent birth. With nineteen days to go until Rosie was due, he became convinced that she was cycling and coming into heat again. Desperate for a second opinion even if it was only mine, he photographed her fanny with his smart-phone, returned to the house and showed it to me while I was eating my breakfast.

Breakfast was a precious moment of the day, allowing me a moment's sanity after Daisy had gone to school and Kit was either playing quietly or at childcare.

'What the hell is is that?' I said, as he held his phone in front of me with a defiant air.

'It's Rosie's fanny.'

'Why would I want to see that?' I put my spoon down in the bowl of cereal before me.

'Don't you think it's more swollen than normal?'

'I don't go looking at her fanny as often as you do so I've nothing to compare it to.' I was feeling rather heated by now. 'Looks perfectly normal to me.'

'I think she's about to come on heat again,' Oliver asserted. At that point I felt rationality slip away from me.

'For god's sake, try to remember that you're not an expert,' I said. 'You have no experience of pigs' fannies whether they're pregnant or not. You certainly weren't examining mine this thoroughly when I was pregnant so you can't compare it to that either.' And then a moment of sheer genius struck me. 'If you're so concerned, why don't you go round the corner and talk to Adrian about it?'

Adrian was a farmer who lived nearby and ran a standard commercial pig farm, keeping his livestock in large airy sheds. He had been more than helpful when we were investigating the idea of keeping pigs, showing Oliver round his farm and giving him a crash course in pigs. Oliver had reported that the farm was clean as a whistle and the pigs seemed content, housed in large sociable groups. If ever there was a man who would know about pigs' fannies and could shed some light on Rosie's through close scrutiny of a photograph, it was Adrian. Plus, it would get Oliver out of my hair, which seemed necessary if our marriage was to survive.

I wasn't unsympathetic. After all, if the girls weren't pregnant, then the past three months had been a waste of time. Oliver was investing a lot of effort in looking after them in an attempt to start a new business, while still continuing to work as a cabinet-maker. No wonder he was a bit glum at the prospect of failure.

Oliver left for Adrian's farm, giving me the chance to think things over. I was concerned for Oliver, and for us. Our future income depended on being able to set up a small farm infrastructure, breed these pigs, create a line of pork product and find some customers. In typical fashion we hadn't done any proper business planning and were testing the waters as we went.

Suddenly concerned about whether these pigs were pregnant or not, I turned to my own source of wisdom and information - the Internet. I opened a search engine and typed in the phrase 'how to recognise a pregnant sow'. I wasn't game to put 'pig vagina' for fear of the resulting spam.

First on the list of results was one of the posts from my own blog. It appeared my search engine optimisation was better than I'd thought. Further down, I came across some answers from a pig keepers' forum on a website called 'Farmer Friendly', which seemed to offer some answers. I saved it on my list of favourites.

Very soon, Oliver was back from his visit to Adrian's farm with a spring in his step, a reassured man. The size, shape and behaviour of a sow's vagina was not necessarily indicative of whether or not she was pregnant. Pigs' fannies were a law unto themselves, as Adrian's sows had demonstrated only too clearly to Oliver.

'Some of their vulvas are like this!' he told me incredulously, his thumbs and forefingers forming a circle the size of a saucer. I tried not to look, concentrating instead on the swirling froth of my coffee. He went on to admit that the swelling and pinkness he'd imagined in Rosie and Bella's backsides signified nothing, and he had been bending my ear about them pointlessly.

I was relieved that what he had learned from another man's porcine vaginas had such a powerful restorative effect on him. Half an hour after returning home, he was happily ensconced in the online pig forum at Farming Friendly, with a new mood of optimism in the air. With nineteen days to go, I reflected, it was harder work than either of my own third trimesters.

Being at home all day in close proximity and with the prospect of running a business together brought a new kind of stress to our life. Our different personality traits and ingrained habits came to the fore as we struggled to find ways of using our respective strengths in our new vocation as pig farmers. During the years I'd spent in various office jobs, I had learned the value of a proactive mindset, and had a rock solid 'glass-half-full' outlook. I was naturally inclined to believe that plans would come to fruition if we worked hard enough on them, and that our sows would probably get pregnant because that's what animals did.

Oliver was a natural pessimist. His glass was not only half-empty, it had rolled off the table and shattered. Thankfully, after Rosie and Bella's first pregnancies, he grew some confidence in his pig-husbandry skills. His sows fell pregnant time after time and he learned to recognise the subtle and nuanced signs that they were 'in pig'.

But it wasn't just Oliver who could wax on about the anatomical aspects of farming. Other small-holders and farming blokes also liked to hold forth on these aspects of livestock breeding. I found it hard to accept that they were the natural custodians of wisdom on the subject.

One afternoon we had a visit from Gavin, a smallholder from across the river. He and his family kept lambs for the most part, but had recently moved into pigs. He'd had several discussions with Oliver when we were looking for ours. Although he was jovial and encouraging about how marvellous Wessex Saddlebacks were as a breed, how easy they were to keep, how luscious the meat was from them, he had been pointedly discouraging about our chances of getting any, and whether it was worth our while farming them. 'Margins are really small on top quality pork. It's really hard to make a business out of it,' I heard him telling Oliver on the phone one day. Perhaps he was referring to the fact that we had only five acres of land and the likely small scale of our operation made it not worthwhile. This didn't really explain why he himself was bothering to farm the same pigs.

He turned up for a 'sticky-beak' one day, and a look at the stock we'd managed get hold of – Rosie and Bella. Oliver had come to believe Gavin was concerned that we might go into business and be competition for him.

'I think that's why he was holding out on us when we were looking for sows.'

'Surely there's enough of a market for everyone?' I said, although in truth I had no idea.

'Well, there's only one other farm up here in the north that's got enough to make a go of it, and that's Jeff. Maybe Gavin thinks a third business is too many.'

Despite this, Oliver felt he had nothing to hide.

We stood at the pens watching Rosie and Bella snuffling around in the long grasses. Rosie stalked around like a small but stately matron, her trotters keeping her up on tippy-toes and giving her a strangely elegant look. As she walked away from us, brushing her flanks against the long grasses, her udders swung between her back legs, growing large now as she neared her due date.

'Ooh, that's some good udders,' remarked Gavin with an envious note in his voice. 'Very even, aren't they?' Rosie paused to scratch one back leg with the other trotter. 'You'll find the piglets all go to the same teat every feed,' he remarked. 'And the runt gets the last one near the hind legs.'

Having been town-born and bred, I had no problem admitting that I knew very little about agriculture. But when it came to udders, I felt I had the upper hand. I was coming to feel there wouldn't be much difference between a sow suckling piglets and a woman nursing a newborn. I might be proven wrong, but no way was I letting a man tell me how these things worked. Feeling a bit bloody-minded about it, I decided to speak up.

'Interesting, isn't it? Our two favoured the right breast first and then went to the left afterwards. That one was always a bit smaller.'

There was silence for a moment. Oliver kicked the dirt at his feet, and Gavin stared at me, his eyes widening. I ignored him and ploughed on. 'Maybe it's to do with finding the best food source.'

In the silence that followed, I had a sudden realisation. A moment ago, Gavin had been quite comfortably thinking about a lovely, soft, black sow's udder, comparing it to his own sows' udders. Now he found himself unexpectedly picturing mine.

I glanced at Oliver, who looked slightly stricken. In despair, I realised that farming men could talk openly about pigs' udders and fannies, but apparently couldn't cope with the thought of human bosoms doing the same job.

'Cup of tea, anyone?' I said brightly, and left for the kitchen. Perhaps it was best to leave the men to their conversation, unimpeded by my own unorthodox contributions. Privately, I believed that if someone started such a conversation, they should be able to follow it through unflinchingly, whatever responses came their way.

But then nursing is not something one sees or reads much about until having a baby. Even then it's often kept hidden, and there's a kerfuffle when a female politician has the temerity to breastfeed her baby in parliament. I felt it should be more familiar to us all, including men. They were sons, brothers and potentially husbands of women who would quite likely breastfeed at some point.

Later on over dinner, Oliver admitted the awkwardness of the moment.

'What on earth did you say that for?' he asked.

'Because I know what I'm talking about!' I exclaimed. 'There's no way I'm letting Gavin tell me how udders work.'

'I think he was a bit embarrassed.'

'If he brings the subject up, he should be man enough to go through with it.' I stabbed a piece of lamb with my fork.

I had little sympathy. I suspected that what it came down to was that men saw pigs' udders as a feeding mechanism for piglets, but they could only ever see a woman's breasts as a set of lovely playthings.

Piglets

If only the last two weeks of pregnancy were always like Rosie and Bella's. Relieved of the need to be examined so frequently, with Oliver willing to accept that nature was taking its course, the girls were left to sun-bake in peace. Usually they did so slumped together in the wintry afternoon light against the tin of their shed, grunting peaceably.

Still novice pig farmers, even we could see that Rosie's belly had dropped, and her udders were now swollen things that ran the length of her abdomen, swaying majestically from side to side as she walked. She could be expected to farrow at any moment.

To Oliver's relief, it was finally obvious that Bella was pregnant too. Her udders were not so uniformly enlarged as Rosie's, but her belly had expanded and dropped. A bigger pig than Rosie, her vast proportions evidently meant a whole troupe of piglets could swim around her insides without being noticed on the outside.

As if to confirm this, Bella started to behave more like a creature in the late stages of pregnancy. She spent most days slumped in a pool of dappled sunlight in the bush block, her rump propped up against a wattle sapling, a bed of native grasses crushed beneath her. Every so often she heaved a great sigh.

'I've felt the piglets moving around inside her,' Oliver murmured in my ear one afternoon as we stood watching her. I looked at him in amazement.

'Gosh, she lets you do that?'

'She's used to being handled, and she can't move that fast now.'

He beckoned me into the pen, and I slung a leg over the fencing wire and crept towards Bella slowly, so as not to alarm her. She had grown into a placid, good-natured sow and as I approached, she moved her head slightly as if in acknowledgement, but kept her snoozing eyes closed. Her tameness was thanks to the gentle, respectful way in which first Jeff and Heidi and then Oliver had treated her. Reaching out, I lifted her huge ear, which flopped over her face. Beneath it, her smiley eye remained closed, apparently in deep sleep, her eyelashes clogged with dirt.

'Hello darling,' I murmured, and she heaved a great sighing huff in response. Slowly I turned and put my gloved hand lightly on her stomach. Instantly, I felt an unmistakable kick as if from a miniature trotter. Taking my glove off, I laid my palm on the soft skin of her flanks, just above her udders. It was less bristly there, soft and warm to the touch. As if in response, I felt the unmistakable fluttering movements of unborn young. Bella blew a series of sighs, great gusts leaving her nostrils and stirring the dust in front of her.

Later that afternoon when the children came home, I told them what I'd felt.

'Can we feel the piglets, Mummy, can we, can we, please?' they begged. So I took them out to see Bella, who had moved to a different tree but continued to bathe her belly in the sunshine. Walking over to the pens was something we often did when Daisy and Kit arrived home from their day. Lifting them over the electric wire of the pen, I showed them how to approach Bella slowly, talking quietly to her so she'd know we were there. Soon there were lots of hands on Bella's tummy and curious squeals as we all felt the piglets moving around inside her. Then Rosie ambled over to join us, as if curious to see what was going on. As pigs often do, she gave a small grunt of inquiry. Bella harrumphed in return. Who knows what was said between them?

'Alright there, dear?'

'They're palpating me again.'

Later that day, Oliver moved Rosie out of the communal pen and into her own pen next door, with a splendid new eco-hut made of recycled materials. He had run an electricity supply down to it from the shed, which powered a heat lamp in one corner, and there was a bed of straw on the floor.

'They'll start building their birthing nests soon,' he said.

'Do they do that?' I asked.

'Some do and some don't, apparently,' Oliver replied. 'It depends how new their surroundings are, and sometimes just on their personality.' Evidently he'd found a wealth of information about it in the online forums. I thought back to all the books I had read about giving birth, none of which really prepared me. Perhaps I should have tried YouTube, like Oliver.

It was hard to imagine what it must be like, being Rosie. As a young gilt, all she'd known in the first few months of her life was snuffling around in our bush block, digging up roots and munching on small green shrubs and grasses. Then suddenly she was off to a strange farmyard to be rudely mounted by a boar, with no prior explanation of what was to happen. Given the sudden onset of these strange events, she showed incredible platitude, I thought.

What went through her head, three months, three weeks and three days later, when she found herself overcome by the urge to nest, I wondered? Not content with the fresh straw Oliver provided for her, she began foraging in the bush late one evening, bringing great mouthfuls of bracken back to the eco-hut, and piling it up inside. She topped it off with a broken branch from a wattle sapling. It was ten feet long and as thick as a forearm. Wrestling one end of it into the hut and shoving it onto the top of the pile, she left the rest of it sticking out of the doorway. It looked like an uncomfortable bed for birthing on, but to Rosie it clearly felt just right.

It was incredible to watch how her instincts made her behave. This nesting was not a conscious thing, but there were deeper instincts at play, ones we couldn't fathom. Somehow, nature was helping her put two and two together, readying her for what was to come.

It happened quite suddenly, one Sunday morning. I was having a quiet breakfast with the weekend newspapers when Oliver wrenched the back door open and stuck his head through the gap. 'Rosie's in labour!' he blurted out. His excitement and agitation was far greater than when our own children were born, I reflected.

'Shall I call the ambulance?' I said.

He scowled briefly. 'I'm going back out there,' he replied, as if he were returning to a battlefield. He nodded at my plate of half-eaten toast. 'You could come out if you like, when you've finished that. I wouldn't mind a second opinion on how it's going.' He slammed the door and was gone in a flurry of mud-stained fleece, gum boots and angst.

'Can't help thinking you're over-reacting a little,' I muttered into my tea, opening the Review section of the paper.

But I couldn't deny my own curiosity or the children's excitement for long. Ten minutes later we were all crowded around the door of Rosie's hut, eager to see our first piglets born on the farm.

Rosie lay on her side across her great bed of leafy shrubs and straw, panting and heaving and doing her best to ignore us. Oliver had removed the branch she had added to her nest, doubtful that it would facilitate a smooth birthing experience. Beyond the fence-line in the next pen, Bella stood poised with sisterly concern, her nose in the air. Oliver leaned on the doorpost of Rosie's hut, ducking inside occasionally to check whether a piglet was arriving.

'Do you have to do anything to help?' I asked.

'I don't know,' he confessed, flushed.

'Haven't you asked anybody?'

'I don't think Adrian does very much, he's always got a sow birthing. He couldn't be there with all of them.' There were two hundred breeding sows on Adrian's farm, Oliver had told me. It was a farming operation on a scale we could barely imagine, and yet it is tiny compared to the monolithic scale of the farms on which most pork is produced.

Some people are planners and organisers, and some people are not, and that was Oliver. It didn't surprise me that his pigs were about to give birth without his researching what might happen or what he should do. But it did annoy me. Surely this was a time when you should know what to expect?

Racing back to the house, I phoned a photographer I knew who had photographed some alpacas for an article I'd written.

He had a small herd of Wessex Saddlebacks himself.

'Sorry to trouble you, Steven,' I said, trying to catch my breath. 'One of our sows is giving birth, and we just wanted to double check whether we need to do anything.'

If Steven was surprised by our last minute preparations, he didn't turn a hair. 'The best thing you can do is leave them to it and not look,' he said. It seemed add advice to offer a woman who'd actually given birth herself. I certainly intended to be at the business end watching the piglets be born if I could.

But it turned out there was good reason for it. Steven hesitated before continuing. 'Sometimes they eat their piglets if they're born dead.' His voice was apologetic. He clearly didn't know I'd heard this before, and didn't relish having to break such news to a novice pig-keeper and a woman he barely knew.

'We've heard about that,' I replied, my voice doubtful. Indeed, the prospect of mother creatures eating their young at birth rang a vague bell; I just hadn't expected to encounter it in my own back yard.

Steven reassured me that it was more than likely they'd be competent mothers who knew instinctively what to do.

'Mostly they shouldn't need any help at all.'

If he was right, this was the perfect outcome. It meant we could stay and watch, and if anything untoward happened, we'd just use common sense, although I couldn't quite predict the exact circumstances.

I told Oliver what Steven had said about them possibly eating their piglets.

'I can't see ours doing that,' he replied, with quiet conviction. 'It only happens with sows that aren't used to being handled. Our two are really tame now.'

His habit of handling Rosie and Bella was deliberate, he explained. Patting and rubbing their flanks and shoulders when they were busy feeding meant that if he needed to get into their pens while they were birthing, they'd be used to his presence. As usual he had a strategy; he'd just kept it to himself.

I looked at Rosie, who still lay huffing on her nest of bush and straw.

'Are you going to leave her to it, or stay and watch?' I asked.

'I'm just keeping an eye on things,' he said. 'I want to make sure the piglets breathe soon after they come out, and that she doesn't lie on them.' Both seemed like good ideas.

We watched from the doorway as Rosie grunted her way through labour and, slowly and miraculously, her piglets began to slip out one by one, flopping onto the straw behind their mother and flapping about in surprise at having been delivered. Sometimes they were tangled in umbilical cord, or covered in shreds of the shiny sac in which they'd grown, which fell away as they moved around.

The children and I watched in quiet awe from the doorway, their eyes wide as they took in all the sloppy debris of birth and the wriggling new forms emerging. From time to time, Oliver slipped into the shed and checked a piglet out, moving it quickly and gently to the vicinity of Rosie's udders if it headed off in the wrong direction. Sometimes, instead of turning one way and finding their mother's udders, they turned the wrong way and began the long trek up her bristly spine, heading towards the back of her head. Oliver saw no problem in setting them right.

'What do they feel like?' Daisy asked.

'They're sort of warm and firm.'

Sometimes two piglets arrived with just a few minutes between, but usually there was more of a gap, allowing some of us to escape to the house for a rejuvenating hot chocolate. Around lunchtime, Oliver finally conceded in coming over for some much-needed sustenance. He was reluctant to leave Rosie's side, but from what we'd seen, nature was taking its course without a hitch.

He had kept count of the piglets as they were born; she was up to six so far, he said. Heading back to the pens after lunch, we found a seventh in the far corner of the shed, lying quietly and coming to its senses. Soon it found its way to Rosie's udders and began trying to suckle, nudging and stretching upwards to the teats, its eyes still half-closed. When the eighth piglet slipped out, we began to get a sense of how resilient they were. Rosie had adjusted where she lay, shoving herself backwards with her feet and shuffling on her side towards the wall of the shed. As a result, this piglet was born onto the top of the railing which ran around the side of the shed. It was too tricky a position for Oliver to get to, and the piglet tumbled down the short drop between the bar and the tin wall of the shed.

'That's not much of a start in life,' I said, as we all sucked in our breath. But the piglet was undeterred, and promptly got up and ferreted its way along the walls until it arrived under the heat lamp, where its brothers and sisters nestled together in a growing piglet pool.

'It's like they're pre-programmed for survival,' remarked Oliver, as we stood marvelling at its perseverance only a few moments into life.

Rosie appeared pre-programmed for motherhood. Every so often she heaved herself up and looked over into the corner, lit up by the heat lamp, where her new offspring were resting, licking and slurping each other. By six o-clock she had birthed nine piglets, and appeared to have finished. Standing up, she turned around in her bed of straw and twigs, which was now rather pulverized. Looking round as if to take stock of her young brood, she swept a couple of errant piglets out of her way with her front trotter, and lay down again with her udders facing the heat lamp corner, where most of the piglets were cuddled up together. Then she began to grunt, making a noise we hadn't heard before, like a Harley Davidson idling, a sort of deep and primal rumbling. As we watched, amazed, the pile of piglets unfurled and made its way underneath the timber bar to Rosie's udders. There they squirmed over each other to find a teat, and began sucking and pulling. Rosie lay compliant, rumbling encouragement as the piglets suckled, some of them nudging her udders in an instinctive gesture to bring the milk down, and some so worn out by their first day of life that they fell asleep on the teat.

'That's amazing that she knows just what to do,' I remarked, thinking back to my own first experience of breast-feeding, over-complicated by advice and hampered by my own lack of confidence.

And then, tired and glowing from all the excitement, we made our way back to the house, leaving Rosie to spend her first night with her new brood.

A few days later it was Bella's turn, and she did things differently. There was none of the foraging for nesting material that Rosie had done. Bella showed no signs of going into labour until Oliver found her in the early afternoon, lying on the dirt floor of her shed, breathing deeply, lifting her back leg and straining occasionally. She had already birthed a couple of piglets before he got there. Oliver grabbed some of the straw she had shoved to one side and rubbed them down with it. Then he arranged some around Bella's back legs to provide a comfortable landing place for the rest.

As three o'clock approached, we realised one of us would have to do the school run. I had been in bed for three days with a bad cold. My sinuses had produced enough bio-hazardous effluent to crust over the bottom of my nostrils, and my hair had formed itself into a large cleft on the back of my head. When Oliver gave me the choice of picking up the kids or staying with the pig in labour, I chose the pig.

All was quiet and warm in the sty after he left. It was a miserable, wintry day, but inside the hut, sitting on the sidewall bar, all was cosy with the smell of straw and the stillness of the shelter. We settled into the quiet of the afternoon, with Bella puffing and heaving, and me wiping my watery eyes every so often, trying to breathe through my nose and blow it quietly so as not to disturb her. Outside, the high branches of the swamp gums were tossed around in the wind, the kookaburras cackling amongst them, oblivious to the drama playing out below.

It was curiously moving, keeping Bella company while she laboured. She lay at full stretch on her side along the far wall of the sty, her head poking out of the door. Bella was a big pig. I lifted up her ear. The expression on her face was pained concentration, brow furrowed, lip slightly curled, her breath coming in and out in great gusts. I had a pang of fellow feeling, more than I might have expected for a pig. As I watched, her breathing deepened and she whined on every exhalation. Then she strained and lifted her tail, her breath caught in her throat. A small black form slipped wetly out of her back end and flopped onto the straw. Its head twitched and lifted, its black ears plastered back onto its body. Gamely, it strained upwards, got up on its unfamiliar legs and staggered around trying to orientate itself.

I had nothing to go on but my own experiences of birth, and that told me to leave things be if all seemed well. I watched as the newborn coughed and wheezed its way to life and nestled into the warmth of its mother's body. Soon its fidgeting seemed to annoy Bella. She grunted and with a sweep of her back leg, shoved the piglet away. I took that as my cue. Quietly stepping to the back of the shed, I got a hand underneath the piglet's form, picked it up firmly and deposited it with its siblings underneath the heat lamp. It looked around for a moment, and then began wriggling and snuffling about. The other piglets gathered around and set about cleaning it up, nibbling away the birth sac, nudging and climbing over it and generally pushing it around until it became more vigorous. I watched, marvelling at this unfolding of new life before my eyes.

Oliver returned with the children, who were eager to see yet another batch of piglets. While we were confident it was safe to be inside the hut with Bella, we kept Daisy and Kit outside the door. A pig is a powerful creature and not to be argued with. But Oliver came into the hut and sat beside me on the rail, making it rather crowded. He blundered past me in the cramped space, taking the warm spot near the heat lamp, while I grudgingly moved along towards the door.

'You can go back to the house if you like,' he offered. 'I'll take over again here.'

'I'll wait and see the next one arrive,' I said, unable to tear myself away. I had the feeling the next piglet would come soon, as Bella was now wheezing again with effort on each exhalation.

'It's an amazing thing,' I remarked. 'She just seems to know exactly how to get on with it even though she's never done it before.'

'Yes, it's a lot less bother than when you had ours,' said Oliver. He leaned over from where he sat, tugged a handful of straw from beneath Bella's rump and spread it out across the floor. Then he half stood and cleared the straw from the bar across the piglets' corner, where it had become clogged.

'There's probably more of a differential between her size and theirs,' he added. He brushed in front of me and fluffed out the straw around Bella's forelegs, which she had swept into a bundle.

Suddenly, Bella heaved herself up on her haunches, shook her head a little blearily and looked round at Oliver. It was exactly as if she'd had enough of Oliver's ministrations and was turning round to ask, 'What the bloody hell are you doing back there?'

My instincts kicked in. 'Why don't you stop bothering her?' I said. 'You're making all this fuss with the straw. She's been lying there peacefully, labouring away, and now you come back and rearrange the bedding. Just let her get on with it!'

'I'm only trying to make her comfortable,' Oliver protested. But it was too late. In my new role as Bella's birth companion, I would brook no argument.

Late in the afternoon her labour slowed down and she delivered the afterbirth, a splat of tissue. Oliver checked to see that its edges looked uniform, and the whole thing had been safely delivered, then scooped it up with a fork and took it away to be buried. We returned to the house for a cup of tea believing it was all over.

An hour later, Oliver returned to the shed, only to find the bodies of two more piglets half concealed by straw, cold and dead.

'What do you think happened to them?' I asked.

'She either lay on them or they were born dead,' he said glumly. 'They arrived after the placenta, so it's possible they weren't supplied with oxygen.' It was an answer based on intuition and guesswork, but it seemed probable. It was a sad sight, the perfect but lifeless form of a piglet, which only an hour before had been fully formed, quite possibly oxygenated and live in utero. With a heavy heart, Oliver took the two small forms away and buried them.

Bella birthed eleven piglets, nine of which lived. We were in awe of the achievement, her first delivery. We knew we'd get both sows pregnant again soon, generating more livestock for our small farm, and believed we would be confident in supervising another delivery and ensuring the newborns were safe.

Where Rosie and Bella knew intuitively what to do, for us it was a learning experience.

Farming

'I want to get my own boar,' Oliver announced shortly after the first two batches of piglets were born.

'Why can't we just use the Mount Roland boar again?' I asked.

'I don't want to keep relying on that,' Oliver replied. 'It's not good biosecurity to move stock around from one farm to another.'

Now that we were working towards keeping livestock for commercial purposes, we were more familiar with the rules on transporting, handling and feeding them. We were determined to keep our pigs well in terms of their contentment and comfort, and obey best-practice too. Moving pigs or any livestock from one farm to another could result in microorganisms being transferred on their coats or trotters, passing on disease. It was unlikely, but good farming practice was not to take the risk.

'Getting our own boar means we'll have a good blood line as well,' continued Oliver. 'I'm looking at a boar in Victoria and it's got genetics that aren't related to ours.'

'How could it possibly be related to ours if it lives in Victoria?'

'They all come from the same breeding pair that were

imported into Australia from England ages ago.'

Oliver was fascinated, and wanted to develop his herd of pigs with good genetics. Pilot, the boar he was considering, was located in Ballarat, Victoria, and was only distantly related to Rosie and Bella, sharing a great-grandfather.

'Rosie and Bella's parents were sired by the same boar that had sired Pilot's sire,' he explained. 'Are you following?'

We couldn't have our new boar Co-Pilot mate with any of Rosie's offpsring if we wanted to register them to the breed. The resulting piglets would come from too close a union. We could, however, use them as bacon. Genetics doesn't affect the eating quality of the pork.

'Bella's actually called Beatrice and Rose is called Sunset,' Oliver continued.

'What the bloody hell are you talking about now?' I asked.

'Those are the blood-line names that they come from.' It transpired that we could have pet names for our pigs, but on paper they would always be named according to their breed, a bit like the landed-gentry of old in England.

'It's not as if it makes any real difference,' I said. 'They only really answer to the call of the feed bucket.'

Determined to have his own boar and not have to rely on others for mating, Oliver purchased the boar sight unseen, and had him shipped from mainland Australia by road and ferry. He and Kit set off early one morning, to meet a truck in a lay-by near Devonport. This would bring the boar from the *Spirit of Tasmania* ferry, and the driver would help Oliver transfer him into our trailer in the layby. Oliver was excited at the prospect of generating a bigger herd more speedily and growing farm operations apace. Rosie and Bella feigned indifference, but we believed they would change their minds when they met their new beau. Spring was in the air, and soon the aroma of boar pheromones would be too.

Co-Pilot was the name Oliver had been given, and soon Daisy and Kit had added 'Bob' for reasons known only to them. This is what happens when children are given naming rights over one's animals. Nicknamed Pilot for convenience, he was given a week to get settled in, housed in a pen close to Rosie and Bella's, separated by a walkway. He was a trim young thing, with a long lean body and coat of long, black, shiny bristles, which rippled in the sunlight. He'd been kept on a three-acre block in Victoria, giving him a large area in which to roam. His pen on our farm was smaller, but he appeared quite comfortable, and tame, as boars go. Oliver assumed this meant he'd had a fair bit of contact with his human keepers, and was pleased about this, as a tame boar was far less intimidating than an untame one.

When we walked towards the pen with a bucket of apples, Pilot approached the fence tentatively. Raising his head and holding his jaws open patiently as we dropped apples into his mouth, he crunched and sucked the juice from them noisily. Once he could see the bucket was empty, he allowed us to rub him on his hairy nose, the tips of his tusks protruding up from his mouth at either side. When we did this, he made a contented huffing sound. 'Oof, oof,' we'd say in return. He was a gentle, handsome creature, and we quickly became fond of him.

A week after Pilot's arrival, Oliver decided it was time he became acquainted with one of the girls. We chose Bella, as she had grown to be slightly bigger than Rosie, and to Oliver this meant she was readier for breeding. She often stood at the edge of her pen with her nose pointed in Pilot's direction and her beady eyes keen under the huge floppy ears while Rosie, the smaller and more timid of the two, huddled alongside her.

Oliver decided to move Bella into Pilot's pen, rather than the other way round. We knew her better and could predict that she would follow a bucket of apples out of her pen and into his. Oliver turned off the electric current supplying the white fencing tapes. Rosie and Bella had learned that those tapes would give them a small electric shock if touched, so they stayed away from them. That meant the current could be switched off when we wanted to move them, and they were none the wiser.

Daisy, Kit and I watched as Oliver backed out through Bella's gate, jostling a handful of apples in a bucket in front of her. He crossed the walkway towards Pilot's pen, where the electric tapes had been switched off and moved aside, leaving a clear path across the dirt and grass. Pilot hung back in the middle of his pen with his nose in the air, as slowly Bella was enticed into his lair. Once she was inside, Oliver dropped the last of the apples on the ground for Bella, and ducked out to re-attach the electric tapes. Then we stood and waited for the sparks to fly.

Pilot approached cautiously, his head swaying from side to side, ears pricked, and began to nose around Bella's backside. At this, there ensued a bit of argy-bargy. After circling away from him, Bella began to chase him round the pen, the pair of them crashing through the grassy undergrowth, snorting and grunting with exertion. After a few laps, Pilot retreated to the far side of the pen, panting and puffing, and then lay down on his side. Bella remained at a distance from him, apparently quite disgusted.

Astonished, we watched as Pilot appeared to take a nap. 'He's not going to sleep, surely?' I said. It was the last thing I had expected, with a paragon of beauty such as Bella in his pen, threatening to trample him.

'He's probably just thinking things over,' said Oliver. This was typical of his pragmatic interpretations of animal behaviour, and he was usually right. We continued to watch curiously, as Bella stayed at the fence-line close to us, tossing Pilot's feed bowl around with her snout, nosing through his droppings, and generally appearing to rearrange things to her liking.

'Probably best to leave them to it,' said Oliver. 'They're not going to hurt each other, and they've got more chance of getting to know each other without us standing here.'

We went back to the house and had a cup of tea, blowing the steam off our cups and wondering what was happening over in the honeymoon suite. A couple of hours later, all four of us crept back to the pens to take a look. The warm, late-afternoon spring sun slanted through the trees as we crossed the bush block. Peering through the saplings and shrubby undergrowth in the pen, we couldn't see any sign of them at first.

'Der dey are!' exclaimed Kit suddenly, pointing. 'Dey's sleeping together!' And indeed they were. Oliver had built a lean-to from recycled tin for this pen, up against a small gum tree. It was the one and only time he built a shelter in such a way, as the gum tree didn't last long when it was used as a house timber and scratching post by two adult pigs. For now though, having overcome their initial doubts, Bella and Pilot were spooning, lying side-by-side in the sun-trap beside the shed's tin wall. They had their backs to us, and we could just make out their rumps alongside each other, warmed by the glow of the afternoon light. Bella's back trotters were curled round Pilot's backside, and his splendid testicles rested softly against her shanks. It was the very picture of marital harmony.

In their first summer as young gilts, Oliver continued to house Rosie and Bella in a pen together, as long as they weren't about to farrow with piglets. Pilot remained across the walkway in his own pen, where he could see, hear, smell and grunt at the girls, but not bother them unnecessarily. Pigs are naturally companionable creatures, and the girls shared their space easily without any acrimony. They appeared to get into a mutually agreed routine. At feeding time, they spent fifteen minutes with their snouts in feed bowls, occasionally swapping places to check whether there was a greater supply in the other bowl. When they were done eating, they sauntered over to the automatic water spout attached to a timber post, and had a good, long drink, pushing the plug with their noses to release a stream of water.

After that, they usually took a dip in their wallow. As the dominant sow, Bella went first. She had grown to be significantly larger than Rosie. We had noticed that she often got to the feed bowls first, and would biff Rosie away with a side-swipe of her head, which was becoming bigger by the day. Rosie would retreat, and lose out on precious eating time; Bella got more feed and so the cycle continued. When it came to taking a bath, there was no doubt over who got first dibs.

The wallow

The wallow had begun as a long, pig-shaped hollow which Oliver had dug with a spade. Over time, Bella continued to excavate with her snout, clearly making judgements about where it needed to be deeper to be exactly the right dimensions. She was in the habit of going in up to her ankles at the edge, as if testing the temperature. Then she lunged forwards, collapsing into the silky brown clay and shallow pool of murky water. Only her head was visible, resting on the bank, her eyes blissfully closed as the dappled sunlight played over her. Rosie sat and watched from the far side of the wallow, waiting her turn. After about twenty minutes Bella would decide she had cooled and soaked for long enough, and would heave herself up and out of the water, her sharp trotters finding purchase on the slippery sides.

Rosie waited until Bella was well clear before taking her turn. As she was now considerably smaller than Bella, we sometimes wondered whether she might go under, but between them they had got the depth exactly right. As Rosie enjoyed her refreshing dip, Bella would position her glistening rump against a swamp gum sapling and rub vigorously, setting the sapling all a-tremble, its crown whipping around in the warm afternoon air and a sharp fragrance shaken from its leaves.

As we stood at the fence line watching this afternoon ritual, Rosie and Bella both watched us watching them, returning our gaze with a benign nonchalance. Perhaps they were wondering what we found so fascinating. Or perhaps they were thinking nothing at all. It's easy to anthropomorphise animals, especially since social media has encouraged the posting of endless pictures of animals forced to masquerade as human. In our experience, what's likely going through any creature's head is nothing like what we humans imagine it to be. It's usually about food, and hardly ever about us, unless you're talking dogs.

Farming brought us into contact with a whole raft of new advisors, amongst them an amiable man called Mike from *Feed n Supplies*. Mike's partner ran the business end of things, taking orders in her home office for everything that the small-scale farmer or acreage owner could want, from chicken wire to star pickets, animal feed and bedding of all varieties. Mike drove a dusty white van at speed around the valley, delivering it all from beneath its creaking rear door. This he had to lift manually because the hydraulics were shot. We watched in awe as he wedged himself underneath it and pressed upwards with one hand, simultaneously gripping a hand-rolled cigarette between his fingers, dropping ash down the front of his wax jacket as his arm shook with the effort required.

Mike helped the local high school care for the livestock on its farm, and occasionally taught the agriculture classes there. His experience and opinions about livestock were wide-ranging, and we came to depend on him for a reliable answer to most conundrums that farm-life presented to us.

One day we asked him about Rosie and Bella's diet, and what we should be feeding them. We had been tossing them vegetable scraps from the kitchen and waste from the vegie garden. We'd noticed that they were fussier than expected, nosing through their feed bowls and turning their snouts up at anything raw.

'They do appreciate it if you cook their vegies up for 'em,' said Mike as we stood in front of Bella's pen watching her eat. With one finger, he pushed the front of his beaten old Akubra hat upwards and scratched his forehead. 'You wouldn't like gnawing through a raw parsnip, would you?'

'But it all gets eaten in the end,' I replied.

'Well yes, they'll eat anything in the end. They're pigs!'

'I've noticed they'll eat lettuce from the garden,' added Oliver. 'I thought they weren't meant to eat that.' We'd heard that lettuce disagreed with pigs and could give them nasty intestinal pain and diarrhoea.

'Yeah, it's not good for 'em,' Mike agreed.

'But they seem to really like it,' Oliver said.

Mike snorted, and plucked the stubby, blackened end of a hand-rolled cigarette from between his lips and waved it in the air. 'Ah, but I like really like smoking, and that doesn't mean it's good for me!'

Back in the kitchen, we agreed there should be no more lettuce for the girls.

'Perhaps we should try boiling some of those sprouts that have gone over for them?' said Oliver. His first attempt at growing Brussels sprouts in the vegetable garden had overshot, and the results were now standing two feet tall in the garden, being enjoyed by caterpillars and aphids. I didn't think I could come at the idea of cooking for the pigs as well as my family, no matter how fond I was becoming of Rosie and Bella. There was only so far I was willing to take this farming thing.

'You're using the term 'we' loosely there, aren't you?' I replied.

'It's probably going to be you that does it, but you seem keen at the moment.'

Oliver was referring to the mania I had developed, temporarily, for self-sufficiency. Inspired by a man called John Seymour and his *Complete Book of Self-Sufficiency,* I had decided that every scrap of food that we grew, bought or produced as a leftover should be used to feed animals or be composted. I had purchased a worm farm, a black recycled plastic tub on legs with a lid and circle of raw woven wool which sat on top of the contents keeping everything contained and the worms insulated from cold or extreme heat. It made a change from my usual purchases of linen clothing and good quality soft furnishings found at second-hand shops and markets. I'd had to order the worms specially, as they were different from garden-variety ones. These special worms arrived by post in a small cardboard box, a mass of slim, red and brown things. Oliver had helped me set the farm up, tipping them into their new home of rich humus so they could build their wormy holes and populate it before we started to top it off with the food scraps they would eat. After a day or two, I rarely saw the worms but would peel back the woollen blanket and marvel at the mess of rotting matter which these tenacious creatures lived on. After a time, turning a tap at the bottom of their cylindrical home resulted in a dribble of dark brown liquid that was rocket fuel for plants, so strong it had to be thoroughly diluted before being applied to the garden beds.

While I appreciated the process in theory, I came to loathe lifting the lid on the farm to dispose of my kitchen scraps, disturbing a mass of tiny flies. As a child of the shiny interior age where hygiene was king, I was conditioned to think of things relating to food preparation as pristine and clean. Employing a worm farm in the cycle of production was a departure for me. I never really got used to it and Oliver was too busy with the pigs and cabinet-making to supervise it. After a year or so, we donated it to the primary school for their kitchen garden.

During my brief self-sufficiency period, vegetable peelings went to the worm farm with a side order of toilet roll tube for their fibre requirements. If the compost heap needed feeding, it got everything except meat. The guinea fowl looked after themselves, as they were pest control and we wanted them to save their appetite for grasshoppers. The hens were fed kitchen waste such as pasta.

We sometimes fed meat leftovers to the dog, Midget, and then her successor Alice, unless it was ham or charcuterie which contains sulphates and additives not good for dogs. Suitable meat leftovers were meted out once or twice daily into the dog's food bowl and never at the table. Even so, Midget became alert to the constant stream of scraps exiting the kitchen in various containers, and helped herself from the chook bucket if she happened to find it in the vegetable garden while I picked veggies for dinner or did a spot of weeding on my way through.

Remembering who ate what and sorting it into the buckets and tubs littering the kitchen surfaces was a constant preoccupation. The prospect of cooking for the pigs could have been a bridge too far but I was still highly motivated by the idea of owning them.

'If I'm already catering for every other form of life on the property, I may as well cook for them too,' I sighed. 'But only until we've used up those sprouts.'

My reading had told me that John Seymour used to brew a pot of spuds on his Aga overnight and feed this to his pigs in the morning. Mike from *Feed n Supplies* suggested simmering potatoes on our wood burner. The problem was that we didn't light the fire in summer. Furthermore, I didn't fancy letting the aroma of root vegetables pervade the house overnight.

'We could pick up a slow cooker from the market,' suggested Oliver.

'We've already got a bread machine, a toaster, a microwave and god knows how many containers for all the different scraps. There's barely any room left for prepping dinner!'

In the end, I cooked up a single batch of overgrown sprouts salvaged from the vegetable garden. I watched them bob around on a fast boil on the stove for ten minutes, drained them, allowed them to cool for a bit, and carted them over to Rosie and Bella who polished them off with alacrity and a great deal of slurping and crunching. Pigs are very appreciative eaters. Trailing back from the pens with my empty colander and bucket, I passed Oliver weeding his asparagus bed.

'How did that go?' he asked.

'They loved them.'

'Plenty more where they came from.' He nodded at the bed where a few sticks of sprouts remained, all torn and holey from the white cabbage moths.

At that point I came to my senses. There must surely be something more productive for me to do than cook leftover vegetables for pigs. There were only so many minutes in the day, and this didn't feel like something that would lead to a linear, satisfying or well-recompensed career. 'Cuisine for pigs ends here!' I declared. 'The sprouts go in the compost from now on.'

There was really no need to cook for the pigs as they weren't short of things to eat. Oliver purchased commercial pig feed and stored it in his cabinet-making workshop. Once considered a sacrosanct space, it now also housed pellets for the chickens, and occasional leftover vegetables donated by a local independent greengrocer. We were fast becoming short of places to keep all the various foodstuffs. There was only one other shed on the property and that already served as a chicken house, and storage for gardening tools, a spare lawn mower, several miles of hosepipe, a winter's supply of firewood and a couple of straw bales. Plus the odd snake in summer.

Once again, Mike from *Feed n Supplies* had the answer. Somebody had given him an old freezer chest, the kind you see in shops with sliding doors on the top and ice creams inside.

'Why did they give it to you?' I asked.

'It's cheaper than taking it to the tip!' he replied. 'It's just what you need; it's rain proof and rat proof!' And with that recommendation he drove off in his van, leaving us to think it over.

'Over my dead body,' I said to Oliver. 'I'm not going to end up on one of those properties that's got all manner of crap dotted around it that people couldn't be bothered disposing of properly.'

'I could clad it in shingles,' Oliver said. I pictured something of that size clad in timber slats, perhaps those ones with a natural, wavy edge. It wasn't unappealing; it would look like a small, country-made container of some sort, which it was. Then I calculated the likelihood of the cladding ever happening. After that, we mutually agreed not to take Mike up on his offer of an ice cream chest.

It was becoming clear that being with each other all the time was both a blessing and a curse for farming couples. Oliver spent much of his day in the workshop. I couldn't see him, but could hear the sound of the table-saw, sander or router emanating from the workshop and echoing amongst the trees. Every so often he returned to the house, getting things out in the kitchen and leaving them scattered across the benchtops, and filling the dishwasher with endless cups from endless tea.

But somehow, he was never around at dinner time, and a five-acre property is a large area to cover when searching for someone. This was prior to us all keeping a mobile phone permanently stashed in some part of our clothing. In the kitchen at the end of the day, having magically wrought a nutritious meal calculated to suit everyone in the family despite our different ages and tastes, with the witching hour upon us and the children tired and cranky, Oliver was rarely in the house. This saw me standing outside the back door and contemplating the gardens, the bush block and the workshop and wondering whether to start looking. Once, my patience shredded by a day conversing entirely with people under five years old, I simply hollered into mid-air, 'Oliver, where the bloody hell are you?' My words bounced off the gum trees in the late afternoon light and echoed across the paddocks towards Bec and Niall's place.

He was most often found not far from the house, but in the vegetable garden, weeding, watering and tending. It was his way of winding down after a hard day, and it came from watching his parents do the same during his own childhood. I couldn't deny him that pleasure, knowing how hard he was working, still building kitchens, wardrobes and cupboards for clients while also starting a pig farm. But I couldn't always be bothered to trudge out to the garden every day to round him up. I contemplated stationing a gong outside the back door, but never got round to it. Often we went ahead and ate without him.

'Oh, I didn't know dinner was ready,' he'd say, when he finally appeared, even though dinner had been served at pretty much the same time in our house every day since we'd been together. We're still getting to the bottom of this conundrum today, and it helps keep the spark alive in our marriage.

Pork

When you have pigs, you potentially have pork. Since this was the ultimate aim of the enterprise we now found ourselves in, Oliver had done some sums and calculated how much it would cost to feed a pig from the time it was born to the time it could be slaughtered for pork. Turned out it was quite a lot. Our product, if we ever got round to selling it, would come with a 'gourmet' price tag reflecting the length of time they had been on the farm.

'Yeah they take a lot longer to grow to size than Large Whites,' Heidi had advised Oliver when they met at Chudleigh, referring to the standard, large white pigs that most pig farmers kept as commercial livestock. 'But it's worth the wait.'

The Saddleback slips we grew on from Rosie and Bella's litters would take longer than a commercial breed to reach the size and weight at which it was worth slaughtering them – around six to eight months. Oliver planned on rearing them in family groups, free-range in pens. The Large Whites on a commercial farm such as Adrian's, he now knew, were bred for their size and fast growth rate.

'They're enormous,' he said returning from one visit to Adrian's farm. 'You just can't believe how big they are, they're a fully grown pig at the age of three months, because they're bred that way.' Three months was the age at which such pigs were typically slaughtered. Keeping them for longer after they'd grown to full size was pointless from a business point of view. Why keep and feed a pig any longer than you had to? That simply meant it was costing you more in feed before you recovered your costs from the meat price. With consumers expecting bacon to be available at the cheapest possible price, the margins achievable were already low.

Three months seemed shockingly young to us. Such pigs had hardly taken a breath before being sacrificed to the demand for bacon and sausage meat, chops and roasts. Still, as meat eaters, having eaten our share of pork in all manner of products, we had no right to complain.

Many people we knew had been interested in our new, unusual venture. Friends Brad and Kat had moved from the valley into the nearby city of Launceston, but still had a keen interest in whether this spurious agri-business conducted on an unfeasibly small parcel of land would be viable. They were especially keen to try the pork.

As Rosie and Bella's first offspring grew to size, we began planning how we might use them, and who might buy them. We knew that to sell pork meat commercially, even if only to friends at first, we had to have our stock slaughtered at a registered abattoir which was audited by State Government inspectors, such as the one at Devonport forty-five minutes away. We were only too happy to concur with this arrangement, being keen to make sure that our livestock met its end in as humane and professional a manner as possible.

Oliver found out that our local butcher did so-called 'service kills'. Local smallholders could have livestock slaughtered at the abattoir and then delivered to him in a refrigerated vehicle, to be butchered into useable cuts. The price was incredibly reasonable. What's more, this butcher was prepared to vacuum-pack it for us.

The stage was now set for us to send a pig to slaughter and have it turned into edible product, to sell to friends as a trial run. The abattoir advised Oliver they would 'process' a pig on a Tuesday. During all the time we ran the business, we used the term 'process', but were never in any doubt what it meant.

The first batch of piglets born to Rosie and Bella was reaching the age of six months. It was the optimal time between six and eight months, to send them to slaughter. Any older and we would be feeding them too long to recoup costs on the sale of the meat. Any younger, and they were too small.

When the day came, Oliver backed the trailer up to their pen, and put their feed on it, rather than in the trough. On the day, several pigs went up the ramp, and Oliver used a large board with a hole cut into it for a handle, to bar the way of the largest one and prevent it from escaping. He had me raise the ramp of the trailer, and he climbed out over the side and secured it. Then he drove off up the road, the pig raising its snout and ears to the air suddenly brushing past. Selfishly, I was glad it was Oliver and not me that was making that journey.

'How was it?' I asked, when he returned. We met in the kitchen over a cup of tea.

'It's not a nice feeling,' he replied. 'You don't really see anything, but it's a bit depressing, leaving your pig in a pen on its own and driving away.'

That feeling never got any better.

But that was Tuesday. On Friday, Oliver drove into Exeter and took delivery of our first cool boxes full of premium pork cuts. It was immediately clear that a Wessex Saddleback pig's diet showed up in the meat, and needed careful control.

'That's a lot of fat,' said Brad when we delivered half a pig's worth of pork cuts to his home in suburban Launceston. He was watching Oliver unload the product onto his kitchen bench tops. Every roast, every section of belly, every pork chop was rimed with a thick white layer of fat. Clearly our pigs were in clover: well fed and lying around in the sun all day. Not only were they living off the fat of the land, they were becoming it. Some fat is traditional, in Saddleback pork, because it is delicious, but not as much as we had produced. Oliver would have some work to do, adjusting their diet and making sure he grew them with a good ratio of meat to fat.

'I've heard that's a trait with Saddlebacks,' he said in the car on the way home. 'They run to fat very easily. I just didn't expect it to be that bad.'

Back on the farm, Oliver began controlling the pigs' diet more rigorously, measuring out the correct quantities for daily feeds using small buckets. He had been supplement feeding them with waste from a feta cheese factory in Launceston. Astonishing amounts of the stuff was available for free, having apparently been produced surplus to requirements or fallen short of quality control. Oliver had been storing it in increasingly smelly vats in the workshop, and adding it to the pigs' feed by the spade.

'I think the feta might not have been such a good idea,' he told me. 'It cuts costs but I think it's just making them even more fat than they already would be.'

The seventeen piglets born to Rosie and Bella would have grown to size very soon and Oliver needed fast results from their new diet. We would also be presented with a new problem: more meat than we could possibly sell to friends. We needed an outlet, and we needed it quick.

We knew the local butchers were not interested in Saddleback or rare breed pork. Despite all the programs on the television spouting about how sensational rare breed meats were, the segment of the population who bought their meat from butchers wanted two things: they wanted Tasmanian, and they wanted cheap. Pork chops were available from our local butcher for about eight dollars per kilogram. Oliver had calculated that if we sold our pork at that price, we wouldn't break even. Nowhere near.

Our pork cost more to produce than the standard pork from a Large White. Rare breed pigs are slower to grow, and smaller all over. Oliver had to raise ours for seven months, feeding them a commercial feed with a cost attached, before they were of a size worth sending to market. Our pork would have to come with a higher price attached. We knew the best market would be the customers at a farmers' market, who appreciated the rare breed cache, wanted free-range meat raised with ethical intent, and were prepared to pay the price.

Oliver continued to sell half a pig at a time to friends, delivering every couple of weeks at the weekend, and fitting in taking the pigs to slaughter between cabinet-making tasks. This allowed him to find out what cuts people would look for, and refine the process of delivery. We had much of the logistics of our business figured out in theory. Now we needed to put it into practice.

Sausages

As a man who loves the sea, the outdoors, adventure and sunshine, Oliver seemed destined to live in Australia. If there was one regret he had about life there, it was the lack of what he saw as a decent sausage, a complaint echoed by countless other Brits.

It was no surprise, then, that he wanted to make sausages from the pork we produced. His thinking was not so much that it made good business sense, or that it would be an intrinsic part of a carefully thought-out plan. No, he planned on making his own sausages because he thought it was the only way he'd get a sausage he wanted to eat. It was, in his book, a problem of national proportions.

'They just don't know how to make them here,' he moaned.

This had been a constant refrain and I had searched the cities of Brisbane and Launceston for a sausage that would meet his strict requirements: not too salty; not too fatty; not too finely minced or too processed; not too gristly; made from quality pork. I tried every sausage known to the consumer: gourmet supermarket versions, fancy butchers' ones. Some contained ingredients I felt were straying too far from sausage territory: who needs a chicken tandoori sausage? Why not just have a chicken tandoori, with some basmati rice and a spinach and potato palak aloo on the side?

Before we entered farming life and started thinking more about what we were eating, we favoured a 'French artisan-style sausage' bought from one of Australia's supermarkets. They were juicy and fat, and kept Oliver's palate occupied for a while. I hoped they weren't made with mechanically-retrieved meat, but feared they might be. Eventually Oliver came to find these too salty and we were off on the hunt for an alternative again.

After we moved to Tasmania, I bought much of our meat in blue plastic bags from the local butchers. Sometimes they could tell us which farm it came from; sometimes it had been purchased as 'boxed' product from a meat wholesaler and possibly came from the mainland. The grass-fed beef that Tasmania is famous for is a seasonal product. Grass isn't prime fodder all year round and in winter, that beef is in short supply. Much of the beef we eat over winter is finished off in central feedlots, at considerable distance from where it is eventually sold.

One of our local butchers made the sausages he sold out the back of his shop, and for a couple of years we particularly enjoyed his Merlot and Cracked Pepper sausages. Popping into the shop to pick up a few one day, I was told he didn't have any.

'No, we ran out of one of the ingredients,' he called, wiping his hands on his apron. Butchers' aprons are black so that they don't show the bloodstains butchers are usually covered in.

'Oh, you drank it all, did you?' I quipped.

'No, we just ran out of one of the ingredients,' he dead-panned back.

I came away crestfallen at my comedy failure and empty-handed, while the butcher went on with his day unperturbed. He had quite the selection of sausages in his cabinets, and won prizes for them, his shop counter lined with gold-plated trophies. This cut no ice with Oliver.

Finally, I found myself at the most expensive butcher's shop in Launceston, purveyors of handmade meat products for people made of money. I came away with a small bag containing four sausages made of chicken breast, the dullest, driest, stringiest, least flavoursome and most expensive meat a chicken can yield, and sun-dried tomatoes, which had no place in a sausage as far as I was concerned. Nestling alongside these were four other sausages made of a beef and stout concoction.

These eight sausages had been handmade in the back of the shop by a gentleman from Bavaria with a magnificent twirled moustache, who had been raised making sausages in the family tradition, by his sausage-making father. If ever there was a mother-lode of sausage-making integrity in Tasmania, I had now mined it.

I placed the precious cargo in an Esky in the back of my car and took the corners carefully all the way home. I cooked those sausages for that evening's dinner and served them with creamy mashed potato and buttery savoy cabbage, keeping the accompanying foods on the dish simple so that these masterful sausage creations could shine at full wattage.

Oliver rejected them both.

'That's really dry,' he complained of the chicken confection, which I had to agree was a fool's errand. Sausages need fat, and chicken breast has none, although presumably the sun-dried tomatoes provided a certain slickness.

'And those are nothing special,' he scoffed, pointing his fork at the beef and stout creations. 'I could make those myself.' Finally it dawned on me that roaming the byways of Tasmania in order to put a satisfactory sausage in front of Oliver was a futile quest.

'Why don't you just make your own bloody sausages?' I challenged him.

Famous last words. Oliver had become convinced that if he could produce a bona-fide sausage which replicated the great English sausages of his youth, our future was secure.

'There's a gap in the market,' he insisted. I rolled my eyes, appalled that we were about to base our future fortunes on this hypothesis. I was guessing that most Australians thought rather less about sausages than Oliver did, and simply wanted something they could cook on a barbecue in the summer with a pair of tongs in one hand and a stubby or a glass of Cabernet in the other. Oliver's thinking about sausages went much deeper.

And on this we based a business.

As the pigs in the paddocks grew to size, the kitchen and house filled up with equipment. Oliver purchased a mincing machine and a small sausage stuffer. Every item was pored over on eBay and discussed endlessly. Finally, he was all set to reproduce the sausages of England.

There's a lot to get right in a sausage. The mince has to be the right consistency. Too fine and it makes for a mealy, soft result. Too chunky, and it makes for an unattractive, lumpy appearance and mouth-feel.

Once the matter of mince is conquered, the meat has to be fed into the sausage stuffer at a rate equal to the speed at which it emerges from the other end, where it is fed into sausage skins through a nozzle. Too slow, and the result is a sausage with air pockets. Too fast, and the sausage casings will be overstuffed and may burst, resulting in disappointment and a very meaty mess spilling across the bench-tops.

Now with access to chest freezers full of pork meat, he spent weekends trying to perfect his art. Gradually, the long stream of pork emanating from his machinery became longer and smoother, and he took great satisfaction from coiling it into a great, flat round of uninterrupted sausage.

Kit and Emily helped out with the early experimenting, standing on boxes at the kitchen bench to ladle the mince into the sausage stuffer, or coiling the sausage as it emerged from the nozzle. When Oliver had twizzled it into sausage lengths, they carefully carried the long, heavy strings to the pantry and hung them over a broomstick propped up on two shelves. There they remained for a brief time, to 'set'.

After watching a few YouTube videos on how to tie bunches of sausages together, Oliver soon became adept at this, holding them up in mid-air and deftly weaving them together as the children cooed in delight. He had experimented with 'natural' sausages skins, which are usually the intestines of lambs. Purchased either from a butcher or from eBay, these arrived in salt water and were slippery and hard to handle. They resulted in lumpy, odd-shaped sausages, presumably the shape of a lamb's intestines. Oliver favoured the collagen casings which are used for almost all commercial sausages. These are artificially manufactured, but still a 'natural' product, as they're made from collagen extracted from beef or pig hides, bones and tendons. We had heard that very little waste comes out of an abattoir, and that all parts of the animals slaughtered are used; now we were learning how.

These collagen casings arrived concertinaed in long tubes and could be stored in a cool, dry cupboard until required. They were significantly easier to use, and produced a sausage with a smooth, regular skin. When Oliver tied them into bunches of three, they made a clean, rasping sound as they passed through his fingers. The children and I watched in awe at this new prowess.

We held sausage-sampling parties at our local park, cooking them on the barbecues and feeding our friends in exchange for feedback. I was the first to admit, the taste was unlike any sausage I had bought. It had less of that salty, artificial flavour one associates with sausages. Instead, it tasted of pork, the succulent, intensely flavoursome Saddleback pork I was coming to know. This was a product set apart from your average sausage, I realised. Oliver was using fine quality meat and careful quantities of herbs and breadcrumbs. Crucially, he wasn't using sulphites, which are used as a preservative in meat products and often obliterate the true flavour. This meant Oliver's product would have a shorter shelf life, but was a purer, gourmet product, made from Wessex Saddleback pork, some of the best pork in the world. The future was beginning to look quite tasty.

* * *

Pork Sausage Casserole

This dish was inspired by our good friends Caro and Chris from Brady's Lookout Cider, who carefully craft a 'methode traditionelle' cider, and are the only cider-makers in Australia dedicated to this means of production. It's fermented a second time in the bottle, like sparkling wine, and results in a delightfully soft and sophisticated drop, equally good to cook with and to drink!

INGREDIENTS
   Good pork sausages from a farm or farmers' market
   Premium sparkling cider
   Onion and apples
   Bacon strips or lardons
   Flour
   Thyme

COOKING
   Heat oven to 160°
   Sear sausages in an ovenproof casserole and remove from pan
   Add onions to pan, then bacon or lardons and sizzle for a while
   Add a little flour and cook for a moment
   Slowly add cider or wine and stir into the mix gently
   Aim for a generous pool of slightly thick saucy liquid in the bottom of the pan
   Return sausages to pan with well-fitted lid and place in oven for 35 minutes
   Remove and rest

WHILE THE CASSEROLE IS COOKING
   Slice apples and fry in a light-flavoured oil and butter

FOR THE TABLE

Add apple slices to top of pan before serving

Plate up with creamy mashed potato (add plenty of butter and cream), seasonal vegetables of your choice, and the rest of the cider or sparkling!

Licensed to Feed

Oliver had determined that he would build all the infrastructure needed on the farm himself. For days upon end, in between cabinet-making jobs, he could be found ankle-deep in trenches, digging them by hand and running water pipes along them. This took water down to the pens, where the pipework connected to water feeders. These were ingenious mechanisms, with a button the pigs pressed with their snouts, generating a flow of water into a small dish below.

To supply the pens with water, he attached a water tank to his workshop, to collect rainwater from the gutters. He sourced a recycled plastic tank from a company who occasionally sold 'seconds', which weren't quite the right colour, or had lumpy seams. It seemed astonishing to us that people would be so exacting about an object which surely was never going to be the subject of close scrutiny. But Oliver was only too happy to drive to the Midlands and collect one for less than the usual cost.

While Oliver took care of the animal husbandry and negotiated the processing of the meat product, I immersed myself in the world of food business registration, and the welcoming arms of our local Council's health and hygiene inspectorate. These unfortunate individuals had a reputation which went before them.

'I think they were turned down by the Gestapo for being too thorough in their approach,' said Jenny, who grew tomatoes hydroponically nearby and had looked into making chutneys and sauces in her kitchen. The weight of bureaucracy had put an end to her ambitions. 'But they get contacted by a lot of tyre-kickers,' she added, telling me about the kitchen of a cattle farmer she knew who wanted to produce burgers from her own beef. 'She's a right slovenly type,' said Jenny, who hailed from Devon. 'Always wandering in and out of the house in her bare feet, dragging dust in. And that kitchen, I wouldn't eat out of it myself.'

Armed with this intel about doing one's groundwork, and mindful of the adage about keeping one's friends close and one's enemies closer, I decided the way to deal with the Council authorities was to develop a good relationship with them from the outset, and show them we were serious. I typed 'Food Act' into the search engine, and began the tedious but essential business of learning how to run a food business safely and hygienically in Australia, and how to get it certified.

Documentation was key. Every operational aspect of the business had to be written out in advance: how you would store meat, make sausages, transport your product. Only then would we stand a chance of convincing the Council that we could operate safely, and not bring the north of Tasmania down with botulism, something we definitely didn't want to do.

On becoming a parent, I'd had all manner of leaflets pressed upon me by services who were keen to see you raise your children on good food, made in a food-safe kitchen. I was already in the habit of using separate boards for vegetables, bread and meat. Oliver held no truck with this and used my wooden boards for anything he liked, and bought plastic ones which he could shove in the dishwasher. Running the business together promised to escalate our arguments over this, because Oliver was a man of habit.

Then it emerged that we would have to undertake Food Safety Awareness training in order to be certified as commercial food handlers. This turned out to be a three-hour course completed online. We sat next to each other for a morning and bickered about the relative merits of a bar of soap versus liquid hand-wash, punching our answers into the program. At the end, we were issued with a certificate to print out, and were fully qualified to run a food business. It seemed like the quickest training in the world for something of such significance, but then we knew it would be backed up by the vigilance of the Council's inspectors.

'I wish my degree had been that simple and given me that kind of vocational training,' I said. I had a Bachelor of Arts in Theatre Studies and Dramatic Arts. Ultimately, it provided me with the analytic and creative skills I needed in my career, but it was a while before this was evident.

'Should have done one of those American ones,' Oliver remarked. 'Anyway, vocational training isn't all it's cracked up to be, I should know.'

I knew he was referring to his five-year degree course in civil engineering. On completing it, he had spent a miserable year as a project manager building a roundabout outside Bournemouth. He spent most of it in a caravan off a slip road, rolling cigarettes with one hand underneath the desk and listening to his team of labourers having disparaging conversations about a woman they referred to as 'the town bike'.

'What did they mean by that?' I asked.

'Everybody's had a ride of her,' said Oliver, glumly.

At last we were armed with food certification and a dossier of information on the way we would produce pork for consumption and bring it to market. This we presented to the Council, whereupon we were visited at home by an understated and mannerly young man we'd been told was the most approachable of the triumvirate that ran the hygiene inspections. He was clearly comforted by our administrative zeal and took it as an indication that we were unlikely to poison people. He was kind enough to give us pointers in areas we hadn't quite covered, and human enough to hold a conversation.

My hunch paid off: we had done our research and knew mostly what we were talking about, and as a result were taken seriously. We'd need to change the light-bulbs in the kitchen to shatterproof ones, the Council's envoy said, and attach a water filter to our taps. Beyond these and a few other tweaks in the administrative systems, he was satisfied with our approach and certified us to run a small food-producing business from our domestic kitchen. Many people were surprised that this was a possibility, but it is.

Our certification stated that our pigs would go from the farm to the abattoir and on to the butcher of our choice by refrigerated vehicle. The butcher would vacuum pack different cuts for us, which would be collected by Oliver in properly cooled Esky containers. The butcher would also mince some of the carcass, for Oliver to make into sausages in our domestic kitchen, which was licensed for this product only. It would all be stored in fridges dedicated to the business, also in our kitchen. Not surprisingly, the dog was not allowed in the house while the sausages were being made. But overall, the Council inspector seemed more concerned about our children accidentally leaving the fridges open. Child-proof locks solved that issue. The temperature of the meat had to be recorded and charted at all stages, and the Council inspectors wanted to see those charts on a regular basis. If we followed this protocol, we were in business. As a result of watching television, talking to some people in the pig world of Tasmania, and reading a few books, we were now farmers and gourmet food producers.

We made sure to maintain our good relationship with the food hygiene inspectors from the Council. Stories about their inspections and unreasonable demands were legendary in the region. They would cite the Food Act, requiring beleaguered chefs to put in monstrous extractor fans or food safe flooring in order to sell coffee and cakes. We still watched episodes of *River Cottage*, in which Hugh Fearnley-Whittingstall would hand out pulled pork rolls from a table in the open air with a cloth covering and not a washable surface or a marquee in sight.

'You'd never get away with that here!' Oliver would exclaim. 'They'd shut us down on the spot.' We couldn't help feeling that the rumours of Australia's food laws being so much more restrictive than elsewhere were probably based in truth. I thought of the stories we'd heard of people closing their bed and breakfast operation because the Council insisted they would need a full commercial kitchen for cooking toast, eggs and bacon. We were lucky to have the licence to operate.

Oliver got onto the Internet to source shatterproof lightbulbs, while I looked forward to having my kitchen floor and surfaces cleaned to sparkling on a regular basis.

Some people we met felt the Council's inspectors couldn't even be counted on to apply common sense, let alone the law. We knew of a bakery owner whose brick oven had been in the kitchen at the back of her commercial property for over a hundred years. The Council inspector expressed concern about the lack of certainty that it was clean and wouldn't have bacterial life hidden inside it.

'I had to point out to her that the temperature inside the oven gets up to eight hundred degrees,' the business owner told me, with undisguised glee.

* * *

Creamy Bacon Carbonara

This dish is a go-to in our household. It came from New Zealand chef and food writer Simon Holst's *Pasta Cookbook* originally and has been adapted for bacon, and the sour cream is our idea.

INGREDIENTS
  Free-range bacon
  Two eggs
  Parmesan
  Sour cream
  Good quality tagliatelle

COOKING

Mix eggs with half a cup of sour cream and half a cup of finely grated Parmesan

Cook the bacon then chop into 1cm strips

Bring a large pan of water to a rolling boil, add salt and cook the pasta

Drain the pasta and add to the pan with the bacon, and toss in the bacon flavours (empty a little of the fat out if there is too much for your taste)

Add the egg mix and toss through gently but thoroughly

Serve immediately

FOR THE TABLE

Tomatoes grilled, roasted or gently fried in olive oil

Mushrooms sautéed in butter and olive oil with fresh dill added after cooking

Extra Parmesan

Black pepper

Evandale

Despite being all set to take our product to market, we didn't yet have a market to take it to. We loved to visit markets as punters, and our favourite was at Evandale, a small, pretty and historic town just south of Launceston. We had been taken with it on our visit to Tasmania as somewhere we'd like to live, largely because it had an English-style pub made of red brick with a shady beer garden out back. A long main street meandered through the village, with shops including an old-fashioned butcher's and a general store with a mile-long counter made of old, timeworn timber.

Every Sunday, there was a market in the grounds of the community hall. It was the brainchild of a local businessman, who had run it for years, and it was popular with both tourists and locals. We had visited ourselves and spent many hours wandering from stall to stall in the dappled sunlight under tall plane trees, picking over everything from garden shrubs to socks imported from China, antiques and bric-a-brac, wicker baskets, vintage furniture and garden ornaments made of rusted steel. There were stallholders making a living from their wares, and casuals selling bits and bobs from the back of their shed.

Evandale was the place to buy gardening tools. You could pick up a pair of vintage shears, their wooden handles worn smooth with use, their steel blades built to last with years yet to give. They were far superior to the cheap imports offered by hardware chains, whose handles came loose and caused painful injuries as our knuckles drove into each other while pruning.

My secret weapon when shopping at markets was Oliver. A typical scenario played out at Evandale one Sunday when Kit, then a toddler, became fixated on a Tonka truck, huge, battered and sun-bleached but big enough for him to sit in.

'I want dat, Mummy,' he moaned, gripped by desire. A peeling sticker on the side put the price at thirty bucks. Quietly I told him we'd get Daddy to have a look at it. I made a play of putting the Tonka truck to one side and picking over a couple of other things on the stall, before moving off in a disinterested fashion. Then I located Oliver and sent him in.

Oliver came from a long line of frugal farming folk and nobody beat him on price. He bartered anywhere it was deemed to be acceptable, and often in places where it wasn't, like department stores. Heading over to the stall and engaging the owner in chat, he got the Tonka truck for twenty bucks, which made him happy for the rest of the day. It made Kit's day too, as he rode pillion in the truck's tray behind Daisy that evening, careening downhill in the back garden on a collision course with the wooden cubby house.

We had noticed there were food stalls at Evandale Market, and Jeff had encouraged Oliver to try it as an outlet for our pork. He and Heidi had begun with a stall there and often did well, he said.

'It was a bit up and down depending on what else was going on, but we had a good spot indoors, and we often sold out.'

Encouraged by this, Oliver contacted Derek, who ran the market. There were no longer any spots inside the community hall, Derek said, because there was a cafe there now, but we could set up and trade from a marquee outside. Taking the plunge, we bought a marquee. This would be our shopfront and our workplace. It had a pointy roof and sides we could zip in for inclement weather. I purchased stripy fabric to make bunting and tablecloths to dress the stall, and we purchased found a chiller cabinet to display the meat. The heavy duty Eskies approved by the Council would transport our precious product. And Oliver bought a small transportable barbecue so that we could cook and sell individual sausages in rolls.

'I reckon the smell of the sausages cooking will get them walking off the shelves,' he said. I hoped he was right. Thus equipped, we began trekking to Evandale and putting our shingle up there every Sunday.

Derek was a straight-talking man with the demeanour you'd expect of someone who'd been up since four talking to people about trestle tables. He ran the market in a no-nonsense style, charging an entry fee for the public of twenty cents per person. Stall fees were also modest, despite the market's huge popularity. This being the case, Derek expected stallholders to sort out their own arguments over pitches, rather than troubling him. Oliver had to rise at an ungodly hour, drive an hour and a quarter to Evandale and manoeuvre the ute into place, set up the marquee and secure our pitch. If a neighbouring stall-holder had already set up two feet to the left, it made manoeuvring the ute impossible. This could result in acrimonious encounters with other stall holders and alarming displays of what Oliver called 'pikey behaviour', mostly swearing and being a bit threatening and obnoxious. Oliver, a peace-loving, good-natured man, found the prospect of these confrontations particularly galling. He came to dread Sunday mornings and got up increasingly early, leaving well before light to get there before everyone else.

I arrived later, bringing the kids and enough packed lunch to see us all through. Daisy and Kit were by now aged nine and six, still not old enough to look after themselves at the market. I had no choice but to cajole Kit into behaving, enlisting Daisy's help, while trying to work the stall and develop relationships with customers. Oliver did the same and managed the barbecue at the back of the stall as well. It was impossible to predict how many hot sausages-in-a-roll we might sell each week. Many times we got it wrong and went home with packets of unused bread rolls, and sausages which we froze and attempted to sell at a reduced price as frozen product the following week, keeping rigorous records about what was made when, when it was frozen and how long for.

The market proved up and down, as predicted. But good things come of every situation. Three stalls along was a young and darkly-handsome chef and his beautifully turned-out girlfriend. They sold food which complemented ours but didn't compete with it. Seeing that we sold pork sausages made from our own pigs, Connor had opted for beef burgers. He was cleverer than us, and had a butcher make them. He combined them with delicious relishes and fresh salad on his stall, and his food walked out the door. Perhaps the fact that he was a trained chef helped.

Our sausages didn't sell as well as we wanted, and perhaps

the fact that sausages are considered a pretty ordinary foodstuff by many people had an impact. Oliver was on a mission to convert people. Perhaps there is still a perception that sausages are made using 'trim', the bits and bobs of meat which come from a carcass when the butcher is breaking it down into the different cuts, which are unwanted for anything else. There's nothing wrong with trim offcuts in this way; they might be a little ragged, not the right shape to sell as premium or even a cheaper cut, but it's perfectly usable meat. So into sausages it goes. Nothing is wasted in skilled butchery and meat production: it's poor business sense and disrespectful to the animal. Vegetarians and vegans would say that killing it in the first place is pretty disrespectful, and that seems like a valid point too.

We usually used shoulder pork to make our sausages, as it's the dark, luscious meat from the carcass, with a good fat content which is useful in sausages. Oliver had continued to experiment and perfect his recipe. He had the butcher mince the trim and shoulder meat, and began stocking bulk quantities of dried herbs and spices. He moved up to a commercial-sized sausage-making machine. Once a fortnight, he swabbed down our kitchen surfaces with food-grade cleaner, and set about making his batch for the next market, filling the kitchen and the house with the scent of herbs and pork.

'Your house has a very particular smell to it,' said one of the kids from next door once, on visiting to play with Daisy. She thought for a moment and then continued. 'Oh yes, it's meaty! Your house has got a meaty smell.' Luckily, that smell didn't sink into the furniture on a permanent basis, and we found it to be quite pleasant and fresh.

It took a while to get the ratio of meat, fat, water and breadcrumbs right, and to hit on a texture that ran easily through the machine, and then cooked well. Another differentiator between our sausages and standard ones was the lack of sulphates. People trained in commercial food production, as opposed to those who have taught themselves sausage-making in their own kitchen, usually put sulphates in their sausages. Sulphate is a kind of salt which acts as a preservative. It's in many processed meat products like sausages, ham and salamis. Some people believe sulphates are the source of digestive problems, and avoid foods containing them. Oliver believed they affected the taste of a sausage, and he wanted to make a small-batch product which would be sold fresh at market, without using sulphates.

Since Connor, our chef neighbour at Evandale market, was only too happy to help, we asked him for advice on how to get our sausages to sell better. If we did any better we'd be competing for his customers, but amazingly, he gave his advice freely anyway.

'Get some really nice toppings out front on the stall to get people's taste buds going,' he suggested. We put some effort into researching and thinking about what to serve with a pork sausage. Caramelised onion seemed an obvious choice, and the smell of it cooking in a pan at the stall would get people's mouths watering. Eventually we happened upon the idea of a red cabbage relish to complement the onions. I made a trial batch, steeping and stewing red cabbage, apples and cider vinegar. It complemented the sausages beautifully. It would look good in a Perspex-lidded tray at the front of the stall too, we decided, and would whet the customer's appetite as we piled it on top of their sausages in front of them.

Soon market goers were stopping at our stall and remarking upon how good it smelt. Plenty of punters still walked past with a Dagwood Dog - a deep-fried garden-variety sausage dipped in batter and then fried and posted vertically on a stick. Nobody in our family has ever eaten a Dagwood Dog, and I doubt we ever will. But some people loved them.

We began to suspect that Evandale wasn't the right market for us. Artisan foodstuffs such as we were making sell best at farmers' markets which are dedicated to food only, and where customers are looking to do their food shopping. Evandale was not such a market. Additionally, it attracted what my sister-in-law in London called 'non-PLUs'. The punters at Evandale simply weren't 'People Like Us'. They had different ideas about how much to pay for a sausage, whether the pigs were free range or not. One Sunday we fared particularly badly. Looking for solace, I went for a wander around the bric-a-brac stalls inside the village hall and blew a significant percentage of our profits on a teapot. Something had to change.

Some Like It Hot

Bloody-mindedness and a surfeit of pork made us determined to find a market for our sausages, and we decided to take our stall to some tourism events. The Tasmanian Craft Fair was held in the springtime every year at Deloraine, a mountain town nearby. The stall fee was more than we had paid up front in advance for anything, but seemed reasonable for a four-day event.

Oliver drove over to set up the stall the day before the fair opened.

'God, it's windy there,' he said on his return. We prayed overnight for our marquee, and when I arrived next day, I looked at the other marquees on the site. A lot of them were heavy-duty white canvas, glossy and obviously weather-proof. Clearly these were owned or hired by people who had been before, whose businesses could afford decent housing.

The craft fair took place at eight venues dotted around the town, in community halls, on fields and sports ovals. Venue Five where we were stationed was the biggest. It had a hall filled with crafted goods and their makers, everywhere a surfeit of Huon pine pots and cheese boards, embroidered quilts, everything that could be crocheted, cow hides made into floor rugs. There was also a cavernous sports hall filled with finely-wrought goods: glassware, fine jewellery, garments woven from Merino wool and the like. A huge, white marquee housed stalls selling foodstuffs, products with truffle, hand-made chocolate coated with Tasmanian wattle seeds, Christmas logs and puddings made to age-old recipes, locally-farmed smoked salmon, cheeses and ice cream made from Tasmania's beautiful milk. Corralled in the middle was the main food area for the craft fair, a ring of twenty food stalls in marquees, food trucks and converted caravans, set to feed the punters for four days.

Coffee stalls, we soon learned, always had the longest queues. Wine stalls weren't far behind them. We were positioned happily between one of each, and two stationary lines of people who had time to be affected by the delicious aromas of onions and pork sausages barbecuing slowly and wafting around them.

As we moved around our stall setting up equipment and signage on the first morning, a tall man in a waxed jacket and a cravat floated by every so often. With the practised geniality of someone in management he introduced himself as Angus, the state manager of the wine company at the stall next to ours.

'Have you got enough fridge capacity? We've got a whole cool room here.' He gestured behind him to a mobile cool room on a trailer, which hummed quietly. Boxes of wine could be glimpsed on the shelves just inside the door. 'Feel free to use it,' he offered. This was a different kind of neighbour than we were used to at Evandale.

As the morning wore on, we eyed up the competition. Jeff and Heidi were opposite us, selling the Pulled Pork Wrap they had won prizes for at other food events.

'They'll do well with that,' I said. 'People will have heard about that win.' Oliver harrumphed in a non-committal manner.

Alongside their stall was Seven Sheds Brewery, run by a man called Willie. I'd read about his former career as a beer writer for a major Australian newspaper, which seemed like a dream job if ever there was one. I resolved to go over and chat to him when time allowed.

When the first customer appeared at our stall and ordered a sausage, it took me a moment to gather my thoughts. But nobody else knew this was the first serving of our product at a major event, and if I put dinner on the table every day for four people with different tastes, how hard could it be to serve someone a sausage in a bread roll?

If Evandale hadn't brought us the sales we wanted, it had given us the chance to refine our operations. Instead of cooking our onion on the barbecue where it became greasy and discoloured, we now cooked it in an electric frying pan, caramelising it slowly to a golden-brown colour. We had two frying pans, so while one cooked, the other kept a supply of onion warm and ready for use. As the first few customers came through the stall, I perfected my assembly technique. On a board at my workstation, I cut a wholemeal roll lengthways along the middle and picked it up using my gloved left hand, holding it with a serviette underneath. Going to the barbecue a couple of steps away at the back of the stall, I used tongs to place a sausage in the roll. Stepping sideways to the electric frypans, I put a good dollop of onions on the sausage, before going back to the customer at the front counter. 'Would you like some red cabbage on that?' I asked them, like a pro.

Between us, we agonised over how to assemble our product.

If I slipped away from the stall for a moment, I could return to find Oliver cramming onion into the bottom of a roll and wedging a sausage on top, as if he were filling a hole in a plasterboard wall. I, on the other hand, arranged the caramelised onion artfully on top, contained by the roll and not obscuring the sausage completely. To me, the look of the thing was important: the sausage should nestle comfortably at the bottom of the roll but still be visible at either end. Van Gogh himself could not have spent more time on the artistry of our sausages.

For the first couple of years we sold just sausages. Then it occurred to us that we could stock cold drinks in the chiller cabinet. We promptly stocked up with bottled water and ginger beer, adding to sand helping customers stay hydrated.

Oliver suffered from the heat too, slaving over a hot barbecue at the back of the stall. 'Jeez, I'm going to have to take my shorts off soon, it's so bloody hot in here,' he told me one warm spring day. He'd already taken his t-shirt off and was wearing just his shorts and an apron. We were learning how to promote our business through social media at the time, and I instantly saw an opportunity.

'Take your shorts off and put your apron back on,' I urged him. He was a little hesitant at having his bluff called, but we waited for a quiet moment with no customers about, and he obligingly dropped his shorts and turned back to tend the barbecue. His apron strings hung down the crack of his bum as he continued jiggling the sausages around busily. I took a photograph with my smartphone, and put it on our Facebook page with a caption about temperatures rising at the craft fair.

'That'll make sales go through the roof,' I assured Oliver, as he pulled his shorts up again. Some years later, I met a vineyard owner who had snapped a similar marketing shot of her husband, pruning their vines dressed only in a strategically placed leather tool belt. Evidently we women in agriculture were instinctively redressing the balance of sexism in marketing and centuries of the chauvinist male gaze in art, by objectifying our husbands. It was passably entertaining for a moment, but it did nothing for our sales figures.

Lunchtime was the main game. The Tasmanian Craft Fair is the largest in Australia, attracting eighteen thousand visitors. Peak sausage sales began just before twelve and lasted non-stop until just after two, when it stopped dead.

That first year, we had a queue constantly for around three hours. I walked in never-ending circles inside the stall, literally beating a path between the front counter, the barbecue and my assembly station. The grass became flattened and then muddy until Oliver finally laid the rubber matting down that we were supposed to have laid anyway for a food-safe stall. I became sick of saying 'Would you like red cabbage on that?' and went to bed at night dreaming of sausages.

One day, with the lunchtime rush over, my legs were trembling and my back ached from leaning over the front counter. Going out the back of the stall, I collapsed into a camping chair in the shade and took a long drink of water. I watched Oliver as he hovered over the barbecue, wiping sweat from his brow with his forearm and prepping a few last sausages. I, for one, fervently hoped there would be no more customers.

Suddenly I looked up to find Angus towering over me. 'How was that?' he asked.

'Knackering!'

He laughed. 'Can I interest you in a glass of something, in exchange for a sausage for myself and Leonie?' He had no need to ask me twice. For the last hour of service I had kept myself going with the promise of what I was going to eat and drink from the surrounding stalls. I heaved myself out of my chair and put together two top-notch gourmet pork-sausages-in-a-roll. And so began a beautiful arrangement which lasted for years, until Angus and Leonie grew tired of pork sausages, and I felt like a change from Pinot Gris.

The craft fair was run by volunteers with the local Rotary Club, and was run with military-style efficiency and excellent communications with stallholders. As a consequence, it was phenomenally successful. At Venue Five, a gentleman called Rodney looked after us. Well into his eighties, Rodney could be seen throughout the day tucking chairs in at tables under the lunch marquee, clearing up lunch detritus, wiping surfaces down and generally keeping the place tidy, always with the same genial manner. Once or twice a day he appeared at the side of our stall to ask how it was going. This wasn't just passing the time of day, but was genuine enquiry. The Rotarians wanted their food stalls to do well, as they knew that keeping customers well-fed was central to the success of the event.

Music added to the festival atmosphere and could make or break the mood. The music marquee was directly opposite ours and right next door to Seven Sheds Ale. A group of young and handsomely-dishevelled young men did feel-good cover versions, the kind to which you know all the words and sing along to without thinking. Oliver and I threw some moves behind the counter, and it made the lunchtime rush seem less onerous.

The opposite effect was also possible. 'Sax Man', as we came to know him, appeared mid-morning on day two, and played until mid-afternoon. He played the saxophone, and played it ably, but repetitively. Occasionally he went for a break and left a recording of himself playing on repeat. Initially we enjoyed the haunting sound, deftly woven around a backing track. But when he finally wrapped up, the stallholders of Venue Five sighed with relief.

Maree, a senior Rotarian who was younger and more feisty than Rod, with more opinions about how things were running, dropped in at the stall.

'Will the saxophone man be playing again tomorrow?' I asked, tentatively.

'If you'd like him to,' answered Maree. Perhaps I blanched visibly, because she added 'What do you think, would you like him to come back?'

At this, Oliver could contain himself no longer. He blurted out his view on the recording being left to play interminably. 'One track sounds exactly like the next when you've been listening to it for hours on end!'

'You're not the first to say so,' replied Maree, stiffening. 'He's not supposed to do that. I'll have a word about him.' The Sax Man didn't reappear after that. We were sorry to have thwarted his festival appearances, but also relieved. We had nothing against the saxophone, and would spend years driving Daisy to rehearsals every Sunday for band rehearsals with her clarinet. But any music can grate on the nerves with over-exposure, and I feared Oliver was about to stuff a pack of sausages up the saxophone if he heard much more of it.

On day four, we got an old-timer singing golden oldies. *Country Road, Take Me Home* was slightly easier on the nerves, but it was a close call.

For the first three to four years, Daisy and Kit were too young to help on the stall, and also to leave at home. We had to depend on the kindness of friends and farm them out for four days in a row. As November approached, I dreaded having to phone people and ask them to take my kids for a long weekend. I dropped them off at the crack of dawn and was gone the whole day. By way of thanks, I did the rounds of the gourmet food marquee, and took food parcels of truffled chocolates and marinated Persian feta to our child minders, without whom we couldn't have managed.

Each year I found a moment to walk around the main hall where the jewellery stalls were: silversmiths making chunky, unusual rings, goldsmiths making finely wrought items like earrings beautifully crafted in silver, fashioned after little Australian gumnuts.

'There's some gorgeous jewellery in there,' I remarked on returning to our stall.

'Put it on your Christmas list!' Oliver said. Seeing an opportunity, I went back to the hall with my smart-phone, and photographed the items I liked and the stall number they were on. Then I texted those photos to Oliver. This worked brilliantly for us both. I got a piece of jewellery for Christmas that I actually liked, instead of a piece Oliver had chosen for some other woman he was having a relationship with in his imagination. And Oliver got a reprieve from the torture of Christmas gifting.

As a couple, we came to enjoy the craft fair as a moment of

reconnection. There was always a sweet spot as the lunchtime rush fell away, and we could hang out side by side behind the counter, people-watching and gossiping. Working hard in small businesses of our own and raising a family at the same time for years, Oliver and I often found we didn't have much time for each other. Standing shoulder to shoulder behind the counter, I rediscovered his mischievous sense of humour and sweet nature. For a few years, it was the closest we came to a hot date.

To Market

Despite being utterly without talent as a gardener, I had booked myself into a workshop on native plant propagation.

In a sunny corner beside a makeshift poly-tunnel, around a half-dozen people gathered around a collection of rustic tables, made from the giant timber spools used for wiring by utility companies. After introductions, a woman called Liz demonstrated the art of pressing seeds from Old Man's Beard, a native climber, into small pots made of toilet roll holders. It was a low footprint kind of workshop. Opposite me in the loose circle and struggling gamely to press the delicate seeds into the soil, was a man called Oscar.

He had introduced himself as a landscape designer with a hobby farm near Patterdale, but he was put together more like a Hollywood film star from the forties: impossibly tall, with a handsome, open face and elegant bearing. My mind wandering in the heat of the day, I was picturing Oscar in a white tuxedo, lighting cigarettes two at a time, one for him and one for me, like Paul Henreid did for Bette Davis in *Now Voyager*. I hadn't smoked for years, and Oscar wore elastic-sided boots and a soiled t-shirt, but I was undeterred. Suddenly my reverie was rudely interrupted when he actually spoke to me.

'Do you do anything with the delicious pork meat you get from your Saddleback pigs?' he asked, his voice warm and gravelly.

'We certainly do,' I replied, dragging myself back to the matter of pigs yet again. I explained that my husband made the pork into sausages, and we sold our product at Evandale market. 'We're getting pretty fed up of going there, though,' I added as an afterthought. 'It's evidently not the right market for the product.'

'You need a proper producers' market,' Oscar said, after listening patiently.

'We do indeed. Do you know of any apart from the big one in Launceston?' I asked.

'As it happens, I'm about to start one in Patterdale,' he replied. He went on to explain that his market would not be strictly food-only, and that there would be artisan goods there as well. But the focus would be on handmade, quality products, with producers present on their stalls to talk to customers. It sounded like a more targeted approach than Evandale, and more likely to attract the customers we were interested in.

'Do you need a website?' I asked. Having built and maintained the website for Oliver's cabinet-making business and a new one for the farm, I was wondering if this was a service I could offer to local small businesses. I could do it from home, take on as much work as suited me, and do it while the kids were at school and childcare.

Oscar's face broke into a grin. 'The website was my next big challenge! If you can help with that, we're definitely in business!'

It was a match made in heaven. I began building a website for Patterdale Market and introduced Oliver to Oscar, who seemed like a manager with his stallholders' best interests at heart.

Patterdale Producers' Market was launched as a fortnightly event. We threw ourselves into it, believing we could help build it from the ground up. Going along that first weekend, we found ourselves in a car-park outside the front of the town's pub. This had been purchased by an enterprising vineyard owner and her husband. Slowly, they were transforming it from a rather characterless pub with a drive-through bottle-shop, into something more ambitious - a providore selling produce like jams, honey and wines from the region, and a cafe with pies and salads made by the in-house chef.

Outside, there was an atmosphere of optimism amongst the new stallholders, who were makers of everything from gourmet dog biscuits to polished concrete furniture; jewellers and knitters. At the front of the car park there were a couple of Shetland ponies and their owner. Rides cost a couple of dollars, and patting was free.

Every fortnight, Oliver now packed the same paraphernalia into the ute, but headed off in a different direction at the crack of dawn on Sunday. As well as the collapsible marquee, the trestle tables, camping chairs, chiller unit, barbecue and tools for cooking, there were now table cloths and signs telling people what we were selling, and a photograph album with pictures of our pigs, including Rosie and Bella. It seemed strange to show people photographs of the pigs and then invite them to buy products made from them, but this was the story of our farm: a small, family-run, free range operation, raising rare breed pigs and producing exceptionally flavoursome pork products. This, we would come to learn, was our all-important 'brand story', which we were encouraged to tell by small business mentors and tourism authorities. We dutifully wove together an idyllic story we believed in wholeheartedly, ignoring the fact that it didn't pay very much.

On a market morning, Oliver left before anyone else was awake, and headed off to set up the stall. I crossed the valley from west to east a couple of hours later, bringing the kids. It takes time to pack a car with two young children and the vital soft toy companions of the day, food and drink to sustain them, and changes of clothing in case of spillages.

I was bowled over by the beauty of the landscape as we drove across from west to east across the Tamar and couldn't wait to see it in all its seasons: still and bleak in winter, lush and green in springtime. From the end of our road in Flowery Gully, we could just see Mount Arthur, the mountain which rose behind Patterdale. It was a quiet, blue presence with slopes rising up to the clouds, and provided a landmark for us to aim at on those Sundays.

Determined to make a success of things for his stallholders and for the town of Patterdale too, Oscar attempted to keep it interesting with a series of initiatives. One Sunday, he invited Matthew Evans, host of television program *The Gourmet Farmer*, to carry out a cookery demonstration. Matthew was a former food critic, and had become the Tasmanian equivalent of Hugh Fearnley-Whittingstall, making a popular television series about his move to Tasmania and his quest for food he had produced himself, or which was produced by someone known to him.

The weather could not have been worse on the day, bucketing down from dawn to dusk. This is the kind of market day when stallholders wake with heavy hearts, and rise from their beds wondering why they're bothering. Customers are thin on the ground on such a day, unless you're at a well-established market with hardened locals who want their weekly market purchases come what may.

To his everlasting credit, Evans didn't miss a beat. Under the shelter of a sodden marquee, he assembled a Cottage Pie using his mum's recipe, and passed around small serves in takeaway dishes for everybody to try. Those of us huddling under the marquee stood transfixed by savoury, mustardy aromas and Matthew's calm demeanour. When the dishes of pie came around, it was warming and peppery, topped by creamy mash.

After the demonstration, Matthew visited the stalls, making a point of meeting every stallholder. His wife Sadie did the same and stopped for a chat about pigs, leafing through our photograph album, and introducing their small son. Only two or three years old, he was getting restless. She tried to distract him with the pictures of our pigs and a carrot to chew on, but he grizzled with discontent.

'He's probably seen it all before,' I said, nodding at the photograph album.

'Yes, and I'm afraid the novelty has worn off,' she sighed, buying a pack of sausages for dinner, and moving on to the next stall. I knew exactly how she felt.

Running a market is a thankless task. With a regular bric-a-brac market already established in Patterdale, the town's population just didn't have an appetite for ours. Oscar and his wife Pauline continued to promote it to people in Launceston, fifteen minutes away by car. But there was little reason for the population there to visit, with a highly successful farmers' market of their own, Harvest, in full swing every Saturday. We had applied for a stall there, but had been told they had too many selling pork already.

As we toiled over to the eastern valley every fortnight, the appeal of the drive faded. Daisy and Kit grew bored. We never knew how well we would do, or whether we could justify driving that distance in two vehicles. At the end of the day, the takings in our plastic box were never enough to warrant doing it for a living.

What's more, the owners of the Patterdale Pub, from whose car park we operated, had employed a new manager for their shop and cafe. This man was unhappy with our selling hot food right outside his door, since it was taking trade from his cafe. Oscar was apologetic when he came to break the news.

'The purpose of the market is really for you to sell produce, rather than cooked food,' he said. It hadn't occurred to us that we were taking trade from someone else; we were simply trying to make the trip worthwhile and make sales. Offering ready-to-eat food had become an important part of our stall's business.

Sadly, that put the last nail in the coffin. There was little point in our being there if we weren't permitted to sell hot food, and the demand for premium pork produce simply wasn't there.

When another farmers' market opened in Deloraine, forty-five minutes away in the opposite direction from Patterdale, Oliver began alternating between the two, in the hope of drawing enough of an income to justify giving up the cabinet-making jobs he still took on. Those had become thin on the ground, as the global financial crisis had bitten hard, and flat-packed kitchens from China had replaced local cabinet-makers and bespoke kitchens. But the farm did not yet earn enough for Oliver to give that business up.

Farming the pigs, manufacturing sausages as well as building people's kitchens was running him ragged. Years later, when we were in the thick of the farm business, it astonished us how some people would ask whether Oliver was 'still doing a bit of cabinet-making', as if it was a gentleman's hobby he kept up on the side. The life of a small business owner and operator is far more complicated, all-consuming and exhausting, than working a regular job for an employer.

With Oliver doing two markets, me running a writing business, and squeezing family life in between, life was a roller-coaster ride. Unless we found a market that put us in direct contact with the right customer base, we knew we may as well give up on the farm business altogether.

Harvest Launceston had been launched a couple of years earlier, when two visionary women had presented to Launceston City Council the idea of a proper, food-only farmers' market in the city-centre. With the Council's support, they brought together a committee made up of producers and community-minded individuals. In their research, they had discovered the Australian Farmers' Market Association's Code of Practice, the recipe for a successful market, and stuck to it like glue. This dictated that the market sell food and nothing else. That food was to be grown or made by local producers. The farmer or producer was to be available on their stall to talk to customers. The code recommended that there be a vegetable stall with a wide variety of produce, which might not be local or seasonal, but which would allow customers to do much of their weekly fresh food shopping, and encourage them to come. Value-added products such as jams or chutneys could be sold if they were made by the producer from local produce. And there was to be careful control over how many vendors of similar foods had stalls.

We had been impressed by the crowds of appreciative customers surrounding the stalls when we visited, and the palpable buzz about the market. Marquees lined the site, a Council car park in the centre of town, and buskers provided the soundtrack. The atmosphere was colourful, fragrant and festive. Bringing new life to the outskirts of Launceston's shopping centre, it proved an attraction for visitors and residents alike, and won the people's choice award from a national magazine in its third year.

We had applied for a stall at Harvest twice, without success. There was only one point in the calendar when applications were accepted, so failure meant exclusion for another year. In our second application we had applied to do a stall once monthly, or perhaps alternating with another supplier. Oliver didn't want to do a weekly market as that would really put the pressure on stock numbers, and him. A monthly or fortnightly stall seemed more achievable, involving a less strenuous production cycle.

There was another thriving farmers' market in Hobart, but we found it hard to countenance the idea of driving three hours each way to set up a stall there, especially with two young children at home. We wanted to keep some of our weekends free to spend as a family, and that didn't seem like too much to ask.

The feedback we'd received from the Harvest committee was that their research showed people just didn't eat that much pork, not enough to warrant allowing another pork stall. In the market's first year, we had counted four stalls selling pork, and now there were two. We didn't know whether two had failed due to a lack of demand, or whether the market could actually support a third stall. Knowing the Code of Practice advocated careful management of parallel product stalls, we had no option but to trust the committee in their assessment of demand. Every producer needed the chance to succeed. We grumbled about the decision, but had to accept it.

One day while the children were at school, Oliver and I had a tense conversation over the dining room table. It began as the weekly meeting when we planned out our time, but soon morphed into a wider discussion about what we were doing with our lives. I felt increasingly fraught, trying to help Oliver with the farm while maintaining my own small business. On a good day, both the kids made it to school. If one was ill or it was school holidays, I got less done. The demands of Patterdale and Deloraine markets kept Oliver busy. I fitted in the food shopping, cooking and laundry and a passing attempt at housework.

Oliver and I sat across the table from one another and sank into a desperate brainstorming session about how to make our farm business work. It wasn't going well; we were running out of ideas and any sense of ambition for what we'd begun.

'Maybe we should just give it all away,' Oliver said suddenly, his voice cracked with emotion. 'Let's just get rid of the pigs and find something else to do.' He stared at me across the table with a slightly manic expression. I sat for a moment, gazing over his shoulder to the paddocks beyond. In the bush block, I could just see a couple of pigs snuffling around contentedly, nose down in the sunshine. Hot tears filled my eyes as I realised that bizarre and unexpected though it was, I had come to love having pigs on our farm. They were such endearing creatures, good-natured and adept at keeping life simple. I thought about how much work we had put into this endeavour, and how proud of it we were, how much I enjoyed working our stall and talking to our customers. It was a business with noble intent, to keep livestock well and bring a great product to market.

'I don't want to give it all away,' I blurted out, astonished to find my bottom lip trembling. I thought of all the work we'd done, the weekends we'd given up, our children putting up with being dragged to markets instead of having a normal day out with their parents. And I thought of the pigs. Unexpectedly, I had come to appreciate them as happy, adaptable creatures who seemed to make the best of every day. 'I love having the pigs,' I said. 'We've come this far, and I want it to work.'

'So do I,' Oliver said. He stared at me, clearly taken aback to find me so adamant. It had to be said, the fact that I wasn't the one feeding them, building their sheds and taking them to slaughter probably had some bearing on things.

We couldn't help bringing to mind a conversation we'd had at the Tasmanian Craft Fair, with a sheep farmer who was selling his rare breed lamb kebabs from a stall. He told us in no uncertain terms that we should apply again for Harvest market.

'It's a mainstay of my business,' he told Oliver, as they stood in the lee of the gourmet food tent. 'I know exactly how many beasts I can take to slaughter, and I can depend on selling the meat that Saturday.'

Scraping together the last of our mettle, we decided to apply one last time. It was the only market worth having a presence at, and it seemed the only way our business would survive. If we didn't have an outlet serving the right customers for our product, we were stuffed.

Our previous applications to Harvest had been correct in every detail but had not really made an argument from the heart. It seemed imperative to make this one stick.

'Let's tell it like it is,' I suggested. 'We've got nothing to lose.'

We wrote a letter to accompany our third application, making points we hadn't made before: that we were more local to the market than other pork-producing stallholders, and that we were a family and dependent on finding a place at markets closer to home. In the world of commercial retailing, this would be neither here nor there. However, according to the Farmers' Market Association's Code of Practice, those were two reasons to support us. We never heard whether this letter had been considered or even read. But our application was successful. This time, they let us in.

Big Time

Harvest Launceston was a proper farmers' market and we were nervous new stallholders. It was obvious that many of the customers were regulars. When we'd been there as visitors, we'd seen them arrive with shopping bags on their arms, making a beeline for stalls they were in the habit of calling at, perhaps weekly. For our business to survive, we needed to capture our own cohort of customers like that. If we didn't do it at Harvest, we wouldn't do it anywhere.

On the Friday before our very first market, we spent all day discussing it and agonising over the details of the stall. Oliver meticulously packed the trailer with our marquee, folding trestle tables, and prepared the Eskies in which he would transport and store the meat, cooling them in advance with freezer blocks. I ducked over to the workshop to check on him from time to time, and prepped lunch-boxes and snacks for the kids, who would now spend alternate Saturdays at another market. Then we set our alarm clocks for early.

Market stall at Harvest Launceston

The Australian guidelines for running a successful farmers' market had been written in the late nineties by Jane Adams, a food writer and marketing consultant. Winning a scholarship to study farmers' markets in the USA, she came back an enthusiast, and banded together everything she had learned in her scholarship report. This formed the basis of the guidelines that markets across Australia went on to use, with universal success. For the next twenty years and more, Jane Adams became a one-woman force for good, heading up the Australian Farmers' Market Association. I once spoke to her on the phone, shortly after we moved to Tasmania and I had considered trying to start a small farmers' market in Exeter, the busy town at the heart of our valley. She was deeply knowledgeable and terrifying in equal parts, no doubt frustrated by my sketchy knowledge and scant research.

Harvest had stuck religiously to Adams' recommendations, and it worked.

Many of the stalls were run by families like us living on rural properties, selling goods with a gourmet element: olive oil grown in their orchard and pressed locally; granola made to an old recipe in the family kitchen; salmon grown in ponds fed by mountain streams. There was a family selling milk from their herd of Jersey cows in traditional bottles, which customers could return to be re-used. They made some of their milk into cheeses produced in traditional European style, in huge wheels which sat on the counter of their stall. I once bought a thin slice of their Cheddar, waxy yellow and dotted with cumin seeds. I never dared reveal to Oliver how much I paid, but it was delicious, with a smooth mouth-feel and creamy flavour, and piquant bursts from the cumin.

With a magic mix of gourmet products, delicious ready-to-eat foods, seasonal vegetables bursting with life and freshness from nearby paddocks, and meats from carefully-reared livestock, the market was bustling. There was fresh, single origin coffee readily available and a seating area with shade, benches and tables, buskers and simple kids' games like quoits, and a Salsa marquee where anyone could have a go at dipping and twirling. All this made the market a social event as well as a shopping destination, somewhere to hang out with other people on a Saturday morning.

We needed electricity for our stall, which meant we'd be just off the centre, in a horse-shoe shaped area. It had the feel of an exclusive enclave. Beside us was Ritual Coffee, whose machines ran non-stop through the morning. A small army of genial operators wrote orders on the side of paper cups at one side of the machine, and a topnotch brew was delivered by a barista on the other. They also sold single-origin coffee beans and blends from great white tins. The coffee grinder was positioned right next to us and the aromas became the signature scent of our market days. If Oliver or I fronted up as a customer, the owner would wordlessly knock a dollar off the price of our coffee. It was a small gesture, perhaps acknowledging the arduous nature of working a market stall, and one we appreciated.

On the other side of us was a woman I had once known as a website designer, who had given up sitting in front of a computer in order to make butter instead. This was not just any old butter; it was cultured butter, made from cream which had been fermented with natural enzymes and Tasmanian sea salt. In the early days of her business, the owner Olivia was operating from a tiny commercial kitchen in the basement of her home, churning, finishing and packing it by hand in handsome gold packaging.

I bought our butter from the supermarket in the biggest packs I could get my hands on, and was new to the idea of cultured products and the cachet they have over their non-fermented cousins. One morning, I sampled Olivia's butter at her stall, where she was spreading it on slices of sourdough baguette for people to try.

'That's nice. How much is it?' I asked.

'Nine dollars for a two hundred gram pack,' she replied without batting an eyelid, prompting me to spray crumbs of sourdough down the front of my apron. In my household, both children would eat cubes of butter cut straight from the pack, and we could easily finish a quarter kilo pack in two days. I estimated my butter bill would be close to fifty dollars a month if we bought this one. Clearly this was a top shelf butter best reserved for special occasions and for Oliver and myself alone, or small households where portions were served in tinier and more exquisite portions than in mine.

Its value was later elevated when the French chef Allain Passard, holder of three Michelin stars, visited the market, and proclaimed it the 'best butter in Australia'. Olivia and he had their photograph taken at the front of her stall, their arms wrapped around each other as if they'd known each other for years and spent most Saturday mornings gabbing over sourdough and a coffee. They stood beaming into the camera, he in his signature scarf flung in Frenchman-like fashion over his shoulder, she in her glossy black glasses and apron.

'I didn't really know who he was,' she admitted afterwards.

The Honey Tasmania stall, in the sunny corner opposite ours, was quite the honey-pot for the bee-keeping fraternity of Tasmania, who all seemed to know each other and use it as a hang-out. The company was owned by Canadians Rebecca and Tristan, and the stall was run by Tristan with a casual élan. His warm Canadian vowels would have been equally at home in a snowy mountain resort as a Tasmanian market in a car park. More often than not, he could be seen chatting at the marquee beside his stall, set up with tables and chairs by the market management, for people in need of a shady sit-down. That was where the honey people hung out, and if they were there, so was Tristan. If someone showed up at his counter, he'd saunter over and serve them in unhurried fashion.

Chatting to him one morning, I noticed a man standing at his counter a few feet away, holding a pot of honey.

'I shouldn't hold you up from your customers. Go ahead and serve this gentleman,' I said, gesturing.

Tristan glanced over at the gentleman, who was well within

earshot. 'Naaah, he's a regular, he'll wait,' he said, and guffawed loudly. The customer beamed back at him. It was a relaxed approach but Tristan's honey and charisma won his customers over.

Managing the market was the ebullient, pragmatic and relentlessly cheerful Chrissie. Originally from the north of England, Chrissie ran workshops for people in the wine trade, specialising in sparkling wines. She was in the right place, as Tasmania's sparkling is now widely accepted as rivalling that of the Champagne region. She managed the market alongside this endeavour and brought considerable sparkle with her. The problem of parking while unloading at the start of the market, and packing up and loading a vehicle at the end of it when everyone wanted to get away as quickly as possible, she took seriously. Issuing everyone with a roster which she'd worked out, she supervised proceedings, and made sure everyone stuck to their fifteen-minute slot, with their vehicle out of the way and off-site in good time.

One particular morning, Oliver had exhorted me to be there on time for the market opening. 'It's when all the regular customers come; I need you there to make sure we get that trade,' he said.

When I turned up, I found Kit alone on the stall, which was only half-ready.

'Where's Daddy?' I said.

'Over there!' He pointed with a piece of the chalk we used to write our goods up on the front of the counter. I looked at the honey stall, and saw Oliver sitting under the marquee, coffee and croissant in hand, engaged in banter with Tristan about how much debt a small food business could accrue before it imploded.

The opening of trade at eight-thirty was heralded by an old-fashioned brass school bell, rung by a volunteer doing a circuit of the market. Well before this happened, customers would be queuing at Sandy's Sourdough. The rest of us had nothing but envy for the roaring trade he did, selling bread and a selection of sumptuous pastries to half of Launceston. His loaves were dark on the outside and off-white inside, nutty in flavour and weighing twice as much as what passes for bread in a supermarket. They were also vastly more expensive than your supermarket loaf, but Sandy was an artisan baker and his bread was the real deal.

A former policeman from New South Wales, he had packed in the force to do something that involved fewer life-threatening situations. He hired an industrial kitchen and baked solidly through Friday night and Saturday morning, the dough having been started days before with a 'mother' from the previous batch. This is the traditional means of making sourdough, originally in Egypt and then spreading north to ancient Greece and on to the Romans and through mainland Europe.

The starter is mixed with the next round of flour and water for the new batch of loaves. It's a living thing containing yeast which can live and regenerate for years, accruing flavour. Some bakers become strangely attached to their starter cultures. I'd heard of an Australian baker moving to England and taking his with him, transporting it in a sock and guarding it jealously from sniffer dogs at airports.

Yeast starters are sensitive to the air around them, which carries pathogens and natural yeasts too. These differ between regions, and add to the mix and the flavours of the final baked or brewed product. The same starter can throw a different loaf in different locations, and good bakers are sensitive to this.

Sandy kept his starter culture in a bucket in his hired kitchen. One morning, he arrived at work ready to make dough for the coming week's bread, only to find the cleaner had thrown it away and washed up the bucket. From then on, he placed the bucket behind a barricade of hazard tape, with 'Do Not Touch!' signs all over it.

After getting to the front of Sandy's queue, it was impossible not to succumb to the lure of his custard doughnuts. Kit was a regular at Sandy's stall, clutching a ten dollar note and returning with a chocolate croissant and a huge smile. It seemed like a crime to drink a coffee without one of Sandy's chocolate sourdough croissants when the two were sold in such close proximity to each other. Sandy's croissants, along with menopause, were responsible for the permanent loss of my waistline.

While I packed snacks and food from home for Daisy and Kit, we allowed them food from stalls but had to monitor the number of pastries they put away, lest they eat their way through the profits. As they grew older, I gave them each twenty dollars and charged them with feeding themselves sensibly, a healthy savoury option, and then a treat. I asked for change, but sadly it was rarely given.

We didn't purchase Sandy's bread often, because Oliver had begun making white loaves and rolls for us at home, spurred on by frugality and the prevalence of bread-making machines in the second-hand goods shops he frequented. Occasionally we swapped a packet of sausages for a loaf or two of sourdough at the end of a market. This worked out well as we arrived home ravenous. Sawing into a sourdough loaf one afternoon, I marvelled at the rich honeycomb of air pockets and light, nutty flavour. Oliver caught me lathering a toasted piece with butter.

'Is that Sandy's sourdough? How does it compare with my bread?'

'That's a loaded question if ever there was one!' I protested. Perhaps I might have dribbled a little butter. Oliver made a grab for the loaf and carved another slice.

'Bloody hell, look at the holes in that!'

I looked. There were indeed gaping holes where the lightness of Sandy's yeast mix and the strong rise his loaves achieved in the oven resulted in an air pocket the size of a dollar coin.

'How much did you pay for this?' Oliver asked.

'Eight bucks.'

He prodded the slice with the bread knife. 'Well that's two bucks' worth of oxygen right there!'

When Sandy's heaving crowd of regulars had been served and his wooden shelves were empty save for a dusting of flour, he was often to be found hanging sleepily from the cross-struts of his market stall, his great bearded head propped up on his arms, trying to stay awake after a hard night's baking.

Competing with Sandy for the length of his queue was the George Town Seafood stall, run by Chris and supplied by his boat, the last family-owned vessel to fish off the coast of Tasmania. Chris had an effusive way with customers, particularly women. Each time I reached the head of his queue, eager for squid tubes and whatever else looked good, Chris would catch my eye.

'There she is,' he would bellow in his deep baritone, as if he'd been waiting for me to turn up all morning. This was a man dressed in a white lab coat and matching white wellingtons, and often a paper shower cap on his head, but his greeting was so effusive, I often felt myself blush and giggle. I'd ask him questions about the fish and take his recommendations.

'Do you want some ice for that?' he usually asked, and I'd marvel at how considerate he was. He'd then hand me over to the teenager who worked his till like a pro. I'd pay up with the satisfaction of a customer who's been singled out for extra-special flirting. Then I'd hear him greeting the customer behind me. 'There she is!' And I'd know I could never depend on Chris's affections being mine alone.

Daisy and Kit were still far too young to stay at home while we were at Harvest, so they had no choice but to come along with us. Soon they got to know two girls of around the same age from the salmon stall. Their father Ben and his family grew the fish in freshwater ponds fed by mountain streams. The four of them formed a gang, and spent the market hours hanging out and stealing disposable gloves from our stall to fill them with water.

I encouraged Oliver to wear a decent shirt to the market, underneath a clean apron. I noticed that when left to his own devices, he could be manning the stall in one of his nondescript fleeces. I made him switch to a woollen jumper in winter and a collared shirt in the warmer months. Oliver added hats and sunglasses and looked presentable. But he never went as far as Ben, sartorially speaking.

Sales in Wurst go up

Ben's family were German. After a trip back to Europe, he occasionally turned up at the market wearing full national costume: Lederhosen, knee-length socks, frilly white shirt and a cocked hat. Not only did he wear it well, he grew the appropriate moustache. It was an effective way of attracting people to his stall, where Ben would greet them deadpan, as if dressed in ordinary clothes. He looked so impressive that I made him visit our stall and photographed him clutching packs of our sausages. Then I got someone else to take the photographs so I could appear in them, with Ben clutching our sausages and kneeling at my feet. Finally it was Ben's idea to dispense with the sausages and hoist me into mid-air on one arm instead.

Shortly after we joined Harvest, it was the market's tenth

anniversary. There was a frisson of excitement rippling through the place, with television cameras and journalists setting up, and some of Tasmania's big names in food walking around. We had already seen Tasmania's famous purveyor of raw and artisan cheeses, a long-time member of the Harvest committee.

'Who's that woman in the stripy top and the black glasses?' I asked Chrissie, of a woman I saw regularly at the market, who always appeared chatting knowledgeably to stallholders as if she belonged in the place. A look of patient indulgence passed over Chrissie's face, and she leaned towards me over the counter.

'That's Kim. She started the market, with Jenny and Mary,' she said. And with that, she strode off on her troubleshooting rounds, her distinctive red Harvest apron flapping around her legs.

I had read about Kim in the newspapers but had never put a face to the name. Originally from Canada, she had married a Tasmanian and come to the island for love. There she promptly helped establish the wine industry and with husband Rod established one of the town's top restaurants, Stillwater. Meeting her properly a few years later to interview her for a magazine, she'd tell me how she sold his car to buy 'the second proper coffee machine in Launceston town'.

I caught up with her at the vegetable stall that morning, as she emerged from the marquee with a huge canvas bag packed with fresh leeks, parsnips and greens. There wasn't much time, as the market was busy and so was our stall, but I wanted to congratulate her on the anniversary, and tell her what Harvest meant to us.

'This market stabilized our business,' I said after introductions. 'We were about to close down the farm, if we hadn't got in.'

Kim's expression softened immediately. It was the story of many small agri-businesses at the market.

'We never knew this would be an economic stimulator,' she said. 'We just wanted a great market! It's so fabulous to hear your story.' Her lusty voice was full of Canadian warmth, good living and generosity. I went back to my stall knowing I'd met one of those people who adds richness to the lives of everyone around them.

There were many stories like ours at Harvest, which put many businesses in touch with a regular, viable outlet with the right sort of customers for their product: the nursery with herbs in huge pots that was able to sell direct to customers instead of through a profit-driven chain-store; the ice cream van that visited in the summer months; the local grass-fed beef farm. We moaned about being there in winter when the cold crept up our legs from the concrete and numbed us, but when the sun was out and it was bustling, there was no better place to be on a Saturday morning, whatever the season, than Harvest.

Events

Buoyed by the success of our stall at the Tasmanian Craft Fair, we added other events to our calendar where we could sell hot food to hungry punters. Gradually, November assumed the same exhausting shape every year.

On the first weekend we set up at the Tasmanian Craft Fair for four days. On the second weekend we went to Gardenfest at Entally House, a historic estate, where people selling plants and gardening wares set up on the decorative lawns in front of the house, and food stalls set up in the stable courtyard. The third weekend saw us at a Festival of Roses at Woolmers, another historic estate, an exhausting one-day event attended by the gardening public. And in later years we joined Farmgate Festival on the last weekend, opening our own farm up to visitors for the day. For this we conducted farm tours and set up the stall outside the house to sell people their lunch. We consoled ourselves with the knowledge that we didn't have to go anywhere for that last weekend. At the beginning of each December, I had a brief nervous collapse, before beginning the end-of-year events at the children's schools, and realising I hadn't done anything about Christmas.

There is no escaping the fact that the settling of Tasmania by

Europeans was a disgraceful time which still haunts the island, with Aboriginal tribes driven from their land and murdered wholesale. This came to mind every year as a counterpoint to the enjoyment we derived from the old historic estates which remain.

Despite their place in Tasmania's dark past, those historic estates of the north are undeniably beautiful. The house at Entally Estate is elegant, built to the old style: pointy roof gables and wide verandas, with oak floorboards and big, cold rooms inside. As the Gardenfest festival was in springtime, the formal walled gardens were filled with spectacular, fragrant blossoms, spires of lupins rising above bushy roses and peonies, jostling for position inside their low box-hedge squares.

Our friends from the 41 Degrees South salmon farm were also there, selling their lake-grown salmon and dried herb mixes. Our kids spent the weekend together, scampering around the gardens, poring over the tadpoles and peeking over the two-hundred-year-old walls at passers-by. Knowing they were entertaining themselves in the safe and beautiful confines of the gardens added to the sense of bucolic bliss.

The Festival of Roses at nearby Woolmers was less predictable. Stalls selling plants and bulbs and gardening accessories filled the grounds, and the magnificent rose garden was at its height, drawing thousands of visitors. Despite the crowd numbers, the first year we attended, only our stall and one other, selling paella, were there to provide food. The queues were terrifying. We cooked and served as quickly as possible so as not to keep people waiting, and thankfully the pleasure of being outdoors on a glorious day in sumptuous gardens put them in a good a mood. Going round in circles at our stall, I felt like a mouse in a wheel. After a couple of hours my brain was so befuddled that I could take someone's order and have forgotten it by the time I got to the assembly table a few steps away. One man felt so sorry for me he went to the stall next door and bought me a coffee.

At the end of service, dazed, a little hysterical and famished, nothing could have possessed me to eat a sausage for my own lunch. So I went to the paella stall to see if they had anything left to eat. It was run by a man called Edrick, his wife Clare and their sons. A classical guitarist from New Zealand, Edrick had discovered paella when studying music in Spain, and had moved his family of six across the world and back in pursuit of perfection. We ate a lot of their prize-winning paella over the years.

'We've only got the scrapings left from the bottom of the pan,' said Clare that day, teetering behind her own stall in exhaustion. 'But it's the bit that Spaniards always want, as it's got the most flavour,' she added.

'I'll have that,' I said, thankful for anything. Clare served me the remaining half a bowl's worth of paella she had left, and refused to charge me for it. The rice was crisp and browned from the bottom of the gigantic flat paella pan and there were morsels of tender salmon and a couple of prawns mixed through it, all coloured and flavoured by local saffron. I wolfed it down right there at the front of their stall, as they staggered around their marquee making futile attempts at clearing up, too bone-tired to accomplish much. We all agreed that a few more food stalls wouldn't go amiss in future years.

When our second year at the Festival of Roses rolled around, Edrick and his family were there again with their paella, and a handful more stalls. Collectively, we fed the crowds without working ourselves into the ground and all had a profitable day.

A year or two after that, the organisers went gangbusters and accepted bookings by every stall-holder and food van that applied. Consequently the place was overrun and there was too much choice for any of us to do well. Becoming hardened food vendors, we took a dim view of this veering from one extreme to the other by the festival committee.

Given light showers or wind, festival goers often still attend an event but perhaps without staying so long. When the weather goes to extremes, everything changes. One particular year, there was torrential rain and wind on the Festival of Roses weekend. Since Woolmers depended on it to raise the cash to maintain the historic estate, they went ahead with the day despite the weather. We had prepared for it by sending pigs to slaughter and, in Oliver's case, making sausages and relish and ordering hundreds of rolls from a local bakery, so we went ahead too. We were unable to persuade Daisy to come with us, but Kit put his waterproofs on and came along.

With the wind whipping across the estate, Oliver had positioned our stall in the lee of the old weatherboard cider house. From there, we had a view of the paddock where visitors parked, and estimated that perhaps sixty vehicles were there at the height of the day. We sold a handful of sausages. The celebrity chef who was cooking under the eaves of the Woolmers homestead, and the television presenter who was interviewing him, did so in front of a handful of onlookers huddled under umbrellas. Rain swept across the river plains beyond the estate, pushing up over the lawns and gardens, saturating us all.

With no customers to serve, Oliver headed off for a look around, and returned in a surprisingly buoyant mood. 'That chef's using my bacon!' he said. 'Reckons he buys it every week from the Devonport Hill Street Grocer.'

It was a welcome endorsement of our product. Back on the stall, however, things were less jovial. Kit was entertaining himself by feasting on sour jelly snakes in lurid colours and then sticking his blue tongue out so I could photograph it for him.

'Good job the pigs like bread,' Oliver said, looking dolefully at the crates of bread rolls underneath the counter. In theory we could have frozen them and used them for a future event, but they were nowhere near as good and we preferred to serve fresh. In such circumstances, we ate as many as we could face ourselves and fed the rest to the livestock. The surplus sausages we did freeze, and then sold at the market at a reduced price, or cooked at future events.

The Examiner newspaper, covering the north of Tasmania, was determined to put a positive spin on the day. Their photographer took shots of Kit and me smelling the roses in a bower between rain showers. We certainly had nothing else to do.

'Blooms brighten gloom at Woolmers Estate' ran the headline, followed by a report about how the 'wet and windy weather didn't stop visitors from attending the sixth annual event.'

'Could have fooled me,' said Oliver, when he saw the article.

Our business depended on the springtime events for an influx of much needed cash, and mostly we did well. That year we made a loss at Woolmers. We lost our stall fee and forfeited the time and effort of manufacturing the product.

But the real loss was suffered by Woolmers Estate. It takes serious money to maintain and run a historic estate, and that loss, followed by the pandemic a couple of years later, put the place in real jeopardy. Ultimately, it was hard to begrudge them one rainy Sunday and the loss of a few bread rolls.

As Daisy and Kit got older, they began helping on the stall. Both of them loved being the cashier; money is very alluring when you're a teenager. They would fight for the privilege of taking cash payment from people and giving out change. That meant doing mental maths at speed and often in front of strangers. It's hard calculating even the most simple change when someone is watching you do it. I had become hardened to this and could blank out the inquisitive stares of customers, my mental maths returning quickly with regular practice. Sometimes I'd do my calculations out loud, at speed. This had the dual effect of befuddling customers, and preventing them from telling me how much I owed them.

With Kit and Daisy, some well-meaning customers would interfere with their mental calculations if they thought it warranted. This didn't help, as it put the kids on the spot and embarrassed them. Nothing was more guaranteed to infuriate me.

'Apparently there's five different ways to do a mental maths calculation, and we all have our own preference,' I said one day, when Daisy was bent over the money box and blushing furiously, completely befuddled by one customer's interference. Fearing that she'd never want to return to the stall again and furious with this man for embarrassing my child, I struggled to remember my manners. 'Let's give the gentleman his five dollars fifty change, and thank you very much,' I said, putting a gentle hand on her back, and fixing him with a gimlet stare across the counter.

As a child of the digital age, Kit particularly enjoyed using the credit card reader. Some customers were clearly alarmed at the prospect of an eleven-year-old waving their credit card over a magic implement and withdrawing funds from their account. Oliver and I kept a close enough eye on things to be seen supervising, and this seemed to mollify most people.

Kit at work

With all four of us on the stall, the orders and money rolled in more steadily. We paid the children, and were glad to do so. What they considered handsome pocket money was highly affordable.

Then we realised that if we had two people assembling food,

the children taking orders, and Oliver cooking the product, we'd be able to do yet more business. We did some rough estimations based on how many more orders we'd be able to knock out, and whether employing someone cash-in-hand would pay for itself. We reckoned it would.

That just left finding the right person, and Patsy stepped right into the role. A short woman with luscious hennaed hair and an equally luscious personality, we'd seen her hanging around Harvest. She had kept me transfixed one Saturday morning with her eclectic conversation, ranging over topics like the importance of bees and feeling confident in one's sexuality regardless of traditional ideas of beauty. She was a burlesque performer so she had a lot to say about this. Having also run cafes and catering operations in various places across the world, she was food-trained, worldly-wise, super-confident, and great with the kids. The burlesque background gave her an insouciant confidence with customers, her approach lying somewhere between red-hot flirting and mild disdain, depending on how clear they'd been about their order.

The first time she came to help out at Gardenfest, she turned up in a denim pinafore that skimmed the top of her shapely thighs, tanned from hours in the garden. Her hair was fixed in two tight knots positioned for maximum cuteness at the back of her head. She proceeded to charm the customers and knock out sausages-in-a-roll exactly as instructed, spending quiet moments clearing the workstations, and treating us to observations from her widely-travelled life, her deep, rolling laugh bouncing off the walls of the marquee.

We gave her as much as she could eat while she was on the stall, and paid her in cash and bacon.

'Is that okay?' I said, handing over a small sheaf of crisp fifty dollar notes.

'Absolutely! I've got a full belly, and next week's groceries paid for,' she said. 'I'm happy.' We loved having Patsy on the stall with us. And we learned a lot about burlesque.

* * *

Slow Cooked Pork with Pasta

This recipe is inspired by the dish prepared for our local Farmgate Festival using our pork. The chef was inspired by the slow cooked pork prepared by his mother. His was better than mine but it brings back memories to cook it.

INGREDIENTS
- Lean pork cut into smallish strips
- Light olive oil and butter
- Small mushrooms, finely sliced
- Onion, finely chopped
- Garlic, crushed
- Red pepper, finely sliced
- Fresh oregano, paprika
- Flour
- Cream, stock and white wine
- Tomato puree

COOKING

Warm oil and butter and cook chopped onion in a large pan until translucent

Add sliced mushrooms and cook until softened, adding garlic midway

Remove from pan

Mix 2 tbsp flour, 2 tbsp paprika, salt and pepper and mix through the pork

Brown lightly in the pan

Push pork to the side of the pan and deglaze with a little white wine and/or stock

Add a spoonful of tomato puree

Gently move pork back into the mix and allow it to thicken and gather

Gradually add more stock and/or wine, and cream, in the quantities of your choice

Return mushroom and onion mix to pan and stir through gently

Add red peppers and some fresh chopped oregano

Place lid on pan and cook on very low heat for 1.5 hours until the pork is tender

FOR THE TABLE

Serve over the best pasta you can find, with Parmesan or Pecorino

Garnish with a little more fresh oregano or parsley

WINE

Pairs well with a zingy Pinot Gris or a more sultry rose

Smokers

On a family holiday to England, Oliver had plundered every shop in his native Suffolk for bacon, doing serious research into the flavours he remembered from his youth, and quizzing butchers on their brining and curing techniques. He wanted to make bacon of his own.

Another fridge appeared in our kitchen, dedicated to bacon. Its bottom two shelves were usually occupied by a slab of belly or a small leg, in a plastic bag. Oliver treated these with a spice rub first, and then added molasses and Guinness to the bag, leaving it for a day or two for the flavours to marinate the meat. Every so often he would crouch in front of the fridges and turn the package over to distribute the mix. With the scent of pork pervading the house on sausage-making days, the additional white-goods and my husband jostling for space alongside me, the family kitchen was becoming a crowded place.

He had also discovered smokers on social media. A smoker was an arrangement of metal chambers welded together by their creator in a man-cave. It would have a fire chamber at one end, connected by a tube to a cooking chamber, in which meat, fish or other foods could be placed to cook gently in the smoke.

Oliver raved about the Americans he came across online who did smoking on a bigger scale than anyone else. 'This bloke can cook twenty-six chickens simultaneously! Think about how many people we'd be able to feed if we had one of those.' I thought about the additional work and expertise to grow the business and do events involving such a lot of product. I thought about how we would find the customers and do the marketing.

'We could do weddings and events!' he exclaimed. I looked at the front of his t-shirt, covered in dust from the pig pens.

You need a broad stable of skills to call upon for running a small business. While we had enough between us to set things up from an operational point of view, raise pigs and make smallgoods, build websites and throw a stall together, neither of us had proper business acumen, we had both come to realise. But that didn't stop Oliver's enthusiasm.

A man with a project and a welder is a happy man, and he began to build smokers in earnest, the noise of metal grinding and sparks flying from the roll-up doors of the workshop in the afternoons. Beginning with a small one, he converted an old air compressor, creating a fire chamber at one end and cutting a tiny door to poke firewood through, and installing a chimney at the other end. Pork sat on a grill in the middle, accessed by another door which hinged upwards from the body of the compressor.

A series of smoked pork roasts began to appear on our Sunday dinner table. They rather over-catered for our needs given that it was just the four of us, including Daisy the vegetarian. A great lump of meat would come out of the smoker looking glossy, charred and unappetising. But once broken open, the pork was rich, meaty and succulent. We ate a small quantity of it, and the rest went into a plastic container in the fridge, infusing everything with its smoky aromas.

Some weeks after building Smoker Mark One, Oliver began work on Smoker Mark Two, converting another air compressor which he had picked up from the tip. This time, he built a cube for the firebox, welding steel plates together, and attaching it 'offset' and slightly lower from the cooking chamber. This he believed would draw the smoke through the chamber more efficiently.

Every so often he would appear in the kitchen full of vim and vigour about his latest innovative design. Each smoker was bigger and grander than the last. Then he brought home an unwanted double fridge from the tip, the sort found in shops, with glass doors and soft drinks inside.

'What the hell is that for?' I asked. We were in the bush block looking at the fridge, which stood in the trailer.

'I'm going to smoke bacon in it.'

'How can you smoke bacon in a fridge?'

'I'll convert it. This will be the smoking chamber. I can hang a whole belly and legs in this, then I can make bacon for the markets.' The light dawned. He was thinking about stepping up production to small-scale commercial quantity.

'Where's it going to go?' I asked.

'Over there, outside the workshop.' He pointed to a spot just outside the vegetable garden. I baulked at this.

'We don't want that sitting around on the property; it'll be such an eyesore!'

'I'll paint it,' he promised. 'And I'm going to see if I can get it passed by the Council and make bacon for the market.'

I gazed at him, wondering if he'd finally lost the plot. 'They're never going to pass something like that for commercial use.'

'It won't look like this when I've finished with it. I can make more bacon, and we can charge more for it.'

Suddenly I saw the sense in his thinking. Value-added products like bacon and sausages, which involved a manufacturing process, were higher in value than straight pork product. We sold pork belly for seventeen dollars per kilo. If we converted it into bacon, sliced it and sold it in small packs, we could double that amount. I looked at the double fridge, sitting with its doors open. There certainly was greater capacity than in any of the other smokers he'd made so far.

'You're not thinking of hanging me in there, are you?'

'Premium meat normally comes from a younger animal,' he replied. I went back to the house feeling reassured that I wasn't going to be suspended by the ankles in a cloud of wood-smoke, after one of our more robust discussions.

As good as his word, Oliver converted the double fridge into his Grand Outdoor Smoker, painting it black, and mounting it on a framework of offcuts found in his workshop so that it towered over us.

'Why is it so high up?' I demanded. 'Did you want it to be noticeable from the road?'

'It's got to be higher than the fire chamber, so that the smoke is drawn up,' Oliver said. He had given the fire chamber a kind of pig face and ears. Smoke was fed from this to the fridge chamber through insulation ducting. In place of the glass doors there were now wooden doors, painted black. When the smoker was in action, a thin drift of smoke emanated from between the doors and up into the trees.

To my utter astonishment, the strictest of all the inspectors from the Council passed it as a food-safe means of smoking bacon in small batches for sale at the market, and licensed Oliver to begin production.

'She didn't like it, but she passed it,' said Oliver, jubilant. 'People have cooked and preserved food like this for thousands of years.'

'Not in a Coke bottle fridge, they haven't.'

Oliver was now able to hang sides of bacon in the Grand Fridge Smoker, monitoring the temperature and making sure it achieved the minimum required for the killing of microbial life. It might have been passed by the Council, but it was still an eyesore, a real Heath Robinson job. It was typical of him, and doubtless many other cabinet-makers: they made beautiful kitchens for other people, but when it came to our own property, he cobbled things together.

'Couldn't you have done something better with that?' I asked.

'I could clad it.'

'Twenty bucks says you never get round to it.'

He shuffled from one foot to the other. I felt for him: as well as maintaining a large house for a demanding spouse, he had to manage the farm, the pigs, the abattoir runs, the manufacturing and the markets. I was constantly amazed by his propensity for hard work. He was often exhausted on a Sunday, the only day when he didn't have to do anything relating to the supply chain, because all the other businesses he dealt with were closed. In order to grow, a business must get more efficient. Ours just seemed to get more complicated, with new, time-consuming processes and projects. No wonder he bodged things together in a hurry, I thought, and resigned myself to living with the smoker as it was.

Good thing too, as that cladding never did get done.

Grand Fridge Smoker

Operating from our domestic kitchen was soon no longer viable. Oliver was often still tying sausages in bundles of nine and packing them in vacuum sealed bags when the kids were coming home from school and wanting their afternoon tea.

Then Oliver found out he was eligible for a low-interest loan available to people operating a small business. He found out I'd be eligible for one too, as the business was run as a partnership. He decided to build himself a processing room, in a shipping container.

'Why are you going to use a shipping container?' I asked.

'You can get them second hand. There's loads of places selling them.'

'Why don't you cordon off a corner of the workshop and build a room in there?' It seemed a much more sensible idea, and quicker to accomplish. But Oliver was hearing none of it. He began the hunt for a container, and insisted we visit an olive grower who had set up his own olive press and bottling room in a container in his backyard. It was an impressive facility, clean and fully kitted out with great chrome vats, chutes and trays.

'I still don't understand why you can't just build a stud wall in the corner of the workshop and build a room in there,' I persisted. This seemed much easier than sourcing a container, finding a spot for it in the bush block and getting a concrete pad laid to put it on.

'But it would be purpose-built,' said Oliver. 'I'm going to see the Council next week to sound them out about it.'

The following week, he returned from his meeting with a jubilant air and refreshed vigour for the project.

'What did they say about the container idea?'

'He suggested building a room in the corner of the workshop,' Oliver replied. 'I never thought of that.'

I waited a moment for a flicker of irony, or a dawning recollection of the conversations we'd had. No flicker of either. I turned back to whatever I was doing in the kitchen.

'We sketched it out together. Do you want to see?' Oliver asked.

'I'm quite busy, actually.' I said. 'I'm sure you've got it all under control.'

Oliver was sanctioned to build a sealed and fully-equipped meat processing room in which he could make as much bacon and sausages as he wanted to. He set about designing it, and sourcing vinyl for the flooring and skirting board. He built the stud frame himself and lined it with wall sheeting. Keeping an eye on the second-hand forums on the Internet, he found chrome shelving and bench-tops from a closing-down café's commercial kitchen, and cut the steel and reshaped it to fit.

Inevitably, when he contacted the Council again for help in understanding how the plumbing should work, the gentleman he had spoken to had left, and nobody there had any record of what he was doing or that he had been given permission to do it. After three months of agonising negotiation and waiting for Council staff to get back to him with answers to questions, we secured a meeting with the new Building Inspector, an eminently reasonable man called Barry, who sorted the whole thing out. Oliver installed sinks, plumbing and drainage that met with their agreement. Finally, a small team of hygiene officers, and Barry himself, came out to do the final inspection. The room was a spacious place gleaming with chrome, three fridges humming in unison to contain our sausage-making empire, and natural light falling in through the large north-facing window. Barry leafed through the documents licensing our operation and leaned on the chrome counter to sign them.

'It was the obvious idea to build it in here instead of in a container,' said Barry, looking up from the papers briefly.

'Yes, it's worked very well,' Oliver agreed. The breeze stirred the treetops outside and I thought about the cup of tea and chocolate digestive biscuit I'd be making for myself later. But perhaps not for my husband.

Pig Lady

For months, we had been taking a small barbecue to Harvest to cook our sausages on. But with so much competition in ready-to-eat food at the market, we only ever sold a handful. Oliver slaved away on the barbecue at the back of the stall instead of serving his customers and had the greasy job of cleaning it at the end of the market.

Eventually, we weighed up the benefits versus all the palaver and inconvenience. After agonising, we dropped serving hot food at the market. We never looked back. It was one of those counter-intuitive decisions that makes a difference you wouldn't expect it to.

It was a burden lifted for Oliver, whose mood lifted as he assumed his position at the front counter. Oliver is a sociable man, and took immense pleasure in telling people how the pigs were kept and the sausages made. He had built us a handsome hardwood front-counter and now, instead of being cluttered with sauce bottles, it was dressed with an earthenware jar of flowers or a basket of vegetables from the garden, and books about pigs.

An unexpected outcome was that our takings went up. We put it down to both of us now being present to maximise sales. As people began to know our product we took pride in the way our stock emptied out of the chiller cabinet and Eskies. Frequently we filled big orders and sold regulars their usual pack of beautiful Saddleback sausages or a roast for Sunday dinner. It was a relief to be handing it over, after all the hard work to get it there.

Without the aromas of caramelised onion and sausage wafting from our stall, we needed another way of providing sensory temptation to market-goers. We opted for sausages cooked in an electric frying pan on the front counter. This sight and smell of these sizzling away drew people in and they came over to peer into the pan and see what smelled so good. We handed out bite-sized pieces on cocktail sticks.

This too had an instant impact on sales. Few people walked away without buying a pack once they'd had a taste. Many asked if we made them with fennel and so we branched out and made two varieties: *Traditional Pork*, and *Pork and Fennel*.

I noticed that women often refused a sample but their husbands would stop for one, and I wondered whether women considered sausages a bit unrefined. Many people told us they never ate sausages or didn't like them. Those who relented and tried a sample of ours frequently had a change of heart. 'I don't normally like sausages but that's different!' they'd say.

Many parents bought them in bulk, pleased to have found a sausage for family dinners which didn't contain sulphates or additives. One day a man with less of a filter than most people gave us our best ever appraisal. 'Wow! That's the crack cocaine of sausages, right there!'

I was taken with his frankness, but it didn't seem quite right as a quote for our marketing material.

I dreaded the day when Oliver might be sick and I'd have to run the stall alone, and inevitably that day came. He developed flu symptoms over the course of a production week, trudging out stoically to feed the pigs, climbing into his overalls and shoving his feet into gumboots. By Wednesday, he needed my help to make it round the pens with the feed buckets, waiting patiently by the barrow hunched against the cold as I poured feed into the troughs. On Thursday, I helped him pack and label the product. He managed everything with as much grace as he could muster, saving his voice for gravelly instructions on how to calculate the prices. On Friday morning, he didn't surface until after the children had left for school and was barely able to stand upright.

'I don't know if I'm going to be able to do the market tomorrow, you know.'

'You don't say.' With his skin the colour of a corpse, there was no way he was selling anything to eager customers.

I knew how to run the stall, but this meant towing a trailer and manoeuvring it on site. Setting up and packing the stall away was heavy work, shifting a folded marquee around, setting out the fold-up trestle tables, and rolling the heavy timber counter and chiller unit on and off the trailer.

'Don't worry about all of that. There'll be plenty of people around to help you,' croaked Oliver. 'The main thing is getting the chiller cabinet switched on so it can cool down, and getting the stock into it.'

On Friday afternoon, we loaded the pork product into the pre-cooled Eskies, and then put all the stall paraphernalia on the back of the ute. Oliver connected the trailer and reversed it up the ramp to the workshop, where we rolled the timber counter onto it. He showed me how to lock the wheels so it didn't roll around as I was driving, and how to fasten the tailgate of the trailer securely.

Saturday dawned. Oliver had encouraged me to set off well before time and get to the site before other stallholders. I'd be able to drive straight up to our spot, unload, and circle around and out to a parking place on the road, all without having to reverse. I was up before five, with the nervous energy of a jack jumper ant on espresso.

At the market, I pulled up at our spot and lowered the trailer's tailgate. The minute the few other stallholders already there saw me on my own, they headed over to help push the counter into place. I thanked them profusely and began unloading the ute. Suddenly a small woman with red hair appeared beside me. I recognised her as Sandy's wife, Glynis. She also had a trailer, and was almost as jumpy as me about getting it into a position to unload. Mine was blocking her way.

After a quick and frantic exchange of views, we calmed down, I finished unloading in a couple of minutes, and drove our ute and trailer off-site out of her way.

As the market got underway, Tim from the coffee stall leaned over and asked me what I wanted, his pen poised over a takeaway cup to take my order. Market volunteers stood in for me on our stall when I needed a bathroom break. And when it was all over, I rolled up the vinyl sign that we slung across the back of the stall, packed the left-over stock back into the still-cold Eskies and looped up the electric cables. Taking the cash box, I fetched the ute and trailer, and packed everything onto it, getting help rolling the counter up onto the trailer again. It was an utter palaver and relentless hard work. I didn't know how Oliver did it so uncomplainingly every fortnight.

Finally, I was almost ready to go, and noticed Sandy packing up his stall. Glynis was hanging around with their kids, keeping him company. We fell into conversation, eager to make amends for our short tempers earlier in the morning.

'I set up for Sandy every Saturday,' she said. 'He's been up since one in the morning baking the bread and it seems like the least I can do to help.'

I hadn't met Glynis before and didn't know much about her. I was betting she had a job of her own and was giving away the opportunity for a weekend lie-in to help her husband out.

'What do you do?' I asked her. 'It's probably nothing to do with baking bread, I bet.'

Glynis looked startled for a moment. 'No, it isn't. I'm an academic. I'm doing a PhD in Clinical Psychology.' There was a brief pause, and then she smiled. 'You've taken me by surprise. Hardly anybody asks about me.'

I laughed. 'I know what that's like. People assume the wife just helps out. They don't always think of you as a person in your own right. I get asked about the pigs all the time and it drives me mad.'

Glynis spluttered. 'Oh I get asked about sourdough as well and I know stuff-all about it!'

'I get called the pig lady!'

Glynis exclaimed in horror and we both fell about.

'Sometimes I don't see the pigs from one week to the next,' I confessed. 'And sometimes I couldn't give a toss about them either!'

This wasn't quite true; I cared deeply about the pigs but it summed up how I often felt about the business.

We chuckled for a while longer about the hilarity of the

patriarchy and its roguish assumptions. Then I pulled myself up into the cab of the ute with aching limbs, and Glynis and Sandy went home to the rest of their weekend with the kids.

A few years later, Glynis and Sandy moved to England when she won a prestigious place on the faculty of a university there. We missed them, and I often wondered what Sandy was getting up to, and whether he was still expanding people's waistlines with his chocolate croissants, having followed his clever wife to another hemisphere.

Providores

It was essential to have different outlets for our products. Oliver found providores and stores which specialised in selling Tasmanian produce were all keen to trial his bacon.

'I knew that would happen,' he said. 'Even vegetarians eat bacon.'

He had established a fortnightly bacon-making routine. Slabs of pork from the leg and belly were marinated in a molasses mix with water and herbs, then the Fridge Smoker would be fired up and they would hang for some hours inside. Since he was now making reasonably large quantities and needed a means of transporting them from fridge to smoker, he saw an opportunity to do some welding. Using wheelbarrow wheels and steel bars, he created a cage on wheels, covered in netting. The pork hung inside this as he trundled it along the garden path to its smoky fate. I wasn't quite clear whether he'd had this part of the process passed by the Council inspector, but she must surely have realised that he'd have to get the pork from the kitchen to the smoker somehow. My days became punctuated by the sight of Oliver passing the windows of the house slowly pulling his pork wagon behind him.

After scouting the local butchers, by a stroke of luck he found one who had a commercial-sized slicing machine that was surplus to requirements.

'It was just sitting out the back. He let me have it for free,' Oliver said. We were running a business which relied upon the kindness of strangers, it seemed.

'But apparently they're a nightmare to clean.'

The food inspector had recommended Oliver get a slicer but had told him they were the worst offenders when it came to harbouring micro-bacterial growth. Oliver diligently took his apart in the workshop, cleaned and polished it, and learned how to keep it in pristine condition. Once that was done, he began slicing bacon into packs of a few hundred grams, labelled and ready for the customer. Once smoked, the bacon was a beautiful product to work with, almost dry to the touch, with a light smoky scent.

Casting around for a name, he struck on Suffolk Smoked Bacon, in deference to all those butchers in his home county whose ideas he had plundered. And so opened another chapter of the business.

A number of local stores began stocking it, including Alps & Amici, a store in the inner suburbs of Launceston owned by local chef Daniel Alps. Not only did they sell fine Tasmanian produce, there was a commercial kitchen in which chefs cooked with the produce and created their own line of ready-to-eat meals. For this, they made their own stock, at scale. Soon after Oliver began supplying the store with bacon, Daniel's chef asked whether the bones from our pigs were available for them to use in stock. Generally, Oliver did not ask for bones to be returned to him, as he had no use for them. Now, he took delivery of them and smoked them in the Fridge

Smoker, and delivered them to the kitchen at Alps & Amici where they were turned into stock and added a flavour bomb to top-notch ready meals.

At the market, the bacon walked off the shelves. It seemed there was a real hunger for bacon made using traditional techniques, with a different flavour from the usual shop-bought fare.

'It's like the bacon my grandfather used to make,' enthused one regular customer.

Reports filtered in from the providores about people timing their fortnightly shopping after Oliver's delivery, and buying multiple packs.

I tried to encourage Oliver to use offcuts from the local apple orchards, so we could say it was smoked with apple-wood, a great story for our marketing efforts. But Oliver held no truck with this, despite his favourite smokers on YouTube tapping into America's rich history of hickory or apple-wood smoked meats.

'What kind of wood do you use to smoke your bacon with?' I'd hear an interested customer ask him at the market.

'I actually just use whatever we've got in the bush block at home,' he'd reply. 'It's usually peppermint gum or some other sort of eucalyptus.' Another branding opportunity zipped past.

'You can't tell them you just use any old piece of wood you've got lying around in the bush,' I'd tell him. 'It really doesn't sound good, and maybe that's why it tastes so strong!'

'I don't mind the taste!' he'd reply.

We had many a discussion about this, but just as you can take a horse to water but not make it drink, you can take a couple to market, where they will run a stall together but constantly bicker over the principles upon which their business is founded.

We saw the same faces at our stall week after week and never took regulars for granted. Everybody had different requirements and we came to know what they would buy, and tailored our newsletters, and the cuts of meat we sold too.

Elizabeth from purchased a large pork roast for her family's Sunday dinner. She asked how best to cook it to get great crackling and make sure the meat was succulent. I gave her some hints.

'Rub salt all over the crackling and put it in the fridge for a couple of hours,' I told her. 'Then rub that off and cover it in thyme or caraway seeds. Those go really well with pork.' Elizabeth continued to listen attentively.

'Cook it for four hours on a really low heat. Then turn the oven up as high as it will go for the last half hour; that's when the crackling cooks. Then take it out of the oven and let it rest; that keeps it succulent.' I made a mental note to write these instructions down on a recipe card, as it was a lot to remember. We could pop one into the bag with each roast purchased.

A couple of weeks after Elizabeth bought her first roast, she turned up at the stall to buy another one, and I asked her how it had gone.

'Oh, I cooked it hard and fast because that's how I cook everything, and it was delicious,' she said. Wessex Saddleback pork was a very forgiving meat.

One cut of pork that didn't sell regularly was fillet, we noticed, and this was a puzzle. Fillet was a favourite in our house, a lean and tender cut from the inside of the ribcage, part of the loin. I liked it seared in an oven-proof pot, then cooked briefly with apple, onion and thyme in the oven, keeping a lid on to contain the flavours and succulence. I sliced it thinly onto warmed plates and served it with wilted greens and mashed potato. It was a quick and sensational meal.

In a flash of inspiration, I wrote the recipe up and published it on our blog and in the newsletter we sent out before each market. That week, Richard and Louise turned up at our stall.

'Have you got any of that pork fillet you wrote about?' I made our marketing up as I went along and was delighted that my attempts had even been noticed. I sold them a modest-sized strip of fillet. At our next market, they came back for more, and raved about how delicious it was and how easy to cook.

The market attracted both young professional couples and families, and we varied the sizes of our packs of product to cater for all. Some of our customers lived alone and simply wanted to look after themselves by eating well. Judy, retired and widowed, turned up to our stall religiously every time we were there and bought a pack of sausages. She took them home and froze the sausages individually, she told us, cooking them one at a time over the next nine days. Then she came back to buy more, raving about them as she packed them away in her shopping-bag on wheels.

A Chinese woman who introduced herself as Miaow purchased our pork ribs. She used them for soups and treated us to descriptions of the careful way she built up flavours in the pot. Every time, we had a serious and detailed discussion about that week's ribs, as she pored over a couple of packets examining them for meat and fat, before taking one away with a look of profound satisfaction.

One young man in particular never purchased anything from us but engaged us in detailed discussion about how each cut should be cooked. Peering intently into our chiller cabinet and never quite meeting Oliver's eye, he absorbed advice about frying bacon in the pan, using lardons for soup, slow cooking ribs in a plum sauce. From his appearance, a black frock-coat, black hat, beard and long sideburns forming ringlets, we were a little mystified by his interest in a stall which sold pork. In the five years we ran our stall, he never made a purchase, but Oliver continued to answer his questions patiently, if a little more briefly.

I had fantasized about making my own ham using one of our own pork legs, picturing myself in an atmospheric barn like the one in that episode of *French Leave*. When it came to it, I had the pinny and the increasingly plump waist to tie it around, but was kept too busy by all the demands on my time. Plus we didn't have an atmospheric barn.

But there was nothing stopping Oliver. He made several hams and prosciuttos, brining and salting them, and hanging them outside our kitchen window so that air could circulate around them. There they would stay for months, getting dryer and smaller and more wizened. When we carved into them though, the results were best served in the thinnest of slivers, salty and delicious, alongside a plate of melon slices. To show off this magnificent product, I purchased a ham holder for Oliver, as a Christmas present. Difficult to source in Australia, the most ornate ones came from Spain, but I settled for simple version which had a heavy base plate, long chrome uprights and screws to hold the ham or prosciutto in place. Once secured, it could be carved into with the sharpest of knives. It made a magnificent centrepiece on our Christmas table, and the main course of Christmas lunch had to be put back after those present gorged themselves on Saddleback prosciutto and were far too full for anything more.

Peak time for market trading was the first two to three hours. It was critical to make the most of this time in sales. If Oliver was serving and another customer was waiting, that second customer had to be prevented from getting restless and wandering off. Most of our friends understood this. When Brad and Kat dropped by for a quick catch-up, Oliver and Brad would often settle in for a long conversation. Soon Kat would realise we needed the time for customers and take Brad away for coffee. We appreciated her understanding that we were there to work. Missing out on sales meant taking our product home with us.

Oliver loves a chat, and often has trouble finishing one. Many times, he would get preoccupied with a conversation and forget that we were there to sell. He and a customer would blithely continue a conversation for ten, twenty minutes or longer. I would duck and weave around him to get to the chiller and the cash box. Sometimes I put my hands on his hips and moved him manually to one side. And sometimes, if I could see that he wasn't going to extricate himself, I gently put a hand on his arm, apologised to both parties, and pointed out that we needed him to serve. People invariably understood.

One couple in particular kept Oliver engaged in long discussions before finally buying a small packet of lardons. They would fuss over which to buy, poring over multiple packs, making us get them in and out of the chiller cabinet so they could choose. Or sometimes they'd buy nothing at all.

As they left with their deep pockets and their tiny packet of bacon, I'd think of the time Oliver had spent making it, steeping the leg of pork in its marinade and turning it daily, drying it overnight in a fridge, smoking it for hours in the bush, carting it back and forth between the smoker and the kitchen, slicing and packing it, loading it into Eskies and heaving them onto the back of the ute, leaving before dawn and setting up in the freezing cold and dark, standing for four hours, selling and talking to people, then packing up and going home exhausted and sometimes defeated.

We always joked that I was the glass-half-full person in our relationship, while Oliver's glass had rolled off the table and shattered, but sometimes even I wondered whether they couldn't buy two packs of lardons instead of one.

* * *

Pork Fillet

Pork fillet is a choice cut, lean and tender. It lends itself to dishes with minimal cooking, cooked gently and simply with a few beautiful herby flavours. It's perfect for a weekday dinner and teams well with all manner of accompaniments, from mashed potato to sumptuous, garlicky, creamy or mushroom sauces.

INGREDIENTS

Pork fillet (one fillet per two people)
Olive oil
Thyme, lemon juice, lemon zest, salt and pepper
One onion chopped or sliced, two cloves garlic, crushed
Chicken or vegetable stock
White wine
Cream

COOKING

Heat oven to 160°

Combine oil with lemon juice and zest, thyme and seasoning

Coat pork in seasoning and marinate in fridge – half an hour or longer

Heat light-flavoured oil and perhaps some butter in ovenproof dish or pan

Sear pork very gently on all sides and remove

Add onion to pan and cook lightly, add garlic

When these are translucent to lightly coloured, add liquids: a little stock to deglaze the pan, then wine, then a little more stock, then a drop of cream. Aim for a small amount of liquid which slightly coats a wooden spoon

Add pork to pan, put lid on and transfer to oven for around 35 minutes maximum.

Remove the pork from the oven and allow it to rest for perhaps ten minutes.

FOR THE TABLE

Slice the pork into 1cm slices and serve a few per plate with sauces

Serve with cauliflower or celeriac puree and vegetables of

your choice such as brussels sprouts, green or yellow runner beans, baby carrots.

Dinner

'We were wondering whether you would like to provide some of your pork to feature in a dinner we're holding.'

The call came through from the general manager of a tenacious organisation set up to support small-scale farmers and producers like us, endearingly named Sprout. They operated mostly by getting producers together so they could learn from each other, but occasionally they organised an event showcasing what those producers made or grew. Jen, a woman whose tiny stature concealed a generous and determined nature, explained that the dinner would be held at Stillwater, one of Launceston's most highly-regarded restaurants. It would be an intimate affair for just twelve people, so the quantity of pork required was not huge, and we would be paid for it. I readily agreed, and arranged to put Oliver in touch with Craig, the chef, to determine what cut of pork he might like.

'You'll have the chance to talk to the people there about your product and what it's like running a small farm, and why you do what you do,' Jen said.

'I'll have to think about why we do it,' I replied. 'I do sometimes wonder.'

I explained to her that Oliver would rather chew his own arm off than do any kind of public speaking, whereas I would be only too happy to have the attention of a whole room of people, so would probably attend on my own.

We kept in touch in the run-up to the dinner, and Jen sent me an invitation by email. The cost was $95, it said, and there was no indication that it would be complimentary for me just because our farm's produce was being presented. Had Oliver wanted to go, I reflected, that would have been a steep outlay for us, as a percentage of our weekly takings. I wondered whether people in other walks of life realised that our so-called idyllic lifestyle meant that eating out was a rarity.

Set against those frugal concerns was the enticing nature of the event. It was to be held in the restaurant's wine cellar, a cosy, brick-lined room probably made by convicts in the early nineteenth century. A few steps down from the bar, it was private, convivial and steeped in atmosphere.

We had been to Stillwater just once before. Oliver and I were in the habit of going out for lunch every so often, but since we spent so much time in each other's company, there was a real danger of us running out of conversation. After we'd dissected our food and had an argument about parenting techniques, we usually ended up talking about pigs. Oliver could talk about them indefinitely but it wasn't my idea of a good time.

With that in mind, we sometimes included another couple who were available for a weekday lunch. John was employed as a senior manager in the oil industry, in Mongolia, and flew there for a three-week shift, then back to Tasmania for two weeks off. Australians have taken commuting to the next level with their fly-in fly-out arrangements.

Some meals are memorable, for the happy symbiosis of company, location and dining, and this was one of those. We settled, the four of us, at a table in the middle of the old mill building, with its wide hardwood flooring and whitewashed brick walls with windows onto the river. Turning our attention to the menu, we all leapt at the entree special: oyster shots. These were oysters, served in shot glasses with vodka, rose water and coriander. We ordered, and found the tenderness of the oyster perfectly complemented by the exotic blend of alcohol and florals. Oliver was not convinced, so the rest of us wolfed down his share before he could change his mind. I followed with a main of ocean trout in a traditional Nicoise salad. This is not such a stretch for a top-notch chef, but I love to eat fish in a good restaurant. Prepared expertly, there's nothing finer on the plate than a fresh catch beautifully presented with its flavours allowed to sing. That day's dish was perfect, the trout tender and pink, with tiny Bintje potatoes nestled amongst greens, and a light dressing marrying it all together.

So I was gleeful at the prospect of dining there again.

I arrived to find our party gathering in the wine cellar, a low room, its brick walls lined with shelves housing the restaurant's wine collection, reputed to be one of the best on the island, put together by an award-winning sommelier. The room was lit with warm lighting which replicated the glow of candles and bounced of the glasses and tableware. White linen created a timeless, elegant look, and Jen had placed gift bags containing complimentary goods on the table, from the producers whose ingredients were being featured: bottles of lavender and saffron from *Campo de Flori* in Tasmania's south; packets of freeze-dried blueberries from *Three Peaks Organics*, snap-frozen on the farm. It was a rainbow of the European flavours which are now grown in Tasmania.

Some of those seated around the table had a connection with Sprout, having completed a mentoring program or thinking about it, and some were simply diners who loved the idea of a special dinner at one of the island's best restaurants. The level of chatter was rising, when Jen tapped the side of her glass gently with a fork to call for quiet, and asked us to take turns introducing ourselves.

'Perhaps you can tell us something you're passionate about, to give us a feel for why you're here,' she added.

No doubt she was expecting some of us to speak about our farms and products, and I wanted to earn my place at the table by whetting my fellow diners' appetites. But I also wanted them to know who I was. I was tiring of being known as 'the pig lady'. I was about to sign a contract with a British publisher for my first book. When it was my turn, I took a breath and tried to be succinct.

'You'll be tasting pork from my farm later on, but contrary to what people think, I'm not that passionate about pigs,' I said. There was already considerable bonhomie around the table and this was greeted with a ripple of laughter. 'I do help my husband with the farm and with running the business, but I'm also a writer. So it's words that I'm most passionate about, myself.'

It was the first time I had introduced myself as a writer with any sort of conviction, but those present appeared to take it at face value. The woman sitting opposite me cocked an eyebrow with interest. She and her husband, who sat alongside her, raised beef cattle on his family's farm, although I was later to find out that they had sensible day jobs as well, and impressive careers in the public service.

Dishes began to arrive on the table. To begin, an amuse-bouche featured the blueberries, reduced to a dark, unctuous liquid dotted around a black plate, with crunchy blueberry sorbet topping a scoop of tangy yoghurt. Such was the artistry of the dish, there was only a hint of resemblance to the plump, matte berries it originated from. Clever and delicious, it awoke our curiosity and our palates in fine style.

Wines accompanied each course and I sipped tentatively, knowing I had to drive home, but appreciating the precise way in which each complemented the different dishes.

When a plate of our pork belly was set in front of me, I had trouble making the link between the dusty little pigs that scuffed around on our farm, the hunks of roast that I put on the table occasionally, and this refined-looking vision. A square section of belly sat amongst salad greens and pickled pear, a shallow puddle of *jus* trickled around it. A reverent silence fell over the table, punctuated by sighs and groans as people tucked in. There was the occasional clink of cutlery as we pulled apart the soft meat fibres. This was a rich and clean version of the Wessex Saddleback meat I had come to know well. The texture and presentation were in a different league to what I ever achieved myself. The dish was melt-in-the-mouth tender, with a diamante crust of crackling. The difference between a home cook and a chef was never clearer to me and it felt like a privilege, suddenly, to have our pork prepared with such finesse.

Beef cheeks were next, and as our appetites were sated and our tongues loosened by wines of impeccable character, the volume of talk and laughter around the table went up, and Rick, the beef farmer from across the table, suddenly addressed himself to me.

'So, Fiona, the question is would you be better off stacking shelves at the supermarket than you are running an artisan farm in Tasmania?'

His cheeks were flushed slightly with Pinot Noir and there was a grin on his boyish face. His wife Liz flinched visibly beside him at the brazenness of his question.

'I have no idea what they pay at the supermarket,' I said, playing for time.

Liz stepped in, half apologetically. 'I think what he meant to ask was whether owning your own business, and running a small ethical farming operation because it's a product you believe in, is rewarding in a *different* way.'

'Well, it probably is,' I shrugged lightly. She had put a good spin on what we did, but I actually preferred Rick's question for its directness. Years earlier in the United Kingdom, I had read of highly-qualified people who built careers in the southern cities of England and then, burnt-out and disillusioned, moved to Cornwall and took jobs doing just what Rick had described: stacking shelves at supermarkets. It was a phenomenon called 'down-shifting', and at times I could easily see myself doing something similar, and relishing the simplicity of that life.

By the time we'd made it through to dessert, a brandy snap with lemon and saffron sauce with a curl of house-made ice-cream, we were all sitting a little further back in our chairs, sated and relaxed. It was at this point, with the kitchens winding down and being cleaned by sous chefs and service over for the evening, that the chef Craig appeared, standing politely at the side of the room in his crisp white tunic. First there was a ripple of applause for the artistry emerging from his kitchen. He nodded modestly, his hard-working hands clasped in front of him, the sheen of an evening's work showing on his face.

After a few questions from around the table, I gathered my thoughts enough to ask how he had cooked our pork. 'I've cooked it myself of course, but what you did with it tonight made it seem like an entirely different meat.'

Craig was standing just behind me and he glanced down thoughtfully. 'It starts with a great product,' he said, meeting my eye. 'That was some of the best pork I've ever cooked with.' There was a murmour of appreciation from the other diners, and I felt a prickle of alertness at this compliment. I knew that to Oliver, responsible for measuring pig feed and diet, getting the quota of meat to fat right, and delivering healthy, happy pigs to slaughter and on to the table, this would mean a great deal.

Craig went on to tell us how he had cooked the pork 'sous vide', meaning 'under vacuum' in French. In this technique, meat is cooked in a vacuum-sealed bag at a precise temperature in a water bath, resulting in unbelievable tenderness. Craig had cooked our pork like this on the lowest possible heat for twenty-four hours. The protein fibres now permanently tenderized, he had refrigerated it until it was required, and then oven cooked it with the greatest of care, to finish the crackling.

As he left, I turned back to the table, slightly dazed and still trying to absorb the distance between the pigs we produced on our humble five acres, and the fine dish we had eaten. As if to drive home the point, Rick pinned me with his most direct gaze and I wondered what challenge he was going to throw my way now.

DINNER

'Your pork was by far the best thing on the table for me,' he said, throwing his napkin onto his place setting for emphasis.

Liz leaned across the table and nodded vigorously in agreement. 'It was exceptional,' she said.

Later, I drove back up the valley in the silky Tasmanian darkness, astonished at the evening's events. Slowly the realisation dawned on me that I would later tell my husband that for one brief moment his pork was the talk of the town.

Oliver is a modest man, not shy, but a little reserved. He obstinately left the 'schmoozing' to his 'marketing department' – me. While I was out that evening doing the schmoozing and imbibing, he was at home with the kids, making them beans on toast for their supper. But without even being there, he had been the star of the show. I thought of him as I followed the gently winding road, with his mad passion for sausages and bacon, and where it had got us. I thought about his obsession with pigs, with getting their diet right. I thought about all the times I'd found him standing in the middle of the kitchen, getting in my way, gazing out of the window and thinking about his precious Wessex Saddlebacks. That evening, I'd seen why it was worth it.

Would I rather stack shelves at the supermarket and have an easier life? Or would I rather continue to beaver away on the farm with Oliver, tussling over who did what, hustling to make the business happen, writing, working and always thinking about the pigs?

We had found the answer to that question once before, when we sat at our dining table in a moment of crisis, almost before our business had even got started. We had found our answer then. And I found it again now.

They say in a small business you wear a lot of hats and

it's rare to find one in which all the necessary skills are present. It had become obvious to me that while Oliver was a natural doer and maker, and I was a natural creative and could just about get by at the marketing, neither of us had proper business management skills.

But what we were better off doing had nothing to do with any such calculation, and everything to do with the value of that dinner and what it had shown me. Suddenly everything we did on our five acres made sense: finding a market for our product, turning up at our food stall at the crack of dawn, trudging out to feed the pigs in the pouring rain and mud. If all of it culminated in that rich, intimate dinner with new friends in an old room, transforming what we did into a noble pursuit we could be quietly proud of, for one brief moment that seemed like enough.

Co-Pilot Bob

Most pigs don't need a pedicure; their nails are worn down by everyday walking and trotting about. But Bella's ankles were such that her hooves tilted backwards, which meant that this wearing away didn't happen. As her toenails grew longer, they pushed her ankles back further and the condition worsened. We didn't want her to be in discomfort, particularly when she was pregnant and carrying extra weight. Cutting a pig's toenails is no ordinary job and sometimes it takes a vet to do it. So between weaning one lot of slips, and getting Bella pregnant again, we called out a vet to clip her toenails.

This meant sedating her. Oliver had tried to do the job himself first. On one of the pig keeping forums, he'd read that if you gave a pig enough cider, it would sedate it sufficiently to clip its toenails, and it would wake up with a headache but a nice set of hooves. Bella out-drank Oliver's expectations, guzzling two casks of cheap white wine with no effect.

When the vet arrived from a local practice that handled farm animals, it was a capable young woman, accompanied by a vet student. Carefully, she gave Bella a quantity of sedative, explaining that she'd like to sedate her gradually with separate doses, to see how they affected her. After about three injections, Bella was buzzing. She wandered up and down the fence-line of her pen, which was next door to Pilot's. He stood there looking puzzled about why this vision of porcine beauty was parading up and down before him. Every so often, Bella stopped to cast him a look. We weren't sure whether it was interest or just blurry eyesight. Eventually, she reclined in the shade of a tree, apparently out cold, and the vet steadily trimmed all her toenails using cutters normally used for horses' hooves.

After they'd gone, I kept an eye on Bella, popping over to the pens from the house every so often. Oliver was out that afternoon, and I wanted to make sure she was okay on my watch. An hour after they left, I found her still asleep but shuddering, and rang the vet to ask what might be wrong.

'She could be hot. Turn the hose on her!' I looked at Bella, whose position beneath the tree was now in full sun. Using some corrugated iron that was lying around, and propping it up on a barrel wedged in place by logs, I built a makeshift shelter to shade her from the sun. Turning the hose on her seemed rather brutal. Instead, I filled a bucket with water, got the large sponge we used for washing the car, and spent the next hour sitting beside Bella literally mopping her brow, squeezing water from the sponge over her neck, ears and shoulders. It seemed to do the trick. Shaded from the sun and cooled by caring ministrations, she stopped shuddering. Later that evening she had slept off the sedative and was up and about again, none the worse for wear and ready for her dinner.

For a couple of days Oliver had been talking about Pilot having a scratch on his foot. 'It doesn't seem to be healing. It never gets the chance as he's always walking on it and it gets dust and dirt in it. I think it might need a couple of stitches.'

Since we'd had such a careful approach by the vet we used for Bella's toenails, we had no hesitation in calling the same surgery, but on this occasion, it was the head of the practice who came to the farm, an older gentleman who was well known in the area. Oliver disappeared out to the bush block with him, and was gone for over an hour. When he returned to the house, he seemed agitated.

'That vet gave Pilot loads of sedative, he's out cold.'

'That's what you want, isn't it?' I replied. 'You couldn't stitch a boar's foot without sedating him.'

'Yes, but he gave him a massive dose all in one go. It just knocked him out.'

I thought of the careful way in which the young woman who'd attended Bella had given her gradual doses of sedative, testing the effect of each dose before administering more.

'Hmm. Well, he must know what he's doing, don't you think?'

'I don't know. He seemed afraid of Pilot.'

'Well, that makes sense. He's a boar.'

'Yes, but Pilot's really well behaved, and he wasn't showing any signs of aggression when this bloke arrived. He never does.' The respectful way Oliver handled the pigs meant they were all quite tame, even the boars.

That evening, Oliver reported that Pilot was still not moving or eating. 'He's just lying there. He's moved once today to a different spot, but he's not getting up and he didn't eat his dinner.'

This was a worry. When pigs go off their food, there's something wrong. I went out to the pens with Oliver to see

Pilot for myself. He was lying on his stomach, his legs curled underneath him, apparently asleep. We approached quietly. Pilot didn't move. The light was fading and night was drawing closer. Oliver had brought a couple of straw bales out from the shed, and built a makeshift house around Pilot for the night, since it appeared he wasn't going to move into his shelter. There's no way you can persuade a pig to move if it doesn't feel like it, particularly a boar. I crouched beside him and tentatively lifted one ear, to see if his eyes were open. Pilot half opened the eye I was looking at, and huffed.

There's no way of telling with such a creature whether they're in pain, or feeling sleepy, or unwell. All you can do is make them comfortable and hope for the best. We put straw bales either side of him, broke up a third one and packed it around Pilot's sleeping form for warmth. Then Oliver threw a tarpaulin over the top and pegged it down on the outside of the bales on three sides, leaving the front open over Pilot's head. That way, if he decided to move in the night, he could. We murmured some encouragement, crossed our fingers and went back to the house. Pigs are hardy creatures. On the few occasions any of ours had been ill, Oliver had found they often just rested and appeared to sleep it off.

'He's probably just sleeping off the sedative, or perhaps he's in a bit of shock.' I tried to reassure Oliver, who was still concerned, and rightly so, as it turned out.

The following morning, I was still in bed when Oliver burst in through the bedroom door. Unusually, he was up before me.

'Pilot's dead,' he blurted out. He looked away from me, wiped his face with his hand, and went over to the window. I sat up in bed, astonished.

'He's dead!' Oliver repeated. 'That vet's killed him. I knew he gave him too much sedative. It was a huge dose!'

I leapt out of bed and threw on some clothes. Together, we headed over to the pens. It was a long walk through the vegetable garden and past the workshop, wondering all the while what I was going to see.

The scene that greeted me looked familiar to the previous night. Pilot lay under the tarpaulin, the straw bales either side of him. He hadn't moved an inch since we tucked him in. But there was a curious silence all around. A light breeze stirred the treetops above us. Below, we crouched again beside our pig. I lifted his ear. The eye was closed. There was no breath, no huffing. Pilot was gone.

It was hard to know what to say to Oliver. I had no particular attachment to Pilot as I would have a family pet. But Oliver did. Feeding his pigs daily, caring for them, watching their behaviours, he grew fond of them. He'd seen how amiable Pilot was when moving from one pen to the other, how gentle he was with the sows. He'd admired the thick coat Pilot grew in the winter months, black and white bristles covering his form in great swirls. He'd dropped windfall apples into Pilot's mouth, avoiding the tusks, listening to the crunchy squelch as an apple was smashed and devoured in seconds by his great jaws. He was distraught at losing this handsome, good-natured creature.

It also left us without a boar. With a breeding cycle that fed the farm with new piglets, which grew into weaners and pigs that went to slaughter and fed the business, that was a bad situation. But it wasn't one that Oliver could face up to that day. All his energy was taken up with the distress of losing Pilot, and fury with the vet.

There was also a stickier problem, of what we would do with Pilot's carcass. We went inside to think these things over with the aid of a cup of tea.

'I'll have to ask Neville to come over with the digger and help me bury him,' said Oliver, facing up to the reality of the situation. I reached across the table and put my hand over his, gnarly and strong from work, the skin increasingly marked and pitted from labouring outdoors.

'Where will we put him?' I asked. We both sat and thought about the available room on our small plot of land. It was all taken up by pens, the bush block across which we walked, and the paddocks where the sheep grazed.

'I'll ask Neville what he thinks.' Draining his cup, he went outside and put the phone to his ear. I heard his voice wavering a little, as he explained to Neville that we'd lost a large pig and needed somewhere to bury it. Coming back in a few minutes later, he said Neville had offered to bury Pilot between the bush and the paddocks on our property where there was ground that would be easy to dig which was not shot through with roots. 'He'll be over in an hour or so. I'd better go and move all that straw and the tarp to get ready.'

He trudged back over to the pens and I let him go alone. I knew he'd need time to process what had happened, and all the consequences for the business, as well as his sorrow at losing this big, hairy porcine friend.

An hour later, I heard the rumble of machinery crossing the paddocks. I stayed inside for a while longer, toying with a job on my laptop, leaving the men to get the digger over to our property and make a plan. After a while, I ducked outside, and went over to the pens. Neville and Oliver had removed the star pickets and lowered the fence wire between our two properties to allow the digger to pass between them. It seemed a flimsy device to keep cows on one side and sheep on the other, but it did its job. Oliver had his arms folded protectively high on his chest. Neville stood off to one side, stroking his beard, as they both looked at the recumbent form of Pilot, stretched out on the ground before them.

As I approached, Neville hopped back onto the digger and fired it up. Catching sight of me, he waved. 'Lost your boar, that's no good!' he shouted above the noise of the engine. I nodded and waved, unable to think of a response, even if he could have heard me. What was about to happen, it dawned on me, was unlike anything I'd had to process before. When my childhood dog was put down, the vet had disposed of him. When Midget our dog had died a few years earlier, Oliver had dug a hole in the garden, and we buried her body wrapped in her favourite towel. That had seemed brutal and inadequate, covering her glossy black and white form with the flimsy fabric and then shovels of soil.

This would be worse. As Neville forced the front of the scoop into the ground before Pilot, the finality hit me. The mechanism had no problem with the soil, compacted as it was, and drove into the ground. Neville worked the levers and scooped up dirt, and Pilot. As he raised the arm of the digger up in the air, it jolted clumsily. Pilot's head lolled over the side of the scoop, and hot tears spilled onto my face, as I was overcome with the sudden loss of this noble creature. In my peripheral vision, I saw Oliver turn away, arms folded, one hand to his face. Blinking, I watched as Neville drove down between the pens, bearing Pilot on a final journey past his offspring in the pens below. The brutality of what we were doing confronted me. Here was one creature killed by a vet's carelessness, and below were other creatures who would be slaughtered so that we could eat them. Truly, our place at the top of the food chain was sometimes an indefensible one.

I stood beside the pens and watched as Neville made his way down through the paddocks and turned to go down the far side of our bush block, out of sight. Oliver trudged behind the digger, head down, his arms hanging listless beside him. They found a spot to bury Pilot, digging a shallow hole and covering him over, then leaving nature and all her creatures to do their work. Neville went down there every so often, curious to see the process. I never did, preferring to imagine Pilot as I had known him, lying on the edge of the bush block under the gum trees, facing the sun as it came up each morning, or raising his big, hairy head to catch an apple dropped into his mouth.

Later that day, Oliver phoned the vet's surgery. He didn't speak directly to the man who had come and injected Pilot with sedative, but to a colleague.

'They were incredibly shocked, but they didn't have an explanation,' he told me. 'They said it's never happened before.'

'Not sure I believe that. They might not necessarily be told about it, and they certainly wouldn't tell us anyway. Did they have anything to say about compensation?' It was rare to lose a fully-grown pig, we knew from other farmers we'd spoken to. We had no insurance for this, as there had never seemed to be the need.

'They said nobody could be sure it was the sedative that caused it,' Oliver replied. 'He might have had a weak heart or something.' I crossed my arms in silence, and looked out over the paddocks and the gum trees. Oliver's face was a picture of anger and sorrow.

'There's nothing we can do, we just have to put up with it,' he added. 'And find another boar.'

He took his cup of tea outside and put it on the table where it sat before him, untouched, for a long time.

Supply and Demand

Dear reader: the following chapter contains passages about the taking of pigs to slaughter and about abattoirs. There is no bloody or grisly detail, but it is still about the deaths of the creatures we raised, and about the meat they became. I have tried to present this in a way which is truthful without being distasteful. It is the reality of the situation we found ourselves in, as farmers and vendors in a meat-eating society. I think we owe it to the pigs we raised to present some of this content here. You may find it distasteful or you may find it fascinating. I leave that up to you, but present this forewarning so that you may be prepared for either.

Many customers came to our market stall because they were in the habit of purchasing meat carefully. Often they wanted to know where our farm was and how the pigs were raised. Central to farmers' markets is the idea that consumers can buy direct from the source, and the producer should be present on the stall and able to tell the customer everything they want to know about how their product came to fruition. It's written into the charter of many markets, the task of educating consumers about food production.

Vegetable growers at a farmers' market can tell you what

kind of landscape and soils their vegetables are grown in, what chemicals they've been sprayed with or whether they're grown spray-free or organically. They can probably tell you when the crop was picked, so you know how fresh it is. If they're dairy farmers, they can tell you whether their cows have been fed with a supplement of hay over the winter months, and whether their calves are allowed to remain with their mothers.

The story of our farm was about raising pigs free-range, outside in family groups, rather than inside in sheds on concrete floors. The pens on our farm kept the pigs in by means of electric fencing, which consisted of a couple of tapes run between star pickets, iron posts which can be hammered into the ground. Pigs are quick learners and keen respecters of electric currents. They learn from their mothers and the others around them not to touch the electric tape. If they do so, the charge delivers a small zap, and they rarely touch it again. This was a key consideration in the first years of developing our farm: this minimal infrastructure was quick and cheap to set up.

Held in these pens under eucalyptus trees, our pigs had shade, space to run about, and in the early days a certain amount of natural bush growth to root about in. This was at the core of what we came to see as our brand, and formed the basis for the marketing story we told in all our advertising. We had gone into the business by accident, without much of a plan, let alone a system of beliefs. But the more we learned, the more convinced we became of supplying meat from pigs that were well treated and housed in a place that felt natural to them.

Our pigs remained outside in all weathers, and in winter

were sometimes deep in mud during long spells of rain. There were metal arcs or rough-built houses for shelter in all the pens, and they slept together in one large, warm heap. Even so, I couldn't help but feel for them.

'Pigs don't mind the weather,' Oliver insisted. 'They live outside in the wild all over Europe.' And indeed, whenever I went over to the pens, they appeared to be thriving, gaining weight and always appearing healthy and content. I came to believe that pigs were adaptable creatures, ideally suited for survival in whatever circumstances they found themselves. Oliver monitored their weight gain scrupulously, and developed a keen eye for whether they were too fat or too thin, and a knack for keeping them just right.

Occasionally our more curious customers asked how and where our pigs were slaughtered. Some expected it to be done on the farm, to minimise the distress of travel for the pigs. Tasmania did indeed have a couple of so-called 'mobile butchers'. We'd seen one slaughter a cow on a farm nearby, lifting its carcass using a crane on the back of his ute, breaking the whole thing down on site, and loading the large sections of carcass into a cool-room on a trailer. This he left parked behind a shed on the farm for two days so the meat could hang, which allows the muscles to relax and the meat to set firmly. Then he returned to butcher it into usable cuts for the family. Once you got beyond the inherent grisliness of the process, it was a masterful process to observe, requiring considerable skill.

But the process of slaughtering pigs includes immersing their carcasses in scalding water to remove the bristles. Mobile butchers cannot transport the equipment required to do this, and so the law dictates that pigs must be slaughtered at an abattoir.

If a customer asked us about the supply chain between a live pig leaving our farm and the end-product of pork in our chiller cabinet, and if we judged them to have the pragmatism to handle the answer, we often told them some of the detail.

Our pigs were driven to an abattoir at Devonport, forty-five minutes away on the north coast, by Oliver. A couple of days' preparation was needed, as it meant loading them onto a trailer. They had to be coaxed onto it, because it was new to them and they were rightfully mistrustful. Oliver would back the trailer through a gate into the pens and get the pigs used to it, usually placing their feed on it for a couple of days before their departure. On the day, he would coax them up the ramp onto the trailer and use boards to block in the ones he wanted, those who had reached optimal weight. Then he drove them to the abattoir.

Devonport City Abattoir was the closest to our farm, and there was not much choice besides. Abattoirs are thin on the ground in Tasmania, and possibly elsewhere too. It's an essential business but not a pleasant one, so it's no surprise that there aren't many about. Often they're owned by large multinationals, and on the mainland, we'd read of abattoirs where the workforce was made up mostly of immigrants being paid a minimum wage with employment conditions that were nothing short of scandalous. That included huge risk of injury and repetitive muscular strain from performing the same physical task for hours.

Although owned by a multinational, the facility at Devonport was run along much more acceptable lines than this, and the workforce drawn from the local community. For many years it had been what's known as a 'service kill' facility, for customers who supplied livestock often in small numbers. They processed around two hundred cattle, six hundred pigs and almost four thousand sheep per week, on demand, for local butchers, supermarkets and niche producers like us. In the world of abattoirs, it was a medium-sized operation. Some in the United States process animals in their thousands weekly. Other small, privately-run facilities all over the world process tiny numbers. Devonport lay somewhere in between.

Smaller abattoirs are often a better option for smallholders, where they're available. With fewer animals being handled, the operators are able to take a more personal approach with both the animal and the farmers using the facility. It can mean better welfare for the animals, a quieter and less stressful end. Oliver had trialled a smaller facility in the hinterlands of the north coast. It was owned by a family and carried out so-called 'service kills' for people who lived on the land and grew their own meat, and small farm businesses like ours. But Oliver didn't like the practice of putting animals from different farms into the same pens where they might fight. It was in a quiet spot between small towns, but a considerable distance from our farm, meaning the pigs travelled further on their last journey. Our pigs were fairly calm and settled down quickly when taken off the trailer at their destination, but Oliver still preferred to minimise travel and lessen stress. This was better for the resulting pork meat, but it was also simply kinder. We owed the pigs that.

This smaller abattoir closed eventually so was no longer an option. We knew of two on the eastern side of the Tamar, but both were small and neither processed pigs. There were two abattoirs in southern Tasmania but the return journey would take up an entire day and such a distance was unacceptable for the pigs' welfare. Nor was it a viable use of Oliver's time. He couldn't afford to take a whole day away from the farm and all the other work to be done there in managing livestock and manufacturing his product. Some might ask why I didn't step in. The simple answer is that our little farm business was not profitable enough to support us as a family, and I spent these years running my own micro-business writing content and providing marketing services for local tourism entities.

One small service that Oliver trialled and was keen to use was a one-woman operation just outside Deloraine. Owned by Janice, her Game Meats service processed wallaby and rabbit for the local butchers' market. Often the animals had been culled by local farmers whose pasture they were eating. This practice is often judged harshly by the public. But common wallabies and rabbits are both plentiful in number, and present a major problem for farmers who want to preserve their pasture for grass-fed cattle or sheep, which in turn make the burgers and steaks and chops that the consuming public largely eats. It is an age-old problem in Tasmania, ever since the first settlers arrived and appropriated the open grasslands that had been cultivated by Aboriginal people, which fed the wallabies which they hunted for food. Now the tables have turned and the land appropriated by colonial settlers is appropriated by wallabies.

Oliver visited Janice's operation in the early days of our business when he was learning about butchering and what to ask for in terms of cuts of meat. Janice was licensed to process pigs but didn't do a lot of them, as her facilities were simply not big enough, so she stuck to smaller animals.

'She wants to expand so she can do pigs for people like us,' said Oliver, returning from his visit with an Esky full of pork from a sample pig which Janice had butchered for him, delivering an impressive range of cuts encased in shiny vacuum-sealed plastic. Janice and her offsider Reg had done a beautiful job, and Oliver was particularly impressed with the small rolled roasts they had made from the shoulder.

'She said this is the best meat for roasts because it's so succulent.' Her processing rooms were spotless, he said, decked out in chrome surfaces with top-notch machinery and workstations where small batches of livestock could be processed with maximum efficiency and ease.

'She's done a fantastic job,' I replied, impressed with the presentation of pink pork in carefully trimmed and labelled packages. But we weren't able to use Janice as our commercial operation grew, as she wasn't taking pigs on a regular basis.

'She'd have to expand to do that, and it costs a bomb to set up properly,' Oliver said. 'Quarter of a million, she told me. She'd need a grant or help from government to do it.' We looked at our beautiful pork in silence, contemplating the difficulties of setting up a much-needed facility which would service the community with one of its essential needs: food. Some years later we heard that doing the paperwork and finding the support had been all too hard for Janice and she had given up on the idea of expanding her impressive operation.

Given the lack of facilities nearby and the logistics involved in getting to more distant ones, there was no real choice for us other than the abattoir at Devonport. It was a large facility by Tasmanian standards and certainly the most substantial on the island. Since we were so dependent upon it with no fall-back plan, we worried constantly that if the unexpected happened and it was to close or become unavailable, our business would be in severe jeopardy.

Once at Devonport, Oliver unloaded the pigs into a pen and gave them a last feed. He usually delivered them the afternoon or evening before they were to be slaughtered, which would be carried out early the next morning. On the few occasions I went with him, the pigs left the trailer without fuss and sniffed around at the smells of the clean concrete stock runs which channelled them into small yard pens. At the Devonport abattoir, they were kept separate from any other farm's stock. This was important for two reasons: one, to avoid our pigs getting mixed up with any others; and two, so that they didn't fight with other, unfamiliar pigs.

Abattoirs are audited regularly by government inspectors, and all their equipment and processes checked. We had met one such auditor at a workshop once, a highly-educated woman with blond hair and expensive dress-sense. She talked to those assembled in a no-nonsense way about the best means of slaughtering different forms of livestock. It was clear that her paramount concern for the length of her career, in which she travelled all over the world to both inspect and learn from different abattoir facilities, was the welfare of the animal at the point of death. We didn't get the chance to ask how on earth someone ends up doing such a job, but I was glad she was doing it with such conviction.

Oliver asked the management at Devonport a few times whether he could accompany his pigs as far as he was able to. He wanted to see for himself how it was done, but this wasn't permitted. He knew that they were funnelled into a narrow pen which contained them, and then stunned with electric zappers to the head, which killed them instantly. From then on, it was into the abattoir building proper, where they were turned from the recognisable creatures we had raised into carcasses for meat, dipped in scalding water to remove their bristles, eviscerated, and their heads removed, before their carcass was sent on into a cool room.

It was never an enjoyable day for Oliver, delivering pigs to the abattoir. In all the years we ran the business, Oliver mostly went alone, because we genuinely both had a great deal to do, and I couldn't spare the time. Of course, given any excuse I was always going to avoid going to an abattoir, and somewhat shamefully, I always did.

But one Sunday, the whole family went. We were meeting friends who lived in the coastal town of Ulverstone, and delivering two pigs to the abattoir on the way there. It was open on Sunday so farmers could drop animals off in the yard, but it was not operational that day so there were no workers present.

It was a deserted place of concrete and steel. Oliver backed the trailer up to the pens and ushered the pigs into them. I watched them snuffling around. Beyond the pens there were low sheds but no sense of what happened inside them. Afterwards, we drove on for pizzas baked in another family's backyard brick oven, stopping along the way at a roadside station for Oliver to rinse the trailer floor of dirt and pig droppings. It seemed a curious mix for an afternoon, and I spoke to another pig-farming friend about it later. 'Ah yes, the family outing via the abattoir. We've done it many times!' she replied.

The time Oliver hated going to the abattoir was calving season, when the male calves were there, unwanted by large commercial dairy organisations who contract farmers to produce milk for the supermarket shelves. I now knew, from talking to dairy farming friends, that they couldn't keep male calves because they draw on the precious milk which is destined for the processing plant. Oliver found it hard to bear seeing them at the abattoir. Beautiful creatures, with huge, watery eyes fringed with lashes, their expression is naturally pitiable. But our society has found no other fate for them than this.

Oliver treated our pigs kindly while they were with us, and made sure their last journey was as stress-free as it could be. He was by no means the only farmer to be affected by sadness at taking his stock to slaughter. One day he came home and told me he'd met Adrian delivering one of his older sows to the abattoir.

'He said her toenails were too long, like Bella's, and she was just getting older and uncomfortable all the time. You could tell he was really fond of her,' he said, ruefully.

On another occasion, he was asked by one of our regular customers to supply a young pig, ideally just two or three months old and recently weaned from its mother. This customer had a milestone birthday coming up and wanted a suckling pig on a spit as the centre-piece of his party. At the time, there was a new litter of twelve slips on the farm.

'I was thinking of letting him have one of those,' said Oliver. 'There are too many of them, they'll all grow to weight at around the same time. It's okay if there's eight or ten of them, but when there's twelve it's a problem.' I could tell he didn't really like the idea of taking such a young pig to the abattoir but he did it, just that once. When he got back, his mood was dark.

'I'm never doing that again. It was revolting.'

'What happened?' I asked.

'Nothing. It was just the idea of it.'

The weaner had snuffled around its concrete pen unperturbed and unaware it was about to die at three months old. Whilst it was not too late, in theory, to back out and bring it home again, to do so would be to let that customer down, and leave him without the centre-piece for his celebratory feast.

'That's a first world problem if ever there was one,' Oliver said, as we stood clutching our cups of tea, looking out over the paddocks and pens. I thought of that young pig, of the short window of its life, and of its fate as the star attraction on a table. It's easy, when one is considering anonymous animals, to forget that each is a small soul that has only one shot at life. As Oliver headed out to feed the rest of the pigs that day, I knew he was remembering the last sight he had of that diminutive black and white form, snuffling in the corners of a concrete stall.

Inevitably, we became more familiar with concepts of slaughtering, carcass breakdown and butchering. If animals were to be eaten, we reasoned, these processes were unavoidable and it was best to know they were done humanely. We still ate meat, our own pork and meat from our local butcher, and sometimes from the supermarket. I bought mostly according to my values and sometimes according to how much time I had, the same as millions of other women bearing the majority burden of running their household.

Knowing we had raised the meat we were eating, being familiar with its living form, seemed a more primal experience than selecting anonymous packages of product. I was comfortable with having seen the living form and eating its meat, but Daisy increasingly was not. Many people could not look at the pictures of pigs on our market stall, and then buy our pork.

They found the idea shocking and distasteful. In my more judgmental moments, I found their squeamishness untenable. It came from a position of privilege, of being able to purchase anonymous meat without having to entertain the idea that it came from an animal. Our compartmentalised society, in which death is largely hidden and the source of our food is a mystery to many, has made many of us uncomfortable with the pragmatism required for farming and producing meat.

In a peculiar and uncomfortable way, I was grateful to be brought face to face so viscerally with where our food comes from, and forced to think about it.

Once or twice we became involved with events and organisations bigger than ours and people cleverer than us who clearly weren't thinking about all aspects of our supply chain at all. When an internationally successful festival from the south of Tasmania proposed putting on a smaller but equally splashy version of itself up north at our end of the island, there was great excitement across town. The event would take place over a weekend at the height of the summer tourist season, we learned at a presentation by the organisers. There was only one problem: their experience of running smaller events in Launceston was that most cafes were either closed on Sunday and those that were open were completely overwhelmed by queues literally around the block so the expected four thousand patrons of the festival potentially had nowhere to have breakfast. I put my hand up, foolishly it turned out, and asked if they had considered asking Harvest whether they would invite their ready-to-eat stalls to put on an extra market, a one-off 'Sunday market' specially to feed the four thousand.

The eyes of the woman presenting lit up and she promised

to take the idea to Harvest's management committee, which she did. They sanctioned it and went to bat doing the extra work of organising an extra market, and finding volunteers and managers who would be there to facilitate on the day. Summer rolled in and the festival came to town. I became involved in an social media event promoting it, a day out courtesy of the festival organisers, visiting the fabulous places of north Tasmania, photographing them and splashing them all over my social media. Back home on the day before the one-off Sunday market, Oliver pointed out that there had been no advertising by the festival of the thirty-something food stalls who would be present in the market square to offer them breakfast. Keenly I looked through the festival's brochure, and found that he was right. I turned to their social media. Again, no mention of the fact that thirty or so stallholders would set up specially to offer delicious hot food, local to the region and artisan produced, especially for the festival.

There was nothing to be done at such short notice and the next day we headed into town with our ute and trailer packed to the gills, set up in good faith and started cooking pork burgers for the expected four thousand hungry people.

Nobody came.

The market is situated on the edge of the shopping district in Launceston. It's central but not so central that you would see it unless you had a reason to be in that part of town. Gradually it became evident that our time had been utterly wasted. The four thousand hungry punters had not been told by their festival that we were there. After several soul-destroying hours we packed up our stall, its infrastructure and our product which had now been turned into food waste, carefully prepared and cooked for no reason, and went home.

Another stallholder passing us in his van as he left wound his window down and asked if we'd sold anything. We replied in the negative.

'What a complete waste of time!' he shouted. To my dismay, he was close to tears.

The next day, I emailed the organiser who had presented to us in Launceston and asked why they had not advertised the event to their mailing list of hungry festival-goers. She rang me later that week.

'We're very careful what we do with our brand and who we align ourselves with' she explained, in confident tones. 'We wouldn't do advertising for another business, like you wouldn't see us advertising Coffee Caff for example, it's up to them to do that.' Coffee Caff were a phenomenally popular and successful café and one of those who had been open on festival weekends and reputedly overwhelmed by demand.

'I see your point,' I told her, and rang off, feeling that I had been on the receiving end of a lecture and somewhat handicapped by my lack of a Master's degree in Business Administration.

It wasn't until later that day, having had time to chew over what she had said, that I came to see that while I could see her point, I didn't accept it at all. Coffee Caff were open for business every Sunday and had a faithful customer base who would make it worth their while being open whether the festival was in town or not. We had put on an extra market specifically to cater for the festival's customers, on a day when we weren't normally there. Every stallholder who had turned up in good faith to honour our proposal that we help the festival out by feeding their patrons, while making a good day's business ourselves, had worked, rearranged their life and potentially a precious day off, for nothing. I thought of the two pigs we had sent to slaughter specifically for that event, and the hours Oliver had spent in the processing room making them into burgers and sausages. In the blink of an eye it occurred to me that one can have a business degree but still not know anything about the perils of running a small business, or an agricultural one. Our business meant life or death for the creatures on our farm. Not everybody, we came to realise, gave much thought to that.

Oliver learned, and repeated to anyone who was interested, that nothing emerging from an abattoir is wasted. Every atom of every carcass is utilised in some way, including the parts we might perceive as waste.

The list of products that arises from the slaughter of a pig is astonishing, and it's said that no other animal provides us with a wider array of goods. Stearic acid comes from a pig and goes into chewing gum and candies. Surgical sutures and violin strings both come from the collagen in a pig's intestines. Porcine glycerine and gelatine is used in matches and marshmallows. The bristles from pigs are used in brushes and the fat from pork bones goes into toothpaste to give it texture. We quickly came to believe that it was only right to use every part of the pig, everything but the oink, leaving no waste.

We also came to realise that pigs are nature's recyclers. Pigs can eat almost anything without ill effect. What we fed them was controlled by law, and we took the clean feeding of our pigs seriously. We fed them our vegetable peelings and bread crusts, but no other kitchen waste, no meat or egg products, and nothing from any commercial bakeries or restaurants, although we were frequently offered waste by well-meaning business owners.

Notwithstanding all the measures put in place to make sure the domestic pig population of a country is fed safely, when left to their own devices, pigs can and will eat almost anything. It was enjoyable watching them eat, as they did so with considerable gusto, and evidently have no digestive troubles.

My father told me that when he was growing up, one or two families in the community, a town in Northern Ireland, always had a pig. After dinnertime, the kids from those families called at every back door in the street for kitchen scraps and food waste, which was then fed to the pigs. That avoided food waste being sent to landfill, and fed the pigs for nothing. Those pigs then became pork which fed most of the people in the street. They still do this in rural Europe and it is a shame it's not still done more widely. Every community should have a few backyard pigs.

The business of being meat-producers inevitably made us think differently about the meat we ate. When we lived in Brisbane, I purchased all my meat at the supermarket, pre-packed and plastic wrapped. If I was buying chicken breasts I chose the free range ones, believing that to be a more humane option than intensively reared chicken. Occasionally I purchased a whole chicken, but more often I purchased drumsticks, thighs or breast. Not often did I give that much thought to what happened to the rest of a carcass on the days when I purchased only a part of it, or what happened to the remaindered bits that nobody purchased. Now in business with a small farm of our own, I thought more about the whole chicken, pig, or cow.

What people saw in our display unit at the market was the different parts of a two pig carcasses. The survival of our business meant ideally selling all of that pork in one market. That was a considerable challenge, as some people never bought, cooked or ate pork. If we had the chance to ask why, we usually did; it was ad hoc market research. Sometimes it was because they had eaten pork in the past and considered it tough or flavourless, and this had put them off. Sometimes it was simply because they weren't in the habit of eating that particular meat.

Before keeping Wessex Saddlebacks, I had purchased pork chops occasionally from a supermarket. I cooked these colourless slices slowly under the grill, perhaps with a blob of herb butter on top. Without exception, they had the eating quality of shoe leather.

Now I came to understand that the rare breed pigs we owned grew more slowly than the commercially raised Long White, which has been bred to grow fast. The eating quality of the meat has become a secondary concern. By contrast, the slow growth of Wessex Saddlebacks and other rare breeds resulted in far more flavour. We saw the proof on our own plates, and were proud to sell it to people.

Having to sell both the premium and the less sought-after cuts was the challenge. The roasts and fillets must sell as well as the sausages and bacon. Our roasts were the hardest sell of all. Not many people want a pork roast for Sunday dinner on a fortnightly basis, no matter how good it is.

We learned to take a smaller supply of roasts to market, and to use the part of the carcass they came from for other purposes: chops, diced pork or occasionally mince. The roasts were made for us by our butcher using shoulder cuts, rolled into a handsome bundle and tied with butchers' knots. Oliver simply asked for smaller roasts, and fewer of them. Sometimes these instructions got through to whoever was doing the cutting, and sometimes they didn't. Those were the odds.

We also sent out newsletters and wrote blog posts with recipes using different cuts of pork. One week, I wrote up the way I had been cooking pork fillet for our family, searing it in a cast-iron pot, then cooking it slowly in the oven on a bed of sautéed onion rings and apple slices, with sprigs of thyme and lemon zest, all kept moist by a pool of wine in the bottom of the pot. Pork fillet comes from the upper back of the pig, and is a narrow loin strip of lean, tender meat. Many people aren't aware of what it is or how to cook it. One couple in particular amongst our customers loved this recipe so much, they purchased fillet from us regularly after that, learning to get to the stall early before others bought it up; we typically had just four packages of fillet to offer per market. They raved about how delicious and tender it was. They had never known what it was or cooked it previously, and I felt proud to have widened their eating repertoire and introduced them to a beautiful product which they valued so highly.

When we came home from a market with leftover stock, particularly roasts, Oliver often minced it, and made it into the sausages we needed for hot-food events, freezing these ready for use when those events rolled around. He got this idea of freezing stock from a local butcher, who saved every leg of pork from every carcass he purchased wholesale from June onwards, storing them in mighty chest freezers out the back of his shop. In December he thawed them out and made hams for Christmas. No doubt many of his customers believed they were eating ham from a pig which had been fattened for Christmas and slaughtered only the other day, not back in June. But how else would a butcher be able to produce two hundred Christmas hams? Pigs only have four legs, and there's a lot of other meat on a carcass. There has to be a way of meeting customer demand, and frozen stock is it.

There's nothing wrong with this practice. If accurate records are kept and stock is kept within the safe temperature range, it falls within all the laws of hygiene and food handling. It's just that as consumers, we often don't think about how our produce is created, and what actually happens sometimes appears surprising, when we do hear about it. Gradually, I came to believe there are many hidden and surprising things about the way our food has come to be produced.

Welfare

After six years of keeping pigs, Oliver and I came to know what was what in small-scale pig farming, and when we were having smoke blown up our arses.

We were half-heartedly watching a cooking show on television one evening. Shows about the good life centering on food were becoming two-a-penny. We were living the reality and it didn't always feel quite so shiny. On this show, two young Australian chefs were touring the land, and were visiting a hobby farm where pigs were kept, 'outdoors and free range as nature intended', as one of the chefs declared. They were chatting to the owner of the farm in her paddocks, hunkered down on the grass with a friendly pig hunkered down alongside them. The camera operator had got down low too, so he or she could fit them all into the shot, with a beautiful lush green grassy foreground. I noticed the pig had a ring in its nose. One of the chefs noticed this too.

'Now why is that, Annabel?' he asked of the farm owner.

Annabel didn't miss a beat and it was clear she had her answer down pat. 'Oh that's just her jewellery, Curtis! Don't you wear a bit of jewellery?' Her laughter tinkled across the paddocks. The two chefs joined in. The pig lay on the grass, not doing much.

There's only one reason why pigs have rings in their noses, and that's to stop them from digging. Their natural instincts are to forage, dig and eat. Some pigs are grazers and it takes acres of grass to keep them. Some are rooters. Once they've eaten all the greenery in a paddock or pen, they'll start turning over the ground for roots. Put them in a pen the size of a double garage, and they'll have eaten everything green within a couple of days. Then they'll start turning the soil over, which takes another few days. After that, they'll continue wandering about and digging, and their trotters will slowly compact the soil over the coming weeks and months until it's hard like concrete.

After years of keeping pigs, our pens were now horribly compacted and devoid of anything green, apart from the vegetable garden waste we threw into them for the pigs to sort through and eat. It's one of the problems of keeping pigs on small acreage: you have to limit the numbers so that you can rotate them through a number of pens, keeping some pens fallow for a while and allowing them to recover. Oliver and I argued perpetually about whether we were doing this adequately. I felt the pens needed to be smaller and the pigs rotated through them more frequently. Oliver was the one who had to put the fences up, so he wanted to leave the pens as they were, giving the pigs more room, and so that in winter there would be dry areas where they could escape from the mud.

The woman in that program might have been keeping her pigs 'free range', but she was hanging on to her lovely green pasture as well. Maybe she had other livestock that she usually grazed in those paddocks. Or maybe she just preferred the look of grass to mud or compacted soil.

'She's not really keeping her pigs in paddocks like that, is she?' I asked Oliver as we watched the chefs gaze suspiciously at the pig, and the farmer gaze warily at the chefs.

'No, I don't reckon. I bet she keeps them in a pen and just allows them out for a nibble at the grass once in a while. Her paddocks wouldn't look like that if there were pigs living in them, even if they have got rings in their noses.'

We looked in silence at the television, both of us thinking about the myths spread about the supposed idyll of keeping livestock on small acreage, and about how different the reality actually was.

Every so often, Oliver would buy in a sow or boar for our farm, from another rare breed farmer, or from sale-yards if he recognised the pig as a rare breed. He usually tried to talk to the person selling it and find out how it had been raised and kept, whether it had been well handled, whether it had come from a small herd or a large, to determine how well it would fit in on our farm. Over time he had become less convinced of the wisdom of raising one breed only, particularly if that was Wessex Saddlebacks, as they ran to fat so easily. After the death of Co-Pilot Bob, he had purchased a Berkshire boar, another traditional breed, from a fellow smallholder with a farm at nearby White Hills. Crossing this boar with our Saddleback sows resulted in a less fatty but equally flavoursome pork. Later, he purchased a Duroc boar, with the same results. The piglets which emanated from the farm's cross-breeding program thrived, having the 'hybrid vigour' which Oliver had heard came from such crosses.

Pigs in the outdoors on our farm

Buying in a pregnant sow from off-farm had an additional advantage. It meant Oliver could raise one of its male piglets born to become a boar servicing the other sows on our farm, as it wouldn't be related to any of them. Pigs are not choosy in their choice of partner for romance; they will mate with any other pig no matter how closely related. In theory, you could raise pigs from such a union and eat the pork with no problem at all. But such a practice completely destroys any sense of integrity in the breeding of good pigs and most likely leads to genetic disorders. We preferred not to allow this to happen, and we thought our customers would probably prefer it not to happen as well. So Oliver continued to introduce new sows to the farm, and raise new boars.

One of the new sows, he called Bunny. He purchased her from another small farm owner, and they met to do the exchange in the car park of Bunnings, the DIY store. 'Bunny' was a Large Black, Oliver was told, an old British breed. She was long rather than large, and a dark, dusky brown colour, with a long face and large, dark eyes.

On Bunny's first evening on the farm, Oliver was nowhere to be seen at dinner time. This was a common problem; late afternoons were when he lost all sense of time and liked to be outside with his herd of pigs, rather than inside with his other herd.

Walking over to the bush block, I found him standing by the gate to the pen where he'd released Bunny. He was holding a hose, running water into a trough and occasionally playing it over the ground closer to her. Most pigs love water during hot weather. They will lie in a wallow regularly, often developing a daily routine as Bella and Rosie had. Some enjoy having water from a hosepipe played gently over their back and sides, shaking gleefully and covering the farmer in muddy splatters.

Oliver used this as thinking time. Standing there holding a hosepipe and looking at one's pigs could make a man ruminative. He's an observant person, and this reflection usually saw him with an insight to share.

'She's had a ring in her nose,' he said, as I arrived beside him and rested my forearms on the gate.

'How can you tell?' I said.

'You see those slits? That's where she's pulled it out.'

I looked at the end of Bunny's snout. Sure enough, at either side of her snout there was a broad slit, which had healed up but left her snout in sections. I recoiled at the thought of her getting a nose-ring caught on roots and ripping it out through her flesh.

'You know, some farmers don't even use a proper ring, they

just stick a bit of old wire through the nose,' Oliver added.

'Oh, god. Do you think it hurts, or is it just like us having our ears pierced?' I tried to picture holding a small pig still while someone drove a piece of wire through its snout. The struggle would be horrific.

'It probably hurts like hell. Their snouts are really sensitive.'

We stood looking at Bunny in silence. She was turned side-on to us, but was watchful, taking the measure of her new home and custodians.

'I think she's pregnant as well,' Oliver said.

I looked at Bunny's tummy. She didn't have the enlarged udders of a sow who has had previous pregnancies. That makes it harder to tell just by looking, whether a sow is pregnant or not. But Oliver was sure. 'If you compare her straight back to her round tummy, it just looks like she's pregnant.'

'I wonder who to,' I said. Over time, Oliver's experience of buying pigs had told him that other owners mixed their breeding too, and if a sow was pregnant when purchased, you never quite knew what you were going to get.

I looked at Bunny. I couldn't tell whether her abdomen looked swollen with the beginnings of a litter or not. But Oliver had a better eye for these things after so long watching. As we stood there, she bent her long snout down to the dust and nosed around at the water puddling there.

'Well, I'm glad to be giving her a home and some comfort for a bit,' Oliver said. Bunny looked back at us. She would have her piglets in a birthing pen with some straw and raise them in an outdoor pen until they were ready to wean. If all went well with this first batch, Oliver would put her in a pen with the boar, and she would have more for us. Every so often, she would be moved into a pen where the grass had regrown, and would graze and dig it over, according to her natural instincts. She would also have the company of sows in neighbouring pens, but the safety of being separated. I knew that we wouldn't keep her on as a pet indefinitely after her breeding years were over, but at least for those years she would be looked after and content.

I knew of just one rescue farm for former farm animals in Tasmania. It was owned by a woman who headed a national retail chain. Alongside her genius for business, she had a thing for animals, and appeared to use her success to subsidise a farm rescue operation. But if every poddy-calf and every sow due for slaughter went there, it would be a very full farm with prohibitive running costs.

During the time we farmed pigs, animal activists gained entry into an intensive pig farm in Australia and filmed sows being held in stalls which confined their movements so that they could not even turn around. The animal rights movement called these 'sow stalls' and made much of the fact that they were used to separate sows from their piglets, preventing the piglets from being squashed when their mother lay on them.

In fact, what they were describing was farrowing crates, which are different from sow stalls. We never used either, but became familiar with the thinking behind them, some of which we understood.

Sow stalls are used on commercial pig farms which often have thousands of sows, and are used to house those sows from the time of their mating, for most or all of their pregnancy. Sows can be highly aggressive towards each other while they are pregnant, and the stalls separate them, preventing them from injuring each other by biting and charging, which might cause a spontaneous loss of the pregnancy.

Such is the pressure for room on commercial farms that sow stalls are small, so narrow that the sow cannot indeed turn around. While pigs are adaptable creatures, confining them like this seemed horribly cruel to us.

We understood the reasoning behind keeping sows separate. We had once introduced two sows into the same pen on our own farm, and watched in horror as they chased each other, trampling and head-butting each other viciously, grunting and squealing, pausing to catch their breath, panting and scraping the dust with their hooves, before attacking all over again. Oliver opened up the pen, dropping the electric fence on one side, and stepped into the pen waving a large board around to separate them. This in itself was dangerous, as pigs can cause horrible injuries by biting, but luckily one of the sows saw sense, and fled the pen, leaving the other one victorious. We never attempted to house sows together again, unless they had known each other from birth.

Strangely, we noticed that sows housed in neighbouring pens, whether they knew each other or not, seemed to be solicitous of each other when one went into labour. Another sow could often be found at the fence-line, looking over as if to inquire of the wellbeing of her companion. Rosie and Bella had always displayed this behaviour, and many of our other sows did too.

Farrowing stalls, the other infrastructure used on commercial farms, house sows as they give birth to their piglets, and for around four weeks afterwards. The stall is made of steel bars which contain the sow, allowing her to stand or lie down, and allowing the piglets to escape between the bars into a separate area. The piglets can still feed from the sow, and have an area to escape to, preventing them from being squashed underneath and crushed to death. Farrowing stalls are undoubtedly cruel in containing the sow in a space barely larger than her own body. They do, however, contain both sow and piglets together and they are an effective system for preventing piglets from being crushed.

Since Rosie and Bella first gave birth on our farm, we had stuck to the infrastructure Oliver had built into our two original pig sheds. Birthing sows were kept in a larger shed near the house which had one corner separated by a low bar, allowing the piglets passage underneath. Above the corner was slung a heat lamp, encouraging the piglets to gather underneath it. Sometimes this worked, but more often the piglets' natural instincts saw them huddling alongside their mother, beside her udders, gathering and sleeping there in one great heap. It was beyond what we could manage to be permanently present in the shed to ensure that no piglets got in the way when the sow got up to turn around, eat from her trough, or change position. Every so often, we lost a piglet, usually in the first few days of its life, when a sow trod or lay on it, and it died from crush injuries or asphyxiation.

As the birthing shed was close to the back of the house where Oliver and I slept, there was a handful of times when I heard the unmistakable screeching of a piglet being lain on. Oliver didn't hear as he slept with his good ear to the pillow. So it was me who dashed out of the house and over to the shed, usually to find that the situation had resolved itself.

On one occasion I found Bella half-reclined, her hind quarters down but her shoulders still up, looking towards her back end as if troubled by something. There was a piglet underneath her rump, its head and shoulders visible. Dressed in my nightgown and gum boots, I got into the stall and straddled Bella, silently thanking god that she was so tame, put one hand under her back-end and heaved upwards. I felt her helping me, and sensing its chance, the piglet freed itself, scrambling away miraculously unharmed.

Other occasions did not end so well. On a number of occasions, Oliver found a tiny carcass in the shed. There was never any way of telling whether it had been lain on or had died from unknown causes, perhaps not properly formed, with birth defects we could not see. There are few things as sad as the body of a new piglet just a few days old, apparently perfect, but lifeless. Daisy and I once nursed a piglet, in some way harmed but still alive, on our laps through the small hours of the morning, until it died just before dawn. As Daisy looked up at me grief-stricken from the sofa, cradling the small black and white form, my thoughts and emotions tangled into a web I was never able to undo. To use farrowing stalls was so cruel for the sow. Not to use them could result in this. The only way to escape both situations was not to eat meat. But if nobody ate pork, there would be no demand for pigs and potentially none would be bred, except as exotic pets or zoo animals, or small herds in villages and small communities kept for private use. And still the dilemma of how to ensure the safe-keeping of newborn piglets would rumble on.

As a result of the campaigning against sow stalls, legislation was introduced to phase them out. Adrian told Oliver it would put him out of business, as he could not afford the cost of rebuilding his pens.

Under the new legislation, the use of farrowing crates was still permitted, protecting piglets in the first few weeks after their birth, but keeping sows penned in narrow confinement.

In my mind, the dilemma of how to save piglets from death by crushing and treat sows well remains unresolved, as few of the options seem to work humanely. I still prefer pork from farmers who keep their stock free-range, as I know those conditions will be the best achievable. I pay more for such pork but have no hesitation in doing so.

Intensive farming with sow stalls and farrowing crates keeps costs as low as possible. The survival of piglets is optimised, which is good for them and for the producer, as every pig is a financial asset.

One thing is certain: wherever you put your money, that's the demand you're creating. Farmers deal with the welfare, life and death of animals every day. Those we met were, without exception, deeply knowledgeable and philosophical about what they did. They're farming in our name, in the style our dollar or pound allows for. They're thinking about profit and loss and operational costs, and they're thinking about their livestock, the animals their livelihood depends upon, about how they're kept and their welfare and wellbeing.

Increasingly, many consumers are also thinking more about the welfare of livestock, whether they're purchasing products from a butcher, a supermarket, or a farmers' market.

And others are not thinking about it at all.

On the Menu

With the Grand Fridge Smoker producing bacon for the market, Oliver decided his Mark 2 Smoker was going to waste just sitting around the property.

'I'm thinking of using it for events to cook the sausages in, instead of the barbecue,' he told me. 'It would be a real feature of the stall.'

Oliver saw the smoker as a tremendous selling point. It would give the meat a delicious smoky flavour, and be a talking point for men with beards who would come and have fascinating conversations with him at the back of the stall. I could picture this happening. I could also picture myself still working my arse off selling sausages up the front of the stall.

I saw the whole idea of using the smoker as a way of making our already fraught business even more difficult, replacing one messy cooking method with another, and necessitating the transport of an unwieldy and heavy piece of equipment, along with a supply of firewood to fuel it. And that was before you started considering the question of safety. How on earth would he persuade event organisers and council hygiene officers that this was a safe way of cooking meat for public consumption?

Smoker Mark 2

But Oliver had the bit between his teeth. Mark 2 Smoker wasn't big enough for events, he said, and he set about building another, larger one that would cook greater quantities of sausage. He got in touch with the Council, and got the idea passed in theory. I thought about the hours he had now spent welding pieces of steel together to build these contraptions and felt we were descending into some sort of steampunk-themed netherworld, losing all focus on making the business work in a sensible, sustainable, easy way. The smokers became the embodiment of my growing frustration. I was proud of the pork, but much of the infrastructure of the business, the smokers, the trailers we towed our stall around in, were welded and held together by bits of rope, literally. Instead of feeling like a polished, modern food business, it had a hodgepodge, thrown-together quality. As I concentrated more on my own business, writing books and freelance journalism, it felt as if the farm business was spiralling out of control.

Smoker Mark 1 had been on our back patio for a year or two now, being tested on Sunday dinners. When Mark 2 came along, Mark 1 was retired, but it was heavy and Oliver had not yet thought of putting wheels on his smokers when he'd built it. Consequently, it didn't make it very far on its journey back to the workshop, and for months sat in a flower bed outside our bedroom window. It was the first thing I saw when I opened the curtains in the morning, which didn't do much to improve the state of our marriage, already under pressure from running an arduous business together.

Smoker Mark 3 was a mammoth structure, with a huge square firebox and great cylindrical smoking chamber the size of a forty-four gallon drum tipped on its side. Showing it to me, Oliver threw open the door which he'd set into the top, giving access to the smoking racks. The door looked heavy and I wondered if he'd given any thought to opening it repeatedly with one hand at events, under pressure and balancing a tray of sausages in the other hand. I decided not to ask.

Mark 3 was large enough to smoke the quantities of product needed for a lunchtime rush, feeding a couple of hundred people. It was on wheels and therefore easily transportable, in theory. He'd also had it passed by the Councils in whose jurisdiction we'd be operating at various events.

A day or two after he'd finished making it and painting it black, he called me over from the house for a grand unveiling. I looked at this new steel monstrosity, matte black with orange handles and legs.

'Help me push it up the ramp into the trailer,' Oliver said, keen to make sure we could manage this when loading up for a market.

'Shouldn't you be able to do that yourself?' I replied. I wasn't always around to help him set up, or even load our equipment onto the trailer from the workshop, as I could be busy elsewhere. 'I thought you'd be making it a size you could manage on your own,' I said.

'It'll be fine, I can always ask someone else to help,' Oliver insisted. It seemed a precarious contingency and was symptomatic of our increasingly different approach. I instinctively felt we needed to streamline everything, take advice and get smarter in how we developed the business; Oliver's approach was influenced more by his determination to make and do everything himself.

Reluctantly, I positioned myself at the back of the smoker, which sat on the smooth concrete floor of the workshop. Oliver had backed the trailer in through the roller doors, and took the front end, pulling it up the ramp while I pushed. Since the ramp was made of steel grid-work, he placed a sheet of plywood on top for the smoker's casters to roll over, tying it on with scraps of rope. As I watched him fumbling with the knots, I couldn't help thinking everything we did was held together in the same tenuous way.

Finally, we were ready to get the beast onto the trailer. As we heaved and swore, it weaved around from side to side on the ramp, veering off towards one side and being heaved back into line by Oliver.

'Why have you made it so bloody heavy?' I gasped from the back, watching Oliver straining to pull it the last couple of feet. He'd had a hernia operation a few years earlier. If he over-exerted himself and burst the repair, the business would have to cease operating. I couldn't run the stall and the farm on my own, feeding the pigs twice daily and managing the production cycle. I had endless admiration for the women I'd met who had run their farms alone in difficult circumstances, but farming was usually in their blood. It wasn't in mine.

Finally the smoker was on the trailer, and looked as if it would only just fit when the tailgate was closed.

'There's not much room for manoeuvre, is there?' I said.

'That's why I wanted to get it on the trailer, to check I've got the length right,' Oliver replied.

'What the hell would we do if it was too long? You've made it now!'

I watched in disbelief as he ushered me off the ramp, fumbled with the rope to remove to plywood sheet, and raised the tailgate into position. It closed, but only just. Oliver dropped the steel pins holding the tailgate closed into place.

'Done and dusted!' he said, jubilant.

I looked at the small steel pin and its housing which held this monstrous contraption on the trailer.

'That's enough to hold it?'

'The brakes are on as well.' He had fitted casters with brakes onto the smoker to hold it in position on the trailer, just as he had with our market stall counter.

I pictured the scene of an accident caused by the monstrous smoker rolling off the back of the trailer as Oliver drove on, oblivious. There had been a report on the news of a driver transporting armchairs on a trailer without securing them properly; one had bounced off and killed the woman in the car behind.

But Oliver, an experienced driver with years of practice in loading utes and heavy transport vehicles, insisted that the tailgate was secure, and the smoker locked in place. Sure enough, we never did lose anything off the back of the trailer, but loading up did nothing for our stress levels.

One good thing came of Smoker Mark 4. It was perfect for cooking pork burgers. For a couple of years, I had been trying to persuade Oliver that we should serve burgers as well as sausages at the stall. It seemed ridiculous to continue to offer one menu item only, even if it was delicious. We had so many repeat customers visit us at the same events every year, it was time to offer them some choice.

I had been watching other food vans and saw that burgers were always popular. They could be topped with a range of substances you didn't have to cook but could simply buy in, such as salad leaves. Significantly, it would require the same amount of meat to make a burger as a sausage, but you could charge more.

Pricing is paramount on a market stall. Too low and you're underselling your product. Too high, and you price yourself out of the market. Instinctively, and through researching other vendors' menus, I knew that we could not charge more than eight dollars for a sausage, even a gourmet one with painstaking farm provenance. We'd hit the glass ceiling for snags.

For a burger, on the other hand, especially a succulent Tasmanian farm-bred pork burger, I suspected punters would pay up to twelve dollars, perhaps more, depending on the event and how much they'd been drinking at the wine and beer stalls.

My problem was the age-old one; Oliver dug his heels in and refused to consider it.

'Burgers are a lot of hassle to make,' he insisted.

'How can they be any more difficult than a bloody sausage? You just shape them into patties and the job's done! There's none of that feeding them into a skin like you do a sausage!'

There couldn't be many business empires built on such conversations, I reflected, and it wasn't even one I felt qualified to have. What did I know about sausage skins? But Oliver couldn't articulate a satisfactory response anyway, and worn out with arguing, we kept letting it drop.

There was a long-standing tradition in our marriage of Oliver resisting things that I suggested. He had dug his heels in about many things: having children, moving to Tasmania, getting a dog. In each case, he would finally relent, and then admit that I'd been right all along. But he still wouldn't remember that for the next time. It drove me to the brink of distraction, until I finally learned to put things into effect without consulting him.

Over the years I puzzled over his difficulty in giving my suggestions credence. One theory, bizarre though it might sound, was that I was too short. There is research indicating that people of less-than-average height are often overlooked, particularly in the world of work: offered lower starting salaries, ignored or interrupted in meetings, finishing their career with less superannuation than people of average or above-average height. I found it hard to countenance the possibility that a man could be so stupid as to find himself a wife who was shorter than him, and spend the rest of his life ignoring her thoughts because of it. But perhaps that's the patriarchy for you.

Another theory was that I was too direct. I've been accused of being blunt many times since we moved to Australia, and had come to suspect it was a cultural thing. In England, we grow up with tabloid newspapers shouting outrageous things from their front pages. Across the channel in mainland Europe, French, German and Italian people not only speak their minds, they shrug, pout and gesticulate freely to drive their point home. But I'd heard it said, and have come to believe, that Australians prefer a more softly-softly approach. That didn't explain what was going on between Oliver and me, as he's as English as I am.

Women through the decades have been encouraged to subtly persuade men that our ideas are actually theirs. I couldn't even begin to imagine how to do this, and anyway, it seemed a ridiculous, disingenuous and misogynistic piece of chicanery which undermined the integrity of everyone involved. If a man had to be pandered to and subtly deceived into believing in his own superior brilliance by his wife, didn't that make him a bit feeble minded? I found the concept so insulting for all parties, it only added to my cantankerousness. Eventually, I even looked at the more straightforward dynamics between the pigs on our farm, and the way they established pecking order in a straight-up manner and 'listened' to one another without resorting to artifice. They had things right, I reflected; there was none of this chicanery and subtle-persuasion shit in their world.

I was raised in a family of people who said what they thought and expected it to be taken at face value. But with Oliver, for whatever reason, my opinion didn't always wash, for reasons I couldn't understand and he couldn't articulate. He always had his own ideas on how to do things, and often dug his heels in about acting on mine.

Luckily, he had other qualities which helped keep us together: like being one of the most thoroughly decent people I know. But at times, during these years, it felt as if the ties that bound us together were money, property, family and the fact that we were too exhausted to go through a separation. Many is the farming relationship I've heard of which has ended up in the same dire straits.

Farming is a difficult, isolated, and often misunderstood business. Running a farm as a couple, especially a marginal business when neither of you has the right skills and you're getting older and tireder, can be problematic in the extreme. I had written about farming women and heard the same story many times: of women going out to work in the paddocks or the stockyard with their men and then returning to the house to cook and care for the family. 'And then you've got to sleep with the bastard too!' as one woman memorably put it.

It was only when these years were behind us that we were really able to find the good in each other again, and be glad that we had stuck it out and remained together. As soulmates, we'd have a rich store of memories to look back on in our old age, as long as we didn't kill each other before we got there.

With our joint decision-making having assumed this level of brinkmanship, I knew how to use every little chink of opportunity. When Oliver decided he wanted to use the smoker for the coming summer's events, I saw my chance for leverage.

I was betting the rough texture of a burger would cook beautifully in the smoker, absorbing a delicious smoky flavour. Wrapped in a wholemeal bun with some springy greens, a dribble of chilli sauce and a dollop of sour cream, this would make for a mouth-watering meal that festival goers could hold in their hand and eat at a table or while they were walking about.

I made my pitch to Oliver.

'If you want to use the smoker at the Tasmanian Craft Fair, then let's do it. But you have to agree to do burgers as well as sausages, so that we can have an actual menu.' This was quid pro quo and Oliver finally relented. With the next batch of pork, he made some burgers for us to try at dinnertime, shaping them with round steel rings he'd picked up at a commercial kitchen supply shop. This seemed to get him over some mental hurdle about how he would manufacture them, and I wondered whether this small matter had been the cause of two years' worth of obduracy. Whatever, they cooked beautifully, and were juicy and delicious, wrapped in paper napkins to catch the succulent juices running down across our fingers.

'They're pretty good, aren't they?' Oliver murmured, gazing at the tender pink meat sandwiched in a wholemeal bun. 'I think these might do okay.'

I turned my gaze to the calm green of the paddocks and took a deep draught of Pinot Gris.

The day before the craft fair opened, Oliver packed up the trailer with the stall equipment, and called me over to help him push the Monstrous Smoker up the ramp.

'Why is it so heavy?' I demanded, as we stood in the bush block staring at it, and catching our breath. 'Shouldn't we be consolidating what we take to markets and making it lighter and more efficient?' I was thinking ahead to a time when we had sufficient assets and custom to sell the business off to another couple, preferably someone who had the youth and energy to actually enjoy it. But Oliver had made the biggest smoker he could, with capacity for the greatest amount of product.

When we began using it at the Tasmanian Craft Fair, the smoker proved to be the talking point Oliver had imagined, and it certainly differentiated our stall having it chuffing away out the back of the marquee. But it was harder work than anticipated.

Oliver had imagined himself stoking the fire chamber with timber, opening the door to poke another log in every so often and intriguing passers-by with his flame-fired contraption. Then, clad dramatically in huge leather safety gloves, he would lift the lid of the cooking chamber, and pull out a rack jostling with sizzling pork product, attracting appreciative oohs and aahs from the crowds. What he had forgotten was that the crowds were at the front of the stall and he'd be at the back, enveloped in a cloud of wood-smoke which blinded him on a windy day. Depending on which event we were at, there could be a cold wind coming off the Western Tiers, and the icy gusts would cool the smoker down, slowing the cooking process, which could be disastrous during a lunchtime rush.

Finally, whilst the carefully styled front-end of the stall

featured flowers from the garden in a rustic stoneware vase, attractive menu signage and a timber front counter which I kept clean and clear of clutter, the back end of the stall now looked like a post-apocalyptic wasteland, with smoke flying, rough-hewn firewood logs spilling out of sagging cardboard boxes, and star pickets driven into the ground with hazard tape strung between them to prevent children from scorching themselves on the hot sides of the smoker. It didn't look like an area designed for the hygienic production of food, and I preferred to stand with my back to it.

Oliver himself took on the appearance of a warrior escapee from a Mad Max film, in a filthy, smoke-and-grease-smeared apron, fireproof glove, and dark glasses and hat, worn in an effort to protect himself from the dual heat of the smoker and the searing sun. As I glanced back at him occasionally from my spot at the front counter, slaving away over his fiery contraption, I had to admire his determination in carrying through with a plan. But surely, I wondered desperately, there had to be easier ways to earn a living.

Despite its cumbersome nature and its replicating of the industrial revolution at the back of the stall, the smoker did enable us to up the ante for the two years we used it, increasing the amount of product we could cook, giving it a unique smoky aroma and flavour. We used slow-cookers to store the sausages and burgers once they were cooked, keeping them up to legal temperature for consumption, while Oliver cooked another batch. On days when we had Daisy and Kit taking orders, and Patsy and myself each with an assembly station, the product walked across the counter.

In our last year of hot food events, we added another menu

item which teamed beautifully with our smoky pork: a local Pinot Gris, produced by a nearby Tamar Valley vineyard. For three days, I worked my way through a series of training videos in an online course, to earn a Responsible Service of Alcohol certificate. Not only did I have to watch videos, I had to video myself, role-playing my responses to clientele who might have imbibed too heavily and had to be refused a further serve.

'I'm sorry, my love,' I said into the camera, its light winking at the top of my laptop screen. 'I think you've probably had one or two more than you should have, and it's against the law for me to serve you more.' I leaned over the desk in my best barmaid manner, finally finding a use for my degree in Theatre Studies.

We approached the owners of Winter Brook Vineyard, and asked if we could purchase their wine wholesale. Owner Nicole recommended their Pinot Gris, which seemed perfect, being the drop that had helped me retain my sanity through the years.

Wine was an easy and obvious addition to the stall. All we needed was storage space under the bench for a box of twelve bottles, some bio-degradable plastic wine glasses with the appropriate measure marked on them, and a wine bucket containing ice which could be displayed on the counter. I myself would be drawn to a stall where I could purchase both my lunch and a glass of chilled white, and it worked. Many customers took advantage of the chance to make their lunch more of an epicurean treat.

At the Tasmanian Craft Fair, Nicole called by and purchased a burger and a glass of her own wine. After dining in the shade of the central food marquee, she swung by again. 'Mm, that burger was delicious, and the acidity of the wine complements that beautiful smoky flavour that you've got going really well.' This was delivered in her warm, smoky Dutch accent, and it was a lovely moment in which all our efforts came together for a brief reward.

* * *

Pork Burgers

Oliver created this recipe basing it on that by Hugh Fearnley-Whittingstall, who inspired us in our love of pigs and the running of our farm, not just burgers. Oliver does tend to go off-piste with herbs and spices; create your own blend to suit!

INGREDIENTS
  Pork mince
  Breadcrumbs or panko breadcrumbs (extra fine)
  Onion powder or finely grated onion
  Garlic powder
  Dried herbs such as sage, oregano
  Allspice, pimento and ginger to taste

PREPARATION
  Mix all ingredients together and form into patties
  For consistent rounds, use steel rings or scone cutters

COOKING
  Cook on the barbecue or in a frying pan with a lid

If your burgers are quite thick, finish them in a warm oven for ten minutes

FOR THE TABLE

Serve in the freshest wholemeal buns you can get with salad leaves, a slice of beef tomato and ranch dressing. If made with rare breed pork, these burgers will pair with the white or red wine of your choice, or beer.

Diversification

In the face of hardship, farmers are often encouraged to do the worst thing they could possibly do in the circumstances: diversify. It's seen as a means of adding income streams when actually it's a means of creating more work and spreading yourselves that little bit more thinly. But we didn't know that.

There was a lot of talk by the tourism authorities about diversifying. We'd be missing a trick if we didn't galvanise ourselves and find an agri-tourism venture as a clever way of adding value to our business. It just meant finding a picker's hut, a straw bale cottage, or an old barn sitting around on your property, and converting it into stylish accommodation.

People from tourism authorities are undoubtedly clever, but they don't know as much about running a small farm as they do about tourism, and that should have told us something. Expanding into agri-tourism sees many a farmer trying to grow a skill set that might not come naturally to them. Some do it brilliantly, running beautiful farm accommodation and feeding their guests pumpkin muffins from a family recipe. To others, it doesn't come so naturally.

We knew life in an artisan farm business was bloody hard, that we worked six days a week and were knackered on the seventh. But we also knew another income stream would be handy.

Offering farm-stay accommodation and sharing our story, however humble, seemed like a good fit with our small-farm enterprise. Ours was a story that many people were curious about: moving from the city and taking up small-farm life. We had an L-shaped house with a double garage and a guest bedroom at one end. We had planned on converting this into a second living area, and sometimes referred to it as the 'west wing', an epithet far too grand for the dumping ground it had become. Slowly, as plans formed, it became known as 'the B&B'.

Over several months, we converted the garage to a spacious living room with a kitchenette along one wall. We replaced the two roller doors with a window and double-door entrance. We chose tiles, painted throughout, and scored some second hand carpet for the bedroom and living area from friends. Our laundry served as a guest bathroom, and we installed a door midway down the hallway, closing off that end of the house while we had guests. It offered us security and privacy, and meant they had a bathroom to themselves. I'd have to do our family laundry between visitors, but we didn't intend on having people to stay constantly, so it didn't seem like a problem. What we should have done was factor in bad weather, and increasing quantities of laundry from children approaching their teenage years. But we didn't know that.

As ever, Oliver did the building work and I did the design. Having relied on this formula before, it should have worked seamlessly, but that didn't account for Oliver's propensity for questioning things.

'Are you sure you want those drawers to be that deep?' he

asked. I'd drawn up a long, low, built-in unit which swept along the entire length of one wall. The television set would sit handsomely on the wall above it, and it would provide ample storage and give the room a well-designed look. I'd taken the idea from a book on Scandinavian design, and knew it would work a treat in this spot and be a real statement piece. Because it stretched the width of the wall, it needed to be a certain depth for the proportions to look right.

For a day or two, Oliver's quibbling made me doubt my plans. I drew the designs up differently, but it just didn't look right, so I stuck to my guns.

'It's time you trusted my design instincts,' I told him, a little pompously. I could tell he still had his doubts but he went ahead and built the cabinets. Everybody who visited commented on how handsome they were.

When the rooms were ready, we looked round with satisfaction at the comfortable space we had created. It was then that the irony struck us: it was a good deal smarter than our own living quarters at the other end of the house. There had never been time to renovate our kitchen or living area. Still, it was some small comfort to know we could put strangers up in style.

We set the place up on a booking site online. I knew it would take time before we'd get any interest; Oliver was ready for instant bookings. On the day our listing went live, he put his head round the door of the office. 'I haven't heard the phone ringing off the hook yet,' he said. 'When do you think we'll start getting some calls?'

'We're unlikely to get calls when people are supposed to book online,' I pointed out. 'Anyway, it's the end of the season so we'll be lucky to get any takers at all.' It had taken us longer than anticipated to prepare the place, and our advertising began just as the summer season was tailing off.

To our surprise, we got a few inquiries, and those translated into bookings. The first couple to visit were from just outside Melbourne and seemed like the perfect guests for a farm-stay. Both foodies, he had just begun working as a cheese maker, and they were touring Tasmania to sample its artisan and handmade cheeses. Oliver gave them a walking tour around the pens, where they exclaimed over the pigs who stood obligingly at their fence lines and snorted softly.

Back at the house, we stood around chatting in the front garden outside the guest rooms. 'You really are living the dream, aren't you?' the woman remarked, looking out over the vegetable garden. Oliver and I both smiled, and I knew we were thinking the same thing: the dream is bloody hard work and it's not paying very well.

Over the next year or two, we had a steady stream of guests, mostly delightful people swept away by the Tasmanian way of life. They took great pleasure in discovering what was hidden away in the folds of the island's landscapes: epicurean treats, spectacular wilderness and places of significance to the Aboriginal community, and outstanding wines with vineyards and cellar doors at every bend in the road. There was the rich colonial history too, early settlers' homes, buildings built by convicts and a sense of the past evident in the landscape, and every so often somewhere brave enough to tell the terrible stories of the vanquishing of the Aboriginal community during that time, which amounted to genocide.

Growing up in England, I had been taken as a child to visit all manner of places where history was visible: the remains of Roman forts; Viking artefacts and places where burial ships had been found, with fantastic museums now on the site; replica Stone Age villages, and humps and circles and curious rings in the landscapes which were the semi-buried evidence of ancient cultures. Thousands of years' history and multiple cultures are visible in Britain's landscape, and I had expected the past to be similarly visible in Australia. I was still astonished to find it was not the case, that the celebration and honouring of indigenous culture had not been widely facilitated, with that culture instead being horribly oppressed. It was a feature of Australian life that made me realise what a young, invasive thing the dominant white European culture was.

Like us, many of our guests had no idea what to expect of Tasmania. Once such couple disembarked from the ferry on the north coast late one evening, and drove from there to our farm, expecting to stop for dinner at some classy little roadside restaurant. There is perhaps one establishment serving food on that route, a quaint cafe in a barn, but it closed in the late afternoon. Our guests turned up at our place hungry, tired and taken aback, prepared to make do with the local cheese and crackers we left for visitors. It so happened that we had made a delicious lasagne for our own dinner, complete with home-made pasta made by Oliver. I cut a couple of generous portions, adding a side of freshly steamed broccoli. Under Council regulations, we were not allowed to cook or serve food to our guests, but it felt satisfying to offer that simple act of freely-given hospitality, as people have done across multiple cultures for thousands of years.

We shared the occasional glass of wine with guests, and fell into a routine, Oliver hosting them on tours of the farm, and me recommending wines, cellar doors, places to eat and routes to take around the island.

Soon the Tourism Officer with the West Tamar Council got wind of what we were doing and generously included us in a photo-shoot of local tourism businesses. He turned up with a photographer and four people recruited as 'talent': locals who were happy to come along for a day out, who could pass for visitors and would model in the photographs. The men were in smart shirts and shiny shoes, and the women similarly stylish. Most of our guests turned up in polar fleece gear and scruffy shoes they'd been hiking in. Still, we cooked up some sausages, bacon and farm eggs on the barbecue outside the guest rooms, the photographer snapped away, and we got some free professional-quality shots, even if the blokes did look like they'd be more at home in a corporate office.

The information sent out by the tourism authorities to anybody running a business catering for visitors made for interesting reading: detailed research on visitors, looking at who they were, what age, what kind of jobs they had, their financial status, whether they were young professionals, couples with children, friends travelling together, or empty-nesters. The research described the typical Tasmanian visitor as millennials keen to explore and grab the newest, most Instagram-worthy experience, or older 'life-long learners'. Both were looking for experiences that money couldn't buy elsewhere, such as walking around a farm with a man who talked compulsively about Saddleback pigs. When I walked out to my gate and met the people who came to stay with us in the flesh rather than on the page, I was often amazed at how closely they fit the profile. I studied the tourism reports more closely and read about the colours, styling and tone of voice that might appeal to those looking at Tasmania as a travel destination, and tried to use those in our own website and entries on accommodation sites.

Not all the visitors we had fit the profile of those pleasant life-long learners, and some were downright strange. One man clearly hadn't got the measure of the sharing economy, in which people like us opened their homes to visitors and treated them less like paying guests and more like friends of friends who happened to be passing. It was strange how quickly you could get the measure of people even from a few lines in their initial message to introduce themselves.

'Visiting family in locality,' this man had written. It was different from the more effusive message most people sent us about how lovely our place looked and how they couldn't wait to explore Tasmania. So I'd had my suspicions about this person from the very first.

'Please ensure you have Seven Up in stock for our arrival, I don't travel well and it settles my stomach,' he wrote me a few days before his arrival.

It was Christmas but I was no longer feeling the cheer, fully occupied coping with family and school commitments at that crazy time of year.

'Unfortunately, I'm not sure if I will make it to the shops, as it's a busy market weekend for our farm,' I wrote back, starting to be thankful that he and his partner were only staying a couple of nights and wondering whether they usually stayed somewhere rather more hotel-like.

'Can you send me the times of local church services as I wish to attend a mass on Christmas Eve,' he continued.

'My apologies, but I'm not sure how to go about finding the

times of services.' I replied. 'Perhaps if you search online you might find that information.' I wasn't normally this unhelpful but he had really got under my skin with his room-service requests.

When he and his partner arrived, they were a breed slightly apart. The afternoon they arrived, I found them wandering through our vegetable garden picking tomatoes for their supper. We often invited people to do this but only if we liked them. When I appeared at the garden gate to say good evening, they ignored me. I noticed that while their clothing appeared quite costly, they themselves appeared sweaty and unwashed. I thought of them using my nice sheets and throw rugs, and shuddered. After they'd gone, I found the cupboard doors in the kitchenette smeared with grease. There were torn pieces of food wrapping on the bench-top and the floor, and empty bottles and cans scattered about.

Determined to reclaim the place as my own, I stripped the beds, washed the sheets on the hottest setting, cleaned every surface until it was immaculate, and opened every door and window to let fresh air circulate. I always did this anyway, but it made me feel better on that occasion.

We always welcomed people with dogs, as we knew it was often hard to find pet-friendly accommodation. As dog owners ourselves, we didn't mind helping out, and at the risk of sounding cynical, it was a potential market for us. But as they say in Yorkshire, there's nowt so queer as folk, and that includes folk with dogs.

One couple had two greyhounds, rescued from the racing industry. We'd looked into doing the same, and knew that greyhounds are intelligent and gentle, but can also be aloof. It had been hard to warm to these bony creatures who sprang soundlessly from the back of the car and loped around the place ignoring any human presence.

'Those people are off their rocker about those bloody dogs,' said Oliver. I had been out to an appointment and came home to find him perplexed. 'They've gone out now, but they asked if they could leave the doors open and the heaters on so the dogs could go in and out in comfort!'

The doors of the guest rooms were at the front of the house and visible from the road. Although our district was quiet and we rarely locked our car doors, there were occasions when the local grapevine would light up with news about a break-in, or strange vehicles turning up on people's properties. Oliver was aghast that these people had thought it reasonable to leave the place open to all-comers, but even more aghast at the prospect of warmth from the oil heaters flooding out of the doors. Oliver has a frugal bent, and expected his guests to exhibit common sense. It drove him to distraction when people left lights on in the guest bathroom, and occasionally the fan too, sometimes overnight. Although the door in the hallway was closed and locked for privacy, it was frosted glass so the light shone through, and any transgressions of this nature were clear to see.

Once, when somebody left the heat lamps on, I decided enough was enough. After lying awake fretting about the heat causing spontaneous combustion in the roof space, I leapt out of bed, unlocked the hallway door quietly, turned off the heat lamps, and retraced my steps back to bed.

'I can't believe you just did that,' Oliver said as I climbed in beside him. 'You never normally like going in there when guests are in.'

'I bet they don't even notice in the morning,' I replied, tersely.

'Anyway, it's my house.'

This was increasingly my view. By our third year we were turning into the Sybil and Basil Fawlty of the southern hemisphere. Putting less effort in, we had fewer guests as a result, and found it nothing short of inconvenient. We had come to enjoy using the second living space ourselves, and no longer wanted it to be off-limits and given over to strangers. There was a piano in there which Daisy liked to play, and a second television. It was a quiet, warm space in the afternoons, perfect for a quick nap if the day was proving arduous. In truth, we simply no longer wanted strangers in our house. Washing all the bedlinen after a one or two-night stay seemed environmentally un-viable. Preparing the place for guests after we had been using it ourselves took many hours, and the puny income stream it offered just did not seem worth the effort.

Our agri-tourism venture came to a close in a way none of us could have foreseen. One day I found Oliver and Daisy sitting in our living room at odd angles to each other and staring at the walls, their expressions clouded over.

'What on earth is the matter?' I asked.

'You can tell her,' Daisy muttered in a mutinous tone.

Oliver looked nonplussed. 'She's been in the drawer of my desk and found something.'

'A bag,' said Daisy. Oliver remained silent.

'For God's sake,' I was becoming exasperated. 'Will someone tell me what's going on?' Oliver was looking increasingly awkward, and Daisy increasingly thunderous. She had grown into a mild-mannered, reserved young woman and I had rarely seen her so cross.

Finally Oliver fessed up. 'She found the bag that bloke gave me,' he said. 'Of weed.'

Like many men, Oliver had spent much of his spare time during his youth smoking dope, rolling joints at the back of the class at his boarding school and growing his own in his parents' greenhouse. It afforded him many laughs over the years, and then it messed with his head, resulting in sudden and profound black moods and a sense of helplessness. We were both glad those days were behind him. But his fondness for his misspent youth meant that when some well-meaning bloke he chanced upon gave him a small supply, Oliver had been unable to throw it away. He had stashed it, for old times' sake, underneath a stationery tray in his desk drawer, where it had stayed ever since.

'That must be years old!' I said.

'It is!' said Oliver, as if this excused its existence.

Suddenly Daisy found her voice. 'If he doesn't get rid of it, I'm calling the police.'

'You can't call the police for a bag of weed!' Oliver protested.

I looked at them both, Oliver shamefaced and Daisy resolute, arms folded, her face set in a filthy stare. It was quite the stand-off.

Unfortunately for Oliver, it seemed obvious that I had to take Daisy's side. She had found him in possession of an illicit substance. We had to back up all that she had been taught at school, and the principles we would now want her to adopt. That didn't include accepting that your dad would keep a little stash for a rainy day, even if he didn't smoke any more.

'I think it has to go,' I said to Oliver.

'No, I want to keep it!' he protested.

'Why?'

'I don't know!'

I was reminded of the time he told me that he didn't want to have a vasectomy in case he decided to have children with another woman. After taking a moment to absorb the fact that he would say this out loud, I had to remind him that it had taken three years to persuade him to have children with me, because being a father just wasn't something he ever saw himself doing. It seemed quite the volte-face.

'Where is this bag of stuff then?' I asked, returning to the breach of legality in question.

'Upstairs,' Daisy replied, the disgust in her voice suggesting the mere fact that it was anywhere inside the walls of the house was an atrocity.

After further protest, Oliver fetched it, storming up to the office and returning with a greasy, brown paper bag and thrusting it at me. I opened it tentatively and was confronted with the sight of a fine brown powder. It had only a faint smell, and didn't look like anything you'd want to ingest into your lungs in a hurry.

'That looks disgusting,' I said, and Daisy harrumphed beside me. 'You couldn't possibly want to smoke that, even if you did still smoke!'

'Well throw it away then!' Oliver shouted. He was unusually agitated, no doubt embarrassed at having been caught out by his law-enforcing teenage daughter. I felt myself becoming cross too, which would undoubtedly be helpful.

'Well I'm not going to throw it in the bin, am I?'

'I will!' Daisy offered.

'No you won't,' said Oliver.

'Well, what do you suggest, then?' I asked.

'I don't see why I should have to throw it away.'

I had a sudden sense of what it might be like to be trapped

in a whirlwind.

'Either it goes or I go,' said Daisy, laying all her cards on the table.

I stared at Oliver, agog.

'When were you planning on smoking it, exactly?'

'Never!' said Daisy.

'I don't know!' said Oliver. He was nothing if not consistent.

'You'd be sick as a dog if you smoked anything like this now. Besides, Daisy's right. You shouldn't have it in the house when we've got two teenagers and we want them to do the right thing.'

'Bury it in the sodding garden then!' he yelled.

'Of course I'm not going to do that, the dog will just dig it up!'

'Well then I'll burn it!'

We had finally painted Oliver into a corner. All of a fluster, he got up and grabbed the bag from where it sat on the coffee table, strode over to the wood-burner, opened the door and tossed the bag and its contents into the flames.

I looked at Daisy, wide-eyed. Her expression was still stern, but there was a smug little smile at the corners of her mouth.

A silence fell over the room, none of us quite certain what to say.

Suddenly Kit appeared at the top of the stairs, stopped and waved a hand in front of his face. 'What's that smell?'

I looked at Oliver, and sniffed. An unmistakable scent was slowly filling the living room.

'Oh Christ, we've got guests in!' I leapt up and dashed upstairs.

'Does this mean we'll all get high?' Daisy wailed behind me.

In the bathroom I grabbed a couple of towels, wetted

them in the sink and wrung them out, then dashed along the hallways and laid them at the bottom of the two doors connecting to the guest quarters. Back in the living room, Oliver was still sitting on the sofa looking as if a thundercloud had clapped over his head. Daisy stood at the top of the stairs, flapping a blanket in the air to drive the smell towards the back door. Kit had obligingly opened the back door and was moving it back and fro, attempting to fan the smell out of the house. It wasn't a task I had ever expected to employ my two children for.

I joined Daisy with another throw-rug from the sofa and together we fanned the scent of ancient, dusty old weed away from our precious guests. It wasn't quite the Instagram-ready picture of muffin-baking, farmhouse-style living the tourism people had in mind for visitors to Tasmania.

We just weren't the right people for the farm-stay accommodation dream. We were already spread too thin and our joie de vivre could not extend to embrace those we didn't know and love. We wanted our house back, and we wanted our teenage daughter to be free of listening to strangers using the bathroom on the other side of the wall from her bedroom. Three years after opening our guestroom doors, we took the welcome sign down and started using the rooms ourselves again. Gradually we managed to stop calling that space 'the B&B' and began referring to it as the rumpus. Daisy took up playing the piano again in the afternoons, Kit joined her on the drums and Oliver moved in with a monstrous rowing machine purchased from a local auction house. The rooms filled up with the stuff of happy family life, and it was another occasion when we didn't look back.

Vale Bella

We were standing where we had stood many times before, watching Bella in labour. We kept a respectful distance a couple of feet away, up to our ankles in some of the straw she had used for the great nest on which she now lay. She reclined on her side in the birthing shed, all black bristly hair and heaving flanks, her short dainty front legs tucked under as if for comfort.

We listened in sympathy to her breathing, each inhalation a quick sucking in, the exhalation a great heaving, straining whine, ending with a puffed-out sigh. She rested in between, the flaps of her ears over her eyes, her head quite still. Her flanks, meanwhile, were a frenzy of activity, twitching and rolling as the piglets inside squirmed with anticipation, raring to get out and escape the contractions squeezing them together in a tight bundle.

Suddenly Oliver broke the silence between us. 'This is probably the last time we can breed from Bella,' he said. 'Her front legs are splayed out worse than ever, and she's gone lame with it this time.'

'What will we do with her then?' I hadn't ever thought about Bella as getting old. Somehow she was still the same little gilt we'd taken delivery of years earlier. But Oliver had to think of these things, as the primary manager of the farm.

'Well, sausages,' he said now. 'I did mention this to you once before, you know.' I stared at him aghast and realised my mistake. In the seven years we'd had Bella, I'd failed to keep in mind that she was ultimately livestock, and would go the way of all livestock in the end.

Earlier in the day I had noticed her limping as she made her heavy way from the trough back to her nest. Her front legs looked kind of caved in at the knee, and no wonder. It was a lot to ask of four short legs, carrying the bulk of her own weight and that of her unborn piglets. She must have weighed twice as much as Oliver.

I thought back to the first time Bella had given birth on the farm, delivering eleven piglets in a fuss-free manner. The first few hours of newly minted motherhood had passed quietly, as she occasionally got up to turn around, shoo the brood out of her way, and lie down on her other side. The piglets slept in a big bundle under the heat lamp or snuggled up close to Bella's warmth, their forms tiny against her massive bulk. Every hour or two she lay back placidly and made the Harley Davidson sound in her throat, and the piglets would wake up, squealing, grunting and scrambling over each other to get to their favourite teat. In their urgency they often clambered over Bella herself, sometimes even over her face and head as that was the area lowest to the ground and easiest to get purchase on. Bella took it all with quiet acceptance.

The doughty Bella

Since they had arrived as our first two small gilts, we had lavished Rosie and Bella with attention, using their names, giving them massages and talking to them. But farming had given us an understanding of how animals are anthropomorphised. We are, as a species, given to imbuing our fellow creatures with character traits that they may not have, but which we think makes them endearing. Social media has provided a natural home for this.

After a few years of caring for pigs, we could see that their intelligence was entirely bound up with access to food, and survival. If Rosie and Bella seemed pleased to see us, it wasn't because they loved us or enjoyed our conversation, but because we brought feed buckets with us. That's why they recognised us.

Bella and Rosie certainly had distinct habits and behaviours which appeared to give them an individual identity. Rosie spent a day nesting every time she gave birth, bringing all sorts of objects into her hut – small shrubs, her feed bucket, and the odd long branch which wouldn't actually fit through the door. Bella didn't bother with any of this, simply lying down and getting on with it on top of whatever happened to be around, unless we had provided some fresh straw, which she would grudgingly make use of.

Rosie loved a scratch. Even if you had just tipped her feed into a bowl in front of her, she would stand still while you scratched her back with a stick, swinging ecstatically from side to side, arching her back and giving little squeals of pleasure.

Bella would look into the camera while you took her photo. In my favourite shot of her, she stood with a feed bowl in front of her, and piglets on both sides suckling from her udders. She was looking directly into the camera from underneath her big floppy ears, as if to say 'Hurry up and take the picture, I'm eating here.'

Sows were the pigs farmers got to know, we had realised, as they were with you for a long time, often years. When a sow's time came, when she could not perform as a breeding sow any more due to age or infirmity, it was a challenging moment and one which farmers faced all the time. From the business's point of view that sow was no longer commercially viable. We were running a commercial operation, a small one with tight profit margins. Every creature on the farm was there for a reason and had to earn their keep. Oliver, it turned out, had suspected Bella's long toenails would effectively shorten her productive life on the farm.

Farmers want what's best for their animals. They may be fond of them, but by necessity they have a pragmatic view of farming life and livestock. They see the reality: that livestock is just that – livestock, not pets.

For us, the reality was that we didn't have a connection with Bella or Rosie as we would with a fully domesticated animal. We had certainly sat beside them while they gave birth to their piglets, and had hosed them down in the summer. We had enjoyed the relish with which they greeted a soaking from the hosepipe, or a feed at the end of the day, or a juicy apple picked out of the dirt. But they were not pets. They were farm animals and our purpose in having them was to breed and raise more pigs, and sell pork.

Some creatures are closer to us than others and that's where we distinguish pets from livestock. A dog will look you in the eye, obey you, fetch things for you, respond to you and get into the back of the car when you're going on holiday because it knows that something is going on. It will even relate to you, because it's clever.

But during our time as farmers, I came to believe that all our relationships with animals are based around the fact that we provide them with food. Even the most intelligent dog is basically doing what it's told because you are the person who feeds it, rewards it, and is the leader of its pack.

A pig will do some of the things a dog will do and people often take great pleasure from the idea that pigs can be trained, or 'tamed', taking it as a sign of their intelligence.

A pig will recognise you because you are the person that brings the feed bucket on a regular basis. Oliver had only to disappear through the door of the workshop, put the lights on and be visible through the windows, moving around inside filling up feed buckets, for the pigs to kick up a fuss, squeal and gather at their troughs jostling for position. If Daisy or Kit went into the workshop looking for straw for their guinea pigs, or trundled down across the workshop paddocks on their bikes, the pigs paid scant heed to them. Those smaller beings with their hands empty of feed buckets meant little to them.

Rosie and Bella certainly enjoyed the sensation of a back rub given by one of us with a handy branch. They responded over the years to the conditions in which we kept them and the frequency and friendliness with which we handled them, by being easier to look after, and easier to move from one pen to another. They were trusting and compliant.

But we always remembered that if the circumstances were right, if Bella were hungry enough and one of us happened to trip and fall and lie unconscious in her pen, Bella would be a danger to us. It wouldn't matter how many of her piglets we had watched her deliver, or that I had mopped her brow, or that Oliver had hosed her down when she was hot. Bella wasn't fond of us, not at all. She recognised us, but that was it.

'What would happen if you were away and I tripped on the electric wire and cracked my head on the side of the trough?' I asked Oliver one day as we stood watching Bella nose through her food bowl. One of our hens often ate with Bella, waiting politely until she had settled into her meal, before hopping into the bowl to one side of Bella's immense head, and pecking delicately at the dusty feed. I wondered vaguely if Bella couldn't see her, as her ears flopped down obscuring her vision almost entirely. But when Wiggles, our cheeky young ram, tried the same thing, Bella smacked him out of the way instantly with one firm swing of her head. We felt she was tolerating the chicken as it clearly didn't pose a significant threat to her food supply.

'What would happen if I was bleeding from a cut on the head and had knocked myself out, and Bella was hungry?' I asked Oliver.

'Well she'd be curious,' Oliver conceded.

'Would she have a go at me?'

'I think she'd definitely be curious about the smell of blood, but I don't think she'd eat you in one sitting, if that's what you're getting at.'

I wasn't so sanguine about this. Even though pigs are not fed meat content in their commercial feed, they are carnivores. I had seen them nose through a bucket of kitchen scraps and peelings often enough to know that they were selective about what they ate, and that they undoubtedly judged food by smell.

Added to which, there was no way Bella would leap the electric fence and trot off to alert the neighbours or Oliver to my injured state, like Skippy the Bush Kangaroo. My guess was that she would nose around me and toss my head about with her snout for a bit, and that when the urge for fresh meat kicked in, she'd take a bite.

The upshot was that we might be fond of Bella, but Bella didn't really care about us.

Perhaps this is one of the reasons farmers are able to detach themselves enough to raise livestock for consumption, put them in a truck and send them off to the abattoir. We don't see them as cute. We might enjoy farming them, we might keep them as well as we can, but at the end of the day we're in the food supply chain, and that gives you a more pragmatic outlook.

As we stood at the open side of the birthing shed looking at Bella, we were still left with the question of what to do with her if we couldn't breed with her any more. Damo had joined us, always a sucker for a new brood of anything, whether it was puppies from one of his hunting dogs, or our piglets.

If we had a pragmatic outlook as farmers, Damo's was about to trump ours.

'Shoot her and bury her here, will you?' he asked.

'Oh my God, no,' I gasped, taken aback at the notion. 'It'd be like shooting your own grandmother!' Pragmatic outlook or not, the prospect of shooting Bella on the farm seemed horrendous. The death there of Co-Pilot had been bad enough.

Oliver spoke up. 'More to the point, we couldn't bury that much prime Saddleback pork in a hole in the ground. In a funny way, it would be an insult to Bella. She's a premium Wessex Saddleback pig. I don't want her to go to waste.'

Even though I couldn't countenance the thought of eating anything made from Bella myself, I knew exactly what Oliver meant. Although she was too old to make prime cuts of pork, she could provide the meat for hundreds of sausages which we would sell at events. It was horrible to think of her as minced pork, but we had to. She was worth thousands of dollars to the business, and that could not be squandered.

We stood silently contemplating this quandary, which farmers face on behalf of a meat-eating public every single day.

'I shoot me own dogs,' Damo said suddenly. 'Had a cattle dog last year, an old boy. My word he'd put some hard yards in. Twenty-two years of service, he gave. Twenty-two years!'

I glanced up at Damo, whose voice had become tremulous as he spoke, and could have sworn there were tears in his eyes. I listened carefully as he told us how he'd taken the 'old boy' out the back of his house and shot him. 'I owed him that much.'

I completely understood the tradition of rural people dispatching their own animals. Damo's dogs rarely went anywhere except on the back of a ute with their mates, out to work cattle or for a day's hunting. To end such a dog's days on a veterinary table in a place completely strange to it would see it distressed and its owner too. This way, the dog would have no idea what was coming. Hard though it might be to shoot his own dog, it was Damo's way of doing the right thing by it to the very last.

There was no getting away from the fact that it would be more difficult being responsible for Bella's death than it had been for any of the other anonymous pigs we had raised. Damo shifted beside me, his brawny hand lifting the filthy cap from his head and scratching his dusty hair as he joined us in thinking through Bella's fate.

'What will you do with her then? Send her to the abattoir?'

'Probably will,' Oliver conceded. In such a huge facility, Bella's end would be a sad and anonymous affair, and it was hard to think of that.

'I wish we had a smaller abattoir nearby that we could take her to,' I said. 'Then Oliver could lead her right up to the moment just before it happened.'

'Yep, you wanna stay with 'em, cause they knows you. That old boy of mine didn't know a thing was coming,' agreed Damo.

'We've thought about sending her to a sanctuary,' I put in. Damo nodded and grunted his assent. He had such a deep respect for his working dogs, I wasn't surprised that he didn't seem to scorn the idea of other people offering creatures sanctuary on a bigger scale. It seemed to tally with the soft-hearted man I knew him to be.

'The trouble with that,' I continued, 'is that her toenails will carry on bothering her, and also, we can't be sure of what would happen to her in the long run, and then how she might be dealt with when her time did come.' Having had responsibility for Bella's life, it seemed wrong and cowardly to hand over responsibility for her eventual death.

All this played through our minds as we stood watching her with what we now thought might be her last litter of piglets. As it happened, she had two more litters over the next twelve months, but the piglets grew inconsistent in size and fewer in number. As Bella began to have more difficulty walking and seemed less active, we made the inevitable decision. We had been thinking about it for a year or more. A year later, we would be thinking about it for Rosie.

Bella went to the abattoir on a terrible day for Oliver. Her carcass made over a thousand sausages which we cooked and sold at the Woolmers Festival of Roses. Perhaps in silent tribute to Bella's magnificent form, Oliver made very long, large sausages and they were unwieldy. As I attempted to place them into bread rolls, they flopped around and nearly slipped from my grasp with the tongs and it seemed like Bella's last stand. I considered taking a raw sausage into the Woolmers' National Rose Garden at the end of the day and burying it underneath a rose bush, but thought this would raise an eyebrow with the keepers of the estate. We made a lot in takings that day but it was a terrible price that we paid – Bella's life, her very body and soul. It was the ultimate test of my mettle as a farmer. I've no idea how I managed to get through that day, serving her as food to our customers, or where I put what we were doing in my consciousness, or how I dealt with it in my emotional life. I can't help feeling we withdrew in the most deleterious way on our karma and will always be the poorer in some great bank of universal goodwill.

We felt the absence of those two familiar creatures on the farm keenly. Despite the potential danger sows can pose, Bella and Rosie had become tamed by us and we could get into their pens and interact with them easily. Pigs are companionable, affable creatures when well kept, and this had got under our skin.

In brief moments when I needed succour and simple companionship, there was nobody for me to visit in the pens after they were gone, nobody whose ear I could lift up and murmur into, rubbing the delicate warm skin behind it, patting the great flanks behind the foreleg, and be tolerated while doing it. Oliver felt their absence more keenly, as he saw it whenever he went out to the pens.

We never lost our fondness for Bella and Rosie and we won't ever forget them. We'll always enjoy that photo of Bella looking into the camera and the video of Rosie squealing with pleasure at a back rub. We'll think back on that time of our lives when those two creatures came to mean so much to us, while treating us with what could at best be described as good-natured indifference. It's a peculiar relationship indeed, farming.

Closure

I was on my way to Launceston library to do some work in a quiet corner, when I bumped into Joseph from the Evandale Berry Farm. We had enjoyed a position as neighbouring stalls at many events and often partook of a large helping of their farm-made berry ice-cream at the end of a lunchtime service. We'd have a yack about how the day had gone with Joseph and his wife Susan, who ran the farm and made the ice-cream. I was pleased to see his friendly face now, although there seemed something hesitant about his mood. Eventually there was a natural pause in our conversation.

'I was thinking about you guys this morning, when I heard that news about the abattoir,' Joseph said. 'That's going to have a real impact in your business, isn't it?'

While Oliver prefers to listen to the news on ABC's Radio National in the mornings, I usually switch to Classic FM, preferring a gentler start into the day. Often I'm distracted by the demands of a family's morning routine, so I hadn't caught a news break that morning, and had no idea what Joseph was talking about.

'Oh my god, you haven't heard?' he said, looking increasingly uncomfortable, and little wonder. Devonport abattoir had been earmarked for closure and Joseph was in the unfortunate position of having to break the news to me. 'The company that runs it is pulling out,' he said. 'I was wondering where you'd send your pigs instead.'

My stomach turned over. If the Devonport abattoir closed, there was no other practical option for us when it came to the slaughter of our pigs. I had no idea what we would do. It was hard to believe it could happen, since many other farm businesses depended upon it, but it could certainly be the end of ours.

The abattoir, it turned out, employed a local workforce but was owned by an international corporation based in Brazil. Unbeknown to us, they already had a certain reputation in the agriculture sector. They had run a small abattoir on King Island, a speck of land with two world-class golf courses off the northwest point of Tasmania. It sounds an unlikely place for either agriculture or an abattoir, but the island provides world class grazing on beautiful soils, with grass blown by sea winds and encrusted with microscopic particles of salt. Livestock all over the world raised on such pastures produces highly-prized meat: Welsh lamb grazed on salt marshes, French lamb raised on the north-coast marshes. The abattoir on King Island had been an essential service for the farmers there and had provided employment. But from the multinational company's perspective, it was a tiny operation and they opted to close it. This left the farmers compelled to ship their livestock across the straits to the Tasmanian mainland, and on a lengthy drive along the north coast highway for slaughter. Many animals are driven much greater distances, but this was an unwelcome solution.

My immediate response, standing on that pavement in Launceston hearing the news from Devonport, was one of panic. I pictured our farm full of pigs, with no way for us to convert them into product. Pigs eat tonnes of expensive feed and need a steady supply whatever your farm's circumstances. The price of that feed fluctuates because wheat is expensive and prey to commodity prices. Over the years, Oliver had done everything possible to supplement the commercial feed he used with free waste that was palatable and added fibre to our pigs' diet and which reduced our feed costs. He'd mixed it with bran mash, a waste product from the local brewery in Beaconsfield, had sourced a supply of undersized seed from an animal feed supplier in Launceston, and of vegetable crop waste from a farmer near Longford. But these still had to be mixed with the main ingredient in our pigs' diet, that commercial grain-based feed, which cost money. So the abattoir might be threatened with closure and our business might fold, but the pigs would still need to be fed for as long as we had them.

Our children would of course need to be fed and clothed too. Panic about how we would sustain ourselves as a family was not far behind.

From the reports he'd seen, Joseph was under the impression that the Tasmanian government would enter into talks with the owners of the abattoir. They would attempt to reach a deal, perhaps offer finance to sweeten it, and keep the thing running. I flew round the corner to the library, opened up my computer and found an ABC news report online. The owners of the abattoir had announced their intention to close the facility at the end of November, I read. More than one hundred people from the northwest would lose their jobs after the shock announcement. And what of the farmers who would lose an essential part of the supply chain that they relied upon? The Tasmanian state government was entering into talks with the company to see what could be done to keep it running, the reports said, ensuring farms across the state still had this service to rely upon.

I rang Oliver. Typically, he was calm.

'Well yes, we'd be stuffed if it shuts down. I'd just have to slaughter all the pigs and freeze the meat, if it came to it.'

'We could never fit it in all the freezers!' I was aghast at the thought, not just of the freezers being crammed full of meat, but of the potential mass slaughter of all our remaining pigs. Would it really come to that?

'If they keep the abattoir running for a few months, we might be able to do it gradually,' Oliver said. 'I don't know how we'd sell more meat than we normally do, though.' There was a pause while we both wracked our brains to try and think of ways to sell more pork. We had utilized every opportunity we'd created or that came our way for the preceding six years, so it was unlikely that another one would magically occur to us now in the heat of the moment.

'Could we do weekly markets instead of fortnightly?' I asked him.

'We'd never get in,' he replied. 'There's too much competition.' Another producer with a stall at the market selling beautifully raised, pasture-fed Angus beef had recently started raising pigs as well, and producing bacon. He had been allowed to sell this at the market, sometimes at a stall alongside ours. Not surprisingly, this had impacted on our sales. There's only so much bacon people want to buy, and we had noticed our customers being confused about which bacon they had purchased, since we were there only fortnightly.

I imagined having freezers stocked to capacity with frozen

pork, and no means of selling it except gradually over weeks, and at a price discounted because it was frozen rather than fresh. It was a poor strategy, and could only ever be an interim measure, designed to cope with the immediate problems posed if the abattoir were to cease operating. It didn't help us with the complete loss of our business.

Oliver could only think of the pigs, however: of the prospect of feeding a whole herd when the means of slaughtering them had gone, and the pointlessness of a farm full of stock with no way to sell it.

'This is how farmers end up shooting their livestock and burying it, you know,' he said. 'Plenty of people do it.' He sounded remarkably sanguine given this appalling prospect. I thought of the farmers across the United Kingdom who had buried entire herds of stock with bloodlines stretching back for generations, because of foot-and-mouth disease. When emergency struck on a farm, the fate of the animals could be terrible, through no fault of their own. It wasn't what I wanted for our farm, or what I imagined when I thought of our bush block, the gum trees, and the pigs snuffling around and snoozing in the dappled sunlight beneath them.

Feeling slightly light-headed, I rang off. Oliver had assured me there was no need to panic just yet. We'd wait and see what the state government managed to achieve in negotiation with the abattoir owners. A committee was being set up to oversee the talks, he said. It would come down to whatever they managed to figure out. Our fate was in their hands.

I realised how dependent we were on the supply chain of operators, from feed producers to the abattoir, to butchers and market managers and customers. Being a farmer had never seemed more parlous.

Tasmania's state government went into battle on our behalf, negotiating with the overseas-based corporation that owned the abattoir, and liaising with the owners of other facilities to see who could provide alternative services. As a business dependent upon the outcome, we were put on an emailing list for updates, and received the occasional email with updates from the Department of Primary Industries.

It emerged that the owners of the abattoir had already been given close to a million dollars several years previously, as an incentive to keep the facility open, and that its closure had long been foreseen by others in the agriculture sector. Over the coming weeks and months, more voices joined the debate. Farmers and politicians made comment in the media, and Oliver was interviewed by a commercial television station, filmed feeding the pigs and talking about how it would be the end of our business if there was no abattoir within reasonable driving distance of our farm.

Every so often there was a development that caused our anxiety to spike. One afternoon we received an email from the meat industry working group set up to pursue a solution. The politician chairing it had written a detailed update on negotiations, and chosen to end it with a political statement about the opposing political party's lack of capacity to provide the same assurances. We were agog to see political point-scoring in such a communication, when our every thought was on the future of our business and the way we would support our family. I wrote a fiercely emotional email in response.

A few days later, my phone rang and I answered it to find a government advisor on the line. I'm not used to receiving calls from bureaucrats. In the United Kingdom it would be unthinkable. But Tasmania is a much smaller place. People working in the same field know one another, and are concerned about each other. It turned out that I had interviewed the woman on the line for a book I wrote about farming women. A few moments into the conversation, it occurred to me that she was genuinely calling to try and reassure me, even in the worst of circumstances.

'The Treasurer is meeting for hours every day with the owners, doing everything he can to figure out a solution,' she told me. It was clear the government recognised the devastating impact the abattoir's closure would have on the farming sector across the north of Tasmania, but I suspected the meetings might be too little too late. If a multinational corporation had decided to pull out of a tiny operation in a state far away from their other operations with a small workforce they didn't much care about, there would be no changing that.

The date was set for the abattoir to close in mid-November. In the weeks beforehand, we limped along hoping for a solution. Inevitably, it changed the way we thought about the farm. Taking our stall to markets and events was hard physical labour, and we had already begun to realise we needed an exit strategy. Now into our fifties, neither of us wanted to work this strenuously for much longer. But our hearts and minds were still occupied with the farm on a daily basis. It was difficult to think sensibly about how to move on, and what other ways we could earn a living, especially when our thoughts were clouded by what was going on in the news.

While a longer-term solution was being investigated, a list was released of alternative abattoirs we could consider using. There were just five of them to service the entire state, most of them far smaller than Devonport. One experienced such rapid growth as farmers sought an alternative service, it began processing in a day the number of animals it had previously processed in a week. It was hard to see how this extra loading could continue to be viable, as they had limited paddocks, yards and cold storage, limiting the work its owners could do, however willing to help.

The geographical spread meant most of the alternatives were too far away for us to use. One was three hours to the south, in the Central Highlands, involving too long a trip down the central highway of Tasmania and then a dog-leg up the Derwent Valley on rural roads, completely unfeasible with two pigs in a trailer. One was even further away in the far south of the island. Of the two closest to us, both were now overrun with demand and twice the distance Devonport was. It was hard to see where the solution lay for us. I spent the days with my heart in my mouth wondering what might happen, while Oliver plodded onwards, feeding and tending his pigs, making his delicious sausages and fielding questions from concerned customers at our market stall.

Only one other facility was close to our farm, under an hour away at Cressy. We had never used it as it was certified to supply the Halal export market with meat, meaning pigs could not be slaughtered in the same facility. But a reprieve came for us when the company which owned it agreed to step in and run the 'pig line' at Devonport for up to two years. This would allow time for another facility to be built or another operator to be found. Both of these options seemed unlikely, but the relief of knowing that we had a period of grace to find an exit from our farm business was phenomenal.

The deadline approached for the handover to these interim

operators, and the drama continued to play out in the media during this period of uncertainty. Change was certainly coming, which unsettled everyone.

'One bloke there told me they're taking down all the chains and equipment,' Oliver told me, after dropping off two pigs. The building had been leased by the former operators, but they owned all the removable equipment, and were now stripping it from the facility. As it belonged to them, they were perfectly within their rights, but it was unnerving for anyone whose livelihood depended on the place to see it happening. Amongst all the uncertainty, we knew one thing for sure: we had two years to exit our small farm business.

A few months after this uncertainty took over our lives, I woke up one Saturday morning with the distinct sensation that I was falling out of bed. Opening my eyes in alarm, I clutched at the bedlinen in front of me. The room in front of me looked normal, the wardrobes were in the same place, I hadn't hit the floor, and could feel the bed firm beneath my body. But the sensation in my head still suggested I was spinning sideways through space. It was terrifying.

I'd had dizzy spells for months but they always passed quickly and didn't seem serious. Now I wondered if they had been a precursor to this new sense of complete disorientation. A wave of nausea hit me as I sat up, steadying myself. Looking down and gingerly putting my feet into my slippers, more dizziness overcame me and I had to sit and wait for it to subside. Slowly, I made my way downstairs and found Oliver preparing to head out to the shops.

'I don't think I'll make it out with you today,' I said. 'Those dizzy spells have got worse. I felt like I was falling out of bed just now.'

'I thought you were sleeping in longer than usual,' he replied, looking at me with concern.

The spinning sensation persisted over the weekend, every time I lay on my right hand side or looked up or down. A visit to the doctor early the next week confirmed that I had vertigo, the benign paroxysmal positional sort. Although the inclusion of the word 'benign' is comforting, it's a pernicious condition in which crystals in the middle ear come loose and rattle about causing all manner of dizziness, discomfort and nausea. There was no magic cure: just rest and a peculiar exercise I could do with the aim of getting the crystals to fall back into place. Called the Epley Manoeuvre, it involved sitting on a bed, turning my head to one side and then lying down on my back, turning my head to the other side, rolling over, and sitting up again. It was highly entertaining for Daisy and Kit to watch, and it helped, with the spinning and dizziness subsiding over the coming weeks.

But having something wrong on the inside of your head is a terrifying experience. What if it didn't come right? This was my thinking and operating tool. Unlike a car engine, one couldn't lift the bonnet and tighten things up or tinker to put them right. Furthermore, I didn't think it was too grandiose to believe that my family and our business depended on me recovering. As the weeks wore on, it occurred to me that I definitely needed to be fully better by November, when the intense round of weekend visitor events happened and we would be taking our stall to each of them.

I mentioned this to Oliver.

'I've been thinking about that,' he said. 'If it came to it, we'd just employ someone like Patsy again, and the kids can help.

We'd manage it somehow. We'd have to.'

I felt myself welling with tears at the fact that he had thought through ways to take the pressure off me.

'You don't have to worry so much, you know,' he said, putting his arm around me. 'You can't think about the farm and your writing all the time.'

The episode brought home to us just how preoccupied we were constantly with what we did for a living. It suddenly occurred to us that there was something else we should be thinking about as the years wore on: our health.

The type of vertigo I had is often associated with other conditions that come with age, such as high blood pressure and hypertension, diabetes and Vitamin D deficiency. The coming months brought further visits to the doctor as I continued to veer between wellness and wobbliness. I was able to work on our stall during the summer events alongside Patsy and the kids, but by the end of the year, I could no longer deny that I had succumbed to my family's tendency to high blood pressure.

My doctor referred me to a pathology centre where I was fitted with a monitor which would record my blood pressure every twenty minutes for twenty-four hours. This was a small box containing a motor and recording equipment, worn round my waste on a strap and hidden under clothes. There was a blood pressure band around my arm and the two were connected by a hose. Every twenty minutes the motor would kick in quietly and inflate the armband, take a reading and deflate again. When I felt it working, I was supposed to stand or sit in a relaxed fashion while the technology assessed me.

It so happened that I wore it on the day of the Harvest

market Christmas party, so I stood in the beautiful back garden of an elegant Georgian house at the top of Launceston, fairy lights twinkling above my head, chatting with friends from other stalls and volunteers from the market, and every so often I would feel and hear the gentle whir of the motor at my waist. I had no idea whether others could hear it or if they wondered why I was suddenly standing quite still with a distant look on my face.

A few days later I was back at my doctor's office being shown some squiggly lines on a graph.

'You can see that your blood pressure is just a bit too high, just a bit too often,' he said. 'And having seen your husband on the television news and knowing the stress that's affecting your business at the moment, it's not surprising.'

It was discomfiting to realise that the cause of my change in health might be for such an obvious reason, and yet one that hadn't occurred to me.

Eleven Days

When our business was at its height, we worked an eleven-day fortnight. Once a fortnight, we spent Saturday at the market, and Sunday recovering. Weekends when we weren't doing a market always seemed to fill up with errands, the stuff of life, or kids' activities. Daisy had band rehearsals on Sundays, so I drove her into Launceston and found a way to occupy myself for three hours. It was too long a drive to go home and return later to pick her up, so I took my computer, parked myself on a desk in a spare room, and wrote or worked.

It was arduous but we made it work. Occasionally we went out as a family. We went on holidays in Tasmania, had friends and family to visit, and created the beautiful memories that families look back on in the stunning landscapes of the island.

I worked in the farm business, keeping up the website, producing leaflets, writing newsletters, helping Oliver make day-to-day operational decisions. Alongside this, I developed my own micro-business, first creating websites for other small businesses, content writing and social media management for tourism businesses, and some hard-won freelance writing. I wrote my first book, and edited a couple for other small business owners who wanted a modest publication they could sell or give away.

Close friends knew that I wrote but many people did not. I'd catch these people, who knew us through the business or saw us at the market, looking at me quizzically sometimes, as if they were thinking 'What does *she* do?' I was still referred to as 'the pig lady' from time to time. I got used to it. It was part of what I did. And the farm business was important to us.

When my first book was published and we included mention of it in a newsletter sent to our farm's mailing list, people began asking about it, and it was like emerging from the shadows.

During that time, I kept our small tribe of four clothed and fed. Oliver's sartorial purchases were mainly hard-wearing trousers from the rural supplies store.

When Oliver's sister visited, she professed herself amazed at how much time I spent on my feet. It never occurred to me to sit down unless it was at my desk. Every moment of the day had to be productive.

Most women know that in the midst of such a busy work and family life, something has to go and it's usually the housework. Our house was chaotic. My efforts were spent on keeping up with the laundry for myself and the kids. Oliver did his own and usually brought everyone's in from the line. Sometimes a wash or two stayed there for days getting extra rinses if it was raining. I did the food shopping and cooking, as it seemed unfair to make Oliver spend yet more time in a kitchen when he was preparing kilos of bacon and sausages. Plus the results were more predictable when I cooked.

The mess that two small children can create with the toys accumulated through infancy was apparent on our floors, which were covered with brightly-coloured clutter. No surface was left unadorned. As a person who depends on things feeling organised in order to stay sane, it occasionally got the better of me.

Winding myself up into a frenzy on a Sunday I'd decided to allocate to housework, I would occasionally find myself exclaiming in sheer desperation, 'This place is a shithole!'

'I hate it when you call it that!' Oliver protested. But scurrying from the living room to the bedrooms with a handful of tiny plastic animals in need of their living quarters, I felt the futility of the exercise depleting my energy levels. I wore a path between my desk, the kitchen and the laundry, and Oliver wore one between the house and the workshop. After six years, we were ready for it to stop.

Exiting a business which occupies your thoughts night and day and which represents a significant part of your family's income is no mean feat. If you've come to the end of the road and find yourself exhausted and uninspired, the idea of doing something else is highly appealing but also daunting, particularly when both adult members of the family work in the business.

'I just don't know how to start making that kind of transition,' I said at one of our Monday meetings.

'We've got to stop doing the market,' Oliver replied. 'We need an alternative outlet.'

This meant finding a third party such as a butcher who would purchase our meat wholesale and sell it on, perhaps value-adding by making other products from it. It was highly likely this would not attract the same price per kilo as our retail price—what we sold the pork for at a market—but it would be a step in the right direction.

'It means we'll still have an income stream, and more time to think about what we're going to do next,' Oliver said. If we weren't spending two days per fortnight making sausages and bacon, building up to a market weekend, and marketing the business, we'd both have the benefit of more time.

Oliver was crestfallen at the prospect of no longer making bacon. To him, it wasn't just a product, but a passion. He made the kind of bacon he wanted to eat, free of nitrates and preservatives, rich in flavour and using the traditions he'd discovered visiting those butchers' shops in Suffolk years before.

'You'll still make bacon for yourself though, won't you?' I asked.

'Probably not, because we'll be selling entire carcasses, so I won't have a leg or a shoulder to make it from.'

Even so, he was convinced this was the way to go, the first in a series of steps which would free us up time-wise, sell off the pigs gradually, and keep money coming in, eventually enabling us to withdraw from the business completely. If we could find the right buyers, people who had a need for an entire pork carcass on a regular basis, we both believed it could work.

When Rick the beef cattle farmer had asked whether I would be better off stacking shelves at the supermarket, it was the start of a beautiful friendship. We visited each other's farms and met for lunch and dinner occasionally, and Rick and Oliver struck up an easy understanding. Although he hadn't inherited his parents' farm as Rick had, Oliver could understand how a farm passed down through generations was at the heart of a family's identity, along with a deeply-held sense of duty.

Liz and I often met at events organised for women in the local business community. At one of these we learned that our views are all influenced by the five people we spend the most time with. Liz and I realised that as rural women based on farms we spent a great deal of time with our husbands. While Oliver and Rick were perfectly nice people, we agreed it would be good to see more of each other as a kind of offset effect. Inevitably, we ended up talking about our husbands, but also our businesses and in my case, the desire for an exit strategy.

'You should look up the Meat Mistress,' Liz said to me one day over an egg sandwich. I choked on my tea and asked what on earth she meant. The Meat Mistress, she told me, was a brand set up by two clever women based in Hobart. Together they ran a butcher's shop which purchased meat wholesale from small, artisan farm businesses like ours, with rare breed livestock and ethical farming practices. Liz and Rick had been selling their beef carcasses to them for some time, she told me.

'I don't know that she has many pork suppliers, so you could be in with a chance.'

I scurried home and told Oliver this news. Typically he went straight to the potential problems.

'I don't know how we'd get the carcasses down to Hobart,' he said. 'And butchers don't like our meat anyway, they like pork to be pale. That's why I've never managed to sell any to the shops around here.'

I noticed a ballpoint pen on the desk beside him and briefly considered stabbing him with it. I'd heard people in the SAS could make do with anything to inflict a wound if they really wanted to.

'This is a completely different kind of butcher!' I carried on, putting my homicidal impulses to one side. 'I've looked them up on the Internet, see? How many butchers do you know who have a disco glitter ball in their shop?'

The two women who owned the business had purchased a traditional butcher's shop and put their own spin on the place. They gave the bricks and mortar shop a makeover with murals on the walls and displays of cookbooks by local chefs, and created an all-female butchering brand under the moniker 'Meat Mistress' by way of a marketing story. Rather than ordering in boxed meats from wholesalers on the mainland, they sourced meat by the carcass from regional and remote farmers in Tasmania and paid a price that realised the value of the product. They butchered the carcasses in the back of the shop, in the way all traditional butchers used to do. That meant finding ways of using and selling the cheaper cuts as well as the premium ones, and they had an inventive line in sausages and other butcher-made products.

Based in Sandy Bay, an old Hobart suburb with strong, longstanding community roots, they'd found a ready customer base, and proudly displayed marketing from their farm suppliers in their shop so that customers could understand the provenance of what they were buying.

When Oliver finally overcame his theoretical stumbling blocks and put in a couple of calls to test the waters, they welcomed the idea of purchasing his carcasses. A couple more calls revealed that the abattoir in Devonport could deliver our carcasses to Hobart, despite that city being at the opposite end of the island. Furthermore, the Meat Mistresses had offered a price that fell short of our retail price, but wasn't a million miles from it, and was certainly more than Oliver had expected.

This new regime would bypass the making of product and running of a market stall by us, and mean far less work than Oliver would otherwise have to do.

'She normally visits farms she's going to buy from but she says we've got a well-established brand,' he said, after his phone call with one of the owners. Having dragged his heels over contacting them at all, he'd chatted on the phone for half an hour, learning all about the business and laying the foundations of a relationship which would be vital to us. Knowing how much he liked a chat, this was no surprise to me, but I couldn't help feeling a little resentful about how hard I'd had to work to get him to make the call in the first place.

I took my disgruntled feelings out on that night's carrots in the kitchen while Oliver carried on regaling me with the success of the new arrangement he'd struck.

'They haven't got a regular pork supplier,' he said, sauntering around the dining room holding his phone aloft as if it were a trophy. 'I think it could work out quite well.'

'You don't say,' I replied, keeping my attention firmly on the carrots and chopping perhaps a little more vigorously than was necessary.

Oliver brought his own contacts to the table as our exit plan came into being. After several years sourcing boars and sows as fresh bloodlines for our farm and chatting occasionally to anyone who was in pigs in Tasmania, he had a good network. He got in touch with the owner of a cookery school just outside of Hobart, the former food editor of a premium glossy magazine who had moved to Tasmania and started a cookery school using ingredients supplied by his own kitchen garden and local farmers. Being a polished individual with phenomenal contacts and knowhow in the world of food, this man had made a rip-roaring success of his new venture, attracting visitors and diners from far and wide and featuring on television screens with his quiet, understated way of talking about growing leafy greens and sharing the joy of locally grown, seasonal foods.

Being completely immune to any sense of show-biz celebrity, Oliver thought of this man not as someone with a former high-flying media career who had achieved success in the rarefied world of Tasmanian fine-dining, but as a bloke he talked to about pigs. He rang and asked if the cookery school would have any use for an entire pork carcass occasionally. It would. The former food editor ran a 'Whole Hog' course in how to break down a carcass and use the entire thing from nose to tail. This lasted a weekend and required not just one, but two pigs. Even better, there was a premium price on offer for a pig of predictably good quality, with the right meat to fat ratio, bred and raised in the Tasmanian outdoors in free-range conditions.

It was quite something to know that our pigs and the pork they produced was of sufficient quality to meet the approval of these two discerning places. Between the Meat Mistresses and their butcher's shop, and the food editor with his agrarian cookery school, plus a few other private buyers we would continue to supply from time to time, we were approaching the point where we could step back from our stall at markets and events, and turn our attention to the next chapter of our lives, whatever that would be.

Politics

Dear Reader
I thought long and hard before including the following chapter. It could be argued that politics does not belong in these pages. But politics is everywhere and affects us all. The event described here caused some debate and consternation in Launceston, and in the market community. I considered omitting it or posting it online behind a paywall. Instead, I have attempted to write an account of it factually and without finger-pointing. Judicious omissions have been made. Trusted people I spoke to about this expressed the view that it's important to tell the whole story. Finally, the events described here formed a milestone towards the end of our business. So here it is.

We didn't know the Prime Minister would be visiting the market until a crowd of media types with television cameras positioned themselves at the gate, looking out expectantly onto the road.

'Who's coming?' I asked one of them. He ignored me. A woman standing behind him with a fistful of leaflets answered instead.

'We think it's the Prime Minister.'

'Ooh, really? How exciting!' I squeaked inadvertently.

What an idiot, I castigated myself. That particular Prime Minister was not someone I had voted for or admired. But a visit from a headlining politician is exciting whether you like it or not, and anticipation rippled through the gaggle of people now assembled at the gate like a bubble of yeast through sourdough.

'There he is!' someone blurted. The people handing out leaflets for the local Peace Festival, the media types, market-goers and stallholders peered at a shiny, unmarked vehicle across the road, around which another clutch of people was gathered.

'Oh, he's brought his girls!' someone said. As we watched, the Prime Minister made his way across the road towards the market, accompanied by two young girls and a cluster of suited men. As they approached, the media types hoisted their cameras more firmly onto their shoulders, raised their furry microphones into the air and began filming.

I went back to our stall, a few metres away. 'It's the Prime Minister,' I said to Oliver, as he finished serving a customer.

Oliver drew himself up to his full height and looked out across the counter. 'Is it really,' he said dryly. Oliver's views of public life are not nuanced and he held no truck with this man, whom he regarded as full of arrogance and bluster.

We had no more time than those few seconds before the whirlwind visit commenced, to form our views on why our Prime Minister might be visiting Launceston's farmers' market. It was as if a spinning top had been set off, its potential to impact the day as yet unknown, but latent. As we watched, he swept past with an entourage of market managers and minders, his two girls just ahead of him looking undeniably self-conscious. Everyone watched their stately progression until the hard-working brewer who was selling his craft beer two spots along from us, gave a shout and attracted the Prime Minister's attention. Smiling, he went over and stopped at the stall. The two men held a genial discussion while the crowd of attendees gathered around. Market-goers either stood amongst the crowd to watch, or attempted to brush past, ignoring the fuss and continuing their ordinary Saturday-morning shopping. Some people used their phones to take photos, and the television camera operators jostled for position. Everyone, it seemed, was looking for an angle.

Seconds later, the Prime Minister was off again, heading on through the market, strolling past the cheese stall, the tomato and garlic stall, the honey stall and the egg stall. Many of the business owners stood gaping at the entourage of people and cameras. We watched as the Prime Minister stopped at the jam stall, the cameras closing in again. It was clear this was no ordinary visit by a man and his family. The market was being used for a public relations exercise, with footage of the Prime Minister as an all-Australian bloke due out on the evening news, no doubt.

Feeling a bit nauseous, I went back to the stall, where Oliver was serving one of our regular customers, a pragmatic woman who ran a farm in the Midlands. 'Well, we had no idea the Prime Minister was going to be calling today!' I said, still feeling a bit silly to be affected by the excitement.

She looked up as she packed her bag with packets of pork. 'No, and some of us probably wish he would just clear off so we can get back to normal,' she said. I began to have an inkling of how the visit might divide people. Most politicians elicit a range of responses: respect, awe, indifference, distaste. Appearing in feel-good photos at a farmers' market was undoubtedly a winning look. But those involved in the market every week as customers or stallholders might feel differently.

This became clear when a debate broke out on Facebook later that day. Television footage on the evening news gave the lie to any notion that the visit might have promotional benefits for anyone other than the Prime Minister. He had gone on to visit a new innovation centre in Launceston, and a football match. These took the focus in the report. The centre-piece shot had him walking statesmanlike through Launceston's newly-revamped Civic Square, flanked by the state's Premier, a newly-elected and widely-respected female member of parliament, and some city councillors. The market was mentioned by name, but no meaningful detail was given.

But if the media hadn't done us any favours, several people on Facebook had stepped in and taken public relations into their own hands. Images began appearing on the platform of the Prime Minister posing with stallholders. The most prominent image showed him gazing thoughtfully at something off-camera, alongside a woman from the stall shared by immigrant families from Afghanistan. I knew a woman from the volunteer group who had helped set this up. It had been a means for the families to earn an income stream, she told me, celebrating their food culture, and helping them integrate into Launceston's community. Now it was being used as a means to show the Prime Minister as a touchy-feely nice guy. Such is politics.

My feelings turned rapidly from a vague acceptance that the Prime Minister would occasionally visit Tasmania and then leave again, to cynicism at the way parts of its community and business life had been appropriated for a publicity stunt. As a form of futile protest, I tapped in a couple of deliberately irreverent comments. 'I notice he went straight from the beer stall to the award-winning whisky marmalade - surely there's a theme emerging here!'

Scrolling through comments left by others, I noticed that the visit had succeeded in one thing, and that was polarising the community. A protracted dispute was taking place about whether he should have been there at all, or not. 'There's a homeless girl sleeping rough in a doorway in the mall. I bet he didn't visit her, did he?' someone had posted. I realised that this person was right. The Prime Minister had flown in and visited the positive stories, the wins. He didn't visit the places where an increasing community of homeless people was spending their nights, or the parole offices visited by people who were released from prison with nowhere to live and scant support in life. He didn't visit the Accident and Emergency department at Launceston's hospital and see for himself the cramped, inadequate facilities, the chronically sick people queuing there because they couldn't get admitted any other way, the ambulance drivers waiting in the office, their vehicle and its occupant ramped outside due to a lack of beds and staff inside. He hadn't met any locals whose offspring couldn't afford to buy a home in Tasmania because successive governments have made houses into things we buy as investments, rather than homes we live in. He had ignored the real challenges many ordinary people face.

As my sense of disenchantment grew, I continued tapping remarks into the platform. 'The people on the egg stall missed their chance as he walked past, didn't they!' I wrote, thinking of the eggs and tomatoes thrown at Thatcher's education minister when he had visited the University of Warwick years earlier, when I had been a student there. I hadn't thrown anything myself, but it had taught me about the anger that people feel when a government loses touch with what's happening for people at grass roots level.

'Suggesting that people actually commit an act of violence like that is ABHORRENT!!!!!' wrote someone else in response, as if I'd been standing there handing out eggs from a box and urging people on, rather than writing a sarky comment on social media.

Social media is an easy place to find trouble, I've come to believe. It's easy to tap in a few remarks from the comfort of your armchair, and get involved in a spat which flares up into public unpleasantness. Looking at that comment, I had a dawning realisation that I was involving myself publicly in a row I wasn't even interested in having. Scrolling backwards through the day, I deleted my comments. As the aftermath of the visit played out in the conflicted thoughts of the community, I stopped watching, as people tussled over what had happened to the market some loved and some never visited, and whether it had been celebrated, or used.

I showed some of the comments and images to Oliver, who studied them briefly and then professed himself disgusted with the entire episode. 'I couldn't care less about it,' he said. 'The sooner we can stop doing the stall the better. I didn't need his visit to tell me that.'

I hadn't realised how disenchanted Oliver had become with the business. Over successive winters, he'd become sick of feeding the pigs in the rain, wind and mud, sick of the effort we had to put in to get away from the farm on holiday, and sick of getting up before dawn to go and set up a stall in darkness in the freezing cold. For my part, I was sick of the brand story I'd created for us, of pretending we were living a small-farm dream when in fact it was running us into the ground.

Perhaps it wasn't surprising that any last, feeble trace of enthusiasm we had for running our stall at markets and events died a death on the day of the Prime Minister's visit. He hammered the final nail into that coffin.

I couldn't help feeling it was such a shame that an ordinary, lovely day at the market had been so besmirched. A good farmers' market has the curious effect of making those involved with it feel a deep sense of ownership. It may be organised by a committee and managers paid to do a job, but in my experience everyone involved, whatever their role, cared deeply about ours. A good market is embedded in its community, and is a community in and of itself too. It didn't seem surprising to me that inviting a politician in through the gates and allowing them to use the place for their benefit had caused discontent.

It was also a shame that social media had magnified that discontent and made it even more public. Talking to the Chair of a public forum later that week, I reflected on that. 'Privately, I think many people would have agreed with you,' she said. 'They just wouldn't say so out loud.' Only stupid people like me did that, I reflected, people who thought you should be able to say what you thought about politicians in a democracy.

The only person who would remain unaffected by the whole sorry affair, it seemed, was the Prime Minister. I doubt he was made aware of a stupid row on social media which broke out after his visit. It probably happens all the time and besides, politicians are used to opinion and debate. It's what some of them thrive on and often seek to incite. Opinion is how they win and lose votes and power. Shortly after this, the

Australian Parliament presided over by this Prime Minister would be revealed as one of the most contentious workplaces in the country, a place where the gloves were off and insulting, combative and often misogynistic behaviour was the order of the day. Many politicians appear to have skins thick enough and advisors protective enough to make it like water off a duck's back. Some appear more human. Perhaps this Prime Minister thought about the farmers' market when he was sitting back with a bottle of that beer later in the day, and perhaps he didn't. Either way, he probably wasn't even aware of the fuss and bother his visit caused. Even if he was, I doubt he gave it a second thought.

End Game

In the early days of our business, we'd had a visit from a state government advisor who mentored small business people and got them up and running in their enterprise. This amiable man gave sage advice to many in northern Tasmania. We were a few years in and looking for a perspective on how to do things in a more business-like manner.

'I can see why you're not making any money,' he told us, sitting at our dining room table. Oliver and I both sat up a little straighter, preparing for an epiphany.

'You don't set any financial targets, do you?'

Although we had a vague sense of what we might earn at a market and how much cash or card takings we'd come home with in our cash box or bank account, we had never calculated how much we should be turning over to support ourselves. Instead, we simply lurched from one month to the next. Sometimes we were flush, mostly we weren't. Our 'cash box' was not an actual till but a plastic box purchased from a hardware store. Designed to contain nuts, bolts and screws, it was adapted by us to hold bank notes and coins. Some fellow stallholders at the market had an electronic till which not only totalled their takings but gave them a subtotal for each line of product they sold, so they could see what was selling best. Oliver and I made those calculations on guesswork and hunches, which was less reliable.

'I can see what he's talking about,' Oliver said after that business advisor left. 'I reckon other people think about the financial side of their business a lot more than we do.'

'Perhaps because they've got actual business skills,' I agreed glumly. Although we both enjoyed running our farm and market stall, we both knew we didn't have the core skills required to make a real go of things, or even to understand whether that was possible based on the land we had and the stock numbers we could support. Perhaps we didn't work harder at getting those skills because we had a hunch it wouldn't work.

Once we were set on finding new and easier ways of earning our living and were at ease with the demise of the business, it took longer to reconcile ourselves to the idea that we would no longer have pigs. It seemed strange to think of the farm without them.

Out in the bush block one blustery summer's afternoon, we were chopping up a fallen tree for firewood. A tall swamp gum, it had fallen across Willow Paddock, the victim of south-westerly winds during a mid-winter storm. I had been sitting up in bed writing, my laptop on a breakfast tray, and heard the crash.

'There goes the pergola roof,' I said to the Charlie the cat, who looked up sleepily from his spot curled on the corner of the bed. Scooping up his warm, furry form, I had gone to the bedroom window and found the tree lying prone across the paddock just twenty metres away. It had fallen behind the cat castle, where we locked Charlie in at night.

'Close shave for you,' I murmured into his ear and he purred in reply. Cats don't give a shit about much.

Oliver and the kids and I worked together to chainsaw the trunk and branches into short logs ready for splitting. As we did so, the last crowd of young pigs snorted and squealed around us, keeping a distance of a few feet away, deterred by the chainsaw's racket. The wind whipped the other trees in the bush block into a frenzy above our heads, their leaves shaking and branches creaking. Foresters have an evocative name for branches which are ready to fall if the wind catches them right: widow makers. They can kill or disable you in a moment if you happen to be below. As we four laboured away, small forms in the face of the wind and noise, it felt like a swan-song for our little farming enterprise. We'd given it all we had and enjoyed the adventure while it lasted. But we didn't want to do it for much longer.

After months planning an exit, we took the plunge. We stopped retailing direct to the public at markets and events, and began supplying our other purchasers with entire carcasses instead. We held our last market stall in the new year, at the height of the Australian summer. We suspected it would be our last, but we made no announcement and created no fanfare. We didn't have the energy for it. Oliver simply sent an email to the market manager cancelling our bookings.

The moment we stopped retailing, the other sales channels came good. Oliver took three pigs to slaughter to fulfil an order from the Meat Mistress. They were trucked down to Hobart and we imagined them being turned into sausages and pork cuts to line the display cases of the beautiful traditional butcher's shop. In return, we received a sum which would top up our accounts and tide us over until the next month, and support us through this transitional phase.

'It still doesn't seem like very much for looking after them and feeding them for seven months,' said Oliver, turning to me from his computer as we sat in the office, each contemplating our new working lives. 'And we've had to kill three animals for that too.'

'That's farming for you though, isn't it?' I replied. 'It's a long slog with hard-won gains.

Oliver nodded. 'And that's the price for a rare breed pig from a butcher who recognises their value.'

We thought about all the other pigs, cattle and creatures being raised for the same fate, most of them spending their lives in giant sheds before rattling their way to slaughter on the back of a truck. The prices their meat fetches in supermarkets and giant chains, where the cost is kept at rock bottom for consumers who expect to buy it dirt cheap on special, devalues those animals' lives catastrophically. The years in our business had taught us that farmers produce ordinary meat at huge scale because the price paid to them is so paltry and the value so low, they have to farm in huge numbers to make it worthwhile. As we gazed out of the office window at the neighbours' sheep in the paddocks, I knew we were both thinking about what a species we've become: reducing the value of our companion creatures' lives so much that they are worth the lowest price possible.

While it felt like the end of an era, it also felt like the beginning of one. Suddenly we had weekends together as a family. Oliver and I had time when we could truly kick back and relax. Scouring online notice boards for bargains, I purchased two small sofas and arranged them with a coffee table, in a part of the living room which had once been occupied by children's toys. I moved in some new shelves behind the sofas and filled them with books to complement those overflowing from the built-in bookcases. An angle-poise lamp lit the area and there were cushions and throws on the sofas. The first time I sat down there and read a book for a couple of hours on a Saturday afternoon, something I hadn't countenanced doing for years, it felt like a life-changing moment.

This soon became a meeting area for the family. No sooner had I gone to sit or lie there with a cup of tea and a novel than one of the kids would join me, scrolling through the apps on their phone and catching up with friends. Smart phones had become an important tool for Daisy and Kit. Living in a semi-remote, rural place, apps like Snapchat were vital for keeping in touch.

Then Oliver would come and sit down, and we'd drag a board-game from the lower shelf of the coffee table, blow the dust off it, and set up a game. We played cards there after supper, with Kit's brazen cheating reducing us to loud laughter. It happened more frequently as we discovered we had the time and energy, a more open mindset and the space to simply come together and enjoy each other's company.

Oliver didn't seem worried about the future. Now that he had purchasers in place for the remaining pigs and a means of reducing his herd down, his mood was surprisingly optimistic. Little did I know, he had further plans in mind.

'I was thinking about renewing my heavy-vehicle licence,' he said to me one morning. One of Oliver's first jobs as a young man had been driving trucks around France, collecting antiques and delivering them to dealers in the United Kingdom. Early in our relationship, he had impressed me with his tales of stopping at roadside cafes on the outskirts of Paris, breakfasting on croissants, coffee and Croque Monsieur.

'You're not thinking of driving trucks, are you?' I asked, thinking of the distances racked up by truckies across the red dirt of the Australian outback.

'No, I've seen a couple of adverts for school bus drivers around here,' he replied. 'They need drivers for the morning and the afternoon runs. It would leave me enough time to look after the last of the pigs, and it would give us some regular income.'

I thought of the affable driver who picked our children up from the bus stop at the end of the road in the morning and dropped them off again in the afternoon. He was one of a group of local men and women who'd driven our local school buses for decades, and I'd often wondered whether it would be a fuss-free means of earning a small income stream locally. Oliver, it turned out, had made some calls. He could do a driving-theory course online as a refresher, and take a test in nearby Devonport. If he passed, it would replace his defunct English licence and see him equipped to turn another corner in his working life.

And then the pandemic arrived.

COVID changed everything for us, as it did for everyone. Harvest Launceston closed, and the relief we felt at having moved beyond dependence on our farm business with no other plans was even more palpable.

Ironically, one of the effects of the lockdown was to secure a market for our last remaining pigs. As people began to rediscover the pleasure of cooking at home, butchers had their best year ever. As the last of our herd grew to size, we supplied them to the butcher's shop in Hobart, which was steadily gaining ground. Our pork was in demand, and we were doing less work than we'd ever done before to supply it.

Running the business on this simplified model gave us a sobering insight into how little we'd been surviving on for the past few years. Whenever he sent pigs to slaughter, Oliver received a statement of their 'dressed' weight after slaughter, and calculated what weight he should invoice the buyers for. In theory, it always seemed like a tidy sum to stash away in the bank. But when balanced out against the costs of feed and equipment and the hours of work required from us both in the old days of running the business full bore, it seemed ridiculously hard won.

In those new and strange days, once the live pigs had left the farm our job was done. There was no collecting the carcass from our butcher for making into sausages or bacon, no labelling of pork product ready for market, and no packing the ute with all the market stall paraphernalia. The meat processing room remained empty and silent, the fridges sat mutely with their doors cracked open for air to circulate. In the workshop, the heavy wooden market stall and chiller cabinet stood immobile, covered in removal rugs to keep the dust off.

Instead, Oliver pursued his course in heavy-vehicle driving, and kept in touch with the man who ran the local school bus company. Schools remained open for the children of essential workers, and bus drivers still drove the routes morning and afternoon. With Oliver having gained his licence just before lockdown, he took over the school bus route that Kit would ordinarily take. Kit was being home-schooled, but some kids still caught the bus, their parents essential workers. The smaller numbers gave Oliver a valuable chance to get used to driving the bus without a full complement on board.

Meanwhile, my freelance writing work disappeared in a puff of smoke, as did the part-time marketing job I had applied for. Everything around us stopped. Daisy no longer caught the early morning bus to college but instead watched her tutors online. We attempted to home-school Kit for a couple of tortuous hours each morning, and then set him free to head out into the paddocks with Caro and Neville's boy from next door. With two small hobby farms to range over, they fished in the stream, kayaked on the dam, made damper and cooked it on a fire in the bush. Occasionally the air would resound to the roar of their dirt bikes as they ploughed up and down the driveways and around the dam, churning up mud.

Tuning in to news broadcasts, we watched aghast as cities like New York imploded, listened in disbelief at the cavalier approach taken by the British Prime Minister, and wondered if we'd ever see our parents in the United Kingdom again. When we looked out of our own doors and windows across the paddocks, the world looked much the same, except the skies were empty and the roads were quiet.

When the Australian government stepped in to support small business owners, we qualified, and stepped completely off the merry-go-round. I did jigsaw puzzles at a large table beside the window, natural light flooding over me and the green of the bush in my peripheral vision, saved from penury.

Oliver took to the kitchen and slowly mastered sourdough. Having baked white loaves and dinner rolls for our family for years, he had saved us a fortune, and now promised to save even more and increase the quality of the bread we ate.

He still fed the pigs morning and afternoon, and once or twice a fortnight drove to collect feed from his suppliers. In theory, he was supposed to be working his way through a list of house renovation and maintenance jobs. In reality, he needed a period of adjustment after leaving the treadmill of pork production. He played the guitar more, strumming away in the office with instruction from YouTube, his thoughts for once engaged in something simple, sweet and joyful.

Only one project management role for a single client came along to occupy me, and that was running the local farming festival, Farmgate. Just before lockdown began, I was given the role of festival coordinator. The festival was planned for November, when visitors would usually begin flocking to the island to explore it during the warmer months. In June, the festival committee decided to bank on it going ahead despite the pandemic. By that time, Tasmania was slowly emerging from lockdown, the island was free of the disease, and open air events were deemed to be less risky than those taking place inside a bricks-and-mortar venue.

While the borders remained closed, the state's tourism authority launched a campaign encouraging Tasmanians to support their own tourism industry, visiting restaurants, places to stay, festivals and attractions across the island as everything reopened. A new campaign was launched to encourage us all with the theme, 'Make yourself at home'.

The phrase seemed ill-chosen to me, a ghoulish reminder of the way colonial invasion had done exactly that with disastrous results for the Aboriginal population. But the sentiment behind it was clear and it had the desired effect. Keen to escape the confines of their own homes, Tasmanians flocked to other places across the state. Flinders Island, a spectacular, unspoilt place off the north-eastern corner of Tasmania, had its busiest tourism year ever, as thousands of retirees who would normally be on European cruises looked for somewhere else to go which felt like overseas.

That November as the Australian summer approached and life felt almost normal again, Farmgate Festival had its best year ever. Visitors flocked to the farms keen to see 'behind the scenes' and learn more about how their produce was grown. The farmers hosting them for short talks and farm tours took social-distancing in their stride, having dealt with biosecurity threats for years. With swine flu sweeping through Australasia long before coronavirus raised its ugly head, we had already adopted the practice of putting hazard tape up when visitors came to the farm, holding them back a few feet from the pig pens. It was little more trouble to put signs up and ask people to remain socially distanced from each other, as well as from the pigs.

In the run-up to the festival, I was asked to make a short presentation to the tourism authorities, on how preparations were going and the farms involved. I did so by Zoom, preparing some slides and sharing them. Farmgate was not a high cache event in the Tasmanian tourism calendar. Even in the best of years, we attracted small numbers of people, largely other Tasmanians, not the national or international visitors the tourism authorities usually aimed at, and I was surprised they were interested in hearing from us at all. At the end of the presentation I offered to answer questions. As I peered into the darkened room on the screen of my laptop showing murky figures sitting in an office in Hobart, one disembodied voice spoke up.

'Can you tell us if any of the farms have developed farm-gate operations as a result of being involved with the festival?'

I had heard a rumour that this was an end-goal perceived by people in tourism: if our festival was a catalyst in the further development and diversification of some farming operations, then somehow it would be justified.

My mind turned to the farmers involved in the festival. I thought of the olive growers, a couple who lived nearby who had opened their farm for the four years of the festival so far. They were typical of the small farming businesses involved in it. He slaved away on the farm, managing the extensive orchard, harvesting and pressing the olives and bottling the oil, running the market stall and selling wholesale to restaurants and other buyers, while she held down a full-time job at management level in a government department to subsidise it all. Somehow they juggled the childcare and parenting of a blended family and children of different ages. The last thing they needed was a farm-gate operation. For a start, the farm was a mile off the highway up a driveway shared with a neighbour. And were they supposed to set up the infrastructure needed to cope with visitors calling in at any time of the night or day, and make themselves available to appear at the farm gate to spend half an hour chatting, dropping whatever else they were doing on the spur of the moment?

I knew exactly what this particular man would say if I asked him whether he wanted to run a farm-gate operation. I could picture his handsome face breaking into a bemused smile. 'How am I supposed to manage that on top of everything else?' he would ask with a wry chuckle.

I thought of the attempt Oliver and I had made at diversifying our farm operation, already feeding pigs twice daily, maintaining the property, making the product and travelling between the abattoir, the butcher and the meat processing room, as well as doing all the marketing, accounting and documentation. I thought of how begrudging I had felt about visitors to our farm in the last year of our accommodation sideline, of how different the welcoming impression we tried to give was from the sense of desperation we felt as our day-to-day life and the demands of the business spiralled.

I thought of how thinly spread everyone was who ran a small farm business in the festival and in our region, and no doubt elsewhere. I wondered what a farm-gate operation looked like in the imagination of the people on the screen in front of me. I suspected it looked different to them than it did to me.

Kit with one of the last boars on the farm

As the pandemic year wore on, Oliver and I slowly emerged from the torpor it sunk everyone into and worked towards exiting from our gourmet farming years completely and moving on to different types of work. We also tried to deal with the psychological and emotional effects of feeling distanced from family in different parts of the country and the world, and from normality.

In all of this, we frequently lost sight of the fact that soon we would have no pigs left on the farm.

Oliver had ended his breeding program, no longer moving the sows into a pen with the boar when they came on heat. Primary production was winding down, and this made the winding up of the farm very real: no more pregnant sows, no more piglets, and no more weaners growing on. Gradually, as the numbers fell, Oliver realised how much a part of his day it had been, going out with feed buckets full to the brim and pouring the mix into troughs while a crowd of grunting, snorting hairy little bodies jostled him, nudging his legs and egging him on to pour the feed and get out of the way. Now, it took him less time to feed the dwindling number of pigs that remained.

'It's like when the guns go silent at the end of a war,' he said on returning from the pens one day. 'It's really quiet out there now.' There were just a few weaners left in the pens waiting politely for their food and snorting and jostling each other with less urgency than the bigger packs we used to have. That he had mixed feelings about it was evident, but as he walked between the paddocks, the workshop and the house, his step seemed lighter. A weight had been lifted from his shoulders.

Oliver drove the school bus on the morning and afternoon runs, and tended the pigs and ran the farm in between. We both understood this would be a transitional arrangement. He had occupied two roles previously, working as both a cabinet-maker and a farmer as we started up our farm operation years before. There are substantial difficulties in juggling two roles. Oliver was left with precious little time for anything else, but the matter of finding good owners for his remaining pigs occupied his mind and had to be dealt with.

He was keen to see his sows and boar go to a good home, and when he advertised them for sale, was pleased to be contacted by a farmer from the north-west. This man lived and worked on his parents' dairy farm, living in a separate house with his own young family. He was slowly growing his own herd of pigs as a separate venture. There would be plenty of space for them, he told Oliver, and they'd be fed with whey from the dairy herd, a practice which had once been commonplace on traditional mixed farms. Whey is wha,t remains after milk solids have been used for cheese-making. Pigs love it and grow well on it, as Heidi had told Oliver all those years before at the Chudleigh Agricultural Show. In Italy the region around the city of Parma is known for both its Parma ham and prosciutto, and its Parmesan cheese, with production of the two happily married together by pigs, which make one produce and eat the waste from the other. It's the perfect example of how traditional farming and production methods can make long-lasting foodstuffs which can feed the world reliably, perpetually, simply and deliciously.

Farmers who can manage a mixed operation of cows and pigs have the benefit of being able to economise on feed costs, feeding their pigs whey and reducing the grain mix they need to purchase. As the cost of wheat increases, this is one of the main barriers to pig farming.

Over two weekends, the sows and the last lovely gentle boar Oliver had raised left the farm, picked up and taken to their new home in a horse box filled with straw. Oliver spent an hour chatting to the man and his wife each time, standing in the shade of the eucalyptus trees. I noticed that he stayed out in the paddocks for a while after they had gone, acclimatising himself to the demise of his herd.

Putting my gumboots on, I went for a walk over to the pens where they had lived. Oliver had taken down the fencing, wound the electric tape up and taken some of the star picket posts out of the ground and piled them up near the workshop. Empty of the pen lines, it was a strangely quiet, bereft and empty place.

At the same time, there was more open space around the trees, which no longer needed to be fenced off for protection so the pigs couldn't use them as scratching posts. The undergrowth would soon grow up and fill the place with greenery at ground level again.

The ground was terribly compacted in places, where successive generations of pigs had eaten the greenery, dug up any roots and subterranean vegetation with their strong snouts, and then compacted the earth with their trotters. We planned to hire a machine and break up the compacted ground, aerating it and allowing seeds to take purchase and new vegetation to flourish. It looked hard-used and downtrodden right now, but we hoped this would change quickly. Facilitated by us, nature would replenish the land, and it would bring a new kind of comfort and joy to us, to see it regenerate.

There was one litter left on the farm, a large one with twelve piglets. As they neared the age of eight weeks when they would be weaned and separated from their mother, Oliver fretted about what to do with them.

'I'm just never going to need that many,' he said, putting his breakfast together after returning from the school bus run one morning. He looked smarter in his driver's uniform than he had looked in the tatty fleeces and Hard Yakka trousers he'd worn for farming, and it was clear his mind was on the different choices he would make for work in the future.

'I might put them on Gumtree,' he said, and I looked at him in silence. Posting livestock for sale on a forum online was a last resort. Usually he found a buyer for surplus pigs through word of mouth, preferring to have a connection, however tenuous, to where they were going. But Gumtree was an effective means of finding a buyer when you wanted one quickly.

Nothing fits the word 'scamper' so much as a crowd of young pigs busily running around a paddock. As piglets outgrow their tiny, vulnerable early stage, they fatten up and become boisterous little characters. In late afternoon, they often have a crazy hour when they let off the remaining steam they have for the day, running in circles around their mother, chasing each other and scampering about. This results in a cloud of dust and lots of good-natured snorting and squealing. If they are bold and curious enough to approach you at this age, and you can pick one up for a few moments, they feel wonderful: warm, firm and round, full of life and vigour as they squirm in your arms. Picking up a weaner of this age when it is not sufficiently tame and might become distressed or annoyed is a bad idea. One such pig urinated over my hands and the smell that seeped into my clothing and skin took multiple washes and rinses to remove. My watch had to be taken to a repair shop for professional cleaning, such was the reek.

Our birthing sows had always been housed in a shed near to our back door. From our bedroom at night we could hear the contented snuffling and grunting of a sow and her litter as they shuffled, fidgeted and squirmed their warm, comfortable way through the soft darkness. And in the daytime we were used to catching their black and white forms in the corner of our eye, as they moseyed back and forth under the eucalyptus trees, sometimes with a friendly hen joining them in their pen.

So it was a shock when I returned home one day to find the sow's shed empty, and Oliver hosing down the pen, pushing the pigs' leavings into a pile and dampening down the dust.

'Where are they all?' I asked.

'Gone!' he replied. 'Some bloke from Gumtree took the lot. He's going to grow them on and sell them to his mates.'

That last crowd of amiable weaners had found they could push under the electric fence and go cavorting around the paddock beyond, which confused our two pet sheep, who watched with dumb expressions. When I had left that morning, they had still been there, running around in the sunshine. Now they were gone and it hadn't occurred to me that they would be our last brood.

Would I have done anything differently if I'd realised? Would I have photographed them, or watched them more intently as they spent their last energy of the day scampering in circles in a dust cloud around their indulgent mother? Probably not. I had thousands of photographs of weaners just like them, and had seen it all before. Even so, it was a sad moment as a new absence fell over the farm.

Over the next few weeks, Oliver sold his last boar and sows to buyers he felt instinctively would treat them well. In the space of a few weeks, our lives changed immeasurably. It wasn't until after we stopped that we realised how like a couple of wrung-out dishrags we felt, and yet how much we were going to miss the pigs.

We had many regular customers for the five years we ran our stall at the market. We knew some of their names and some of them by the conversations we had with them and the cuts of pork they bought. We continued to be grateful for their support.

After winding up our business, we occasionally bumped into one of them.

'I haven't seen you at the market lately,' one woman said when we encountered each other two years after our last stall. 'Are you still farming the pigs?'

I was always glad to say that no, we weren't farming anymore and had moved on to other, more reliable ways of making our living.

Mostly there was a resounding silence from our customer base, and we assumed they were busy re-inhabiting their lives in those peculiar times the pandemic brought, as we were.

Suddenly we had more time to look after our home and to create comfort for our family. The household chores that were often left undone and kept the house in disarray during our farming years, were now done quickly and energetically by us all. Daisy revealed a talent for laundry, hanging it out willingly and bringing it in ready-folded. Kit trundled to the woodshed with the trolley and brought back firewood, loading armfuls of it into a basket by the fire.

One morning, up before everyone else and making my way quietly downstairs, I came upon our living room with its flowers and plants, piles of books on side-tables, sofas with throw-rugs folded over the arms, a half-done jigsaw puzzle, condiments and napkins in their basket ready for use by us or by guests. I had a sudden, palpable sense of contentment, of being in a welcoming home which we now had the chance to enjoy.

Both Oliver and I had quite a journey to make as we turned the corner leaving our farm business behind and heading off into new employment adventures, but eventually we found roles we were comfortable in. A new chapter began for us both, one in which we had proper jobs, a sense of achievement and salaries.

'Should have done it years ago,' Oliver said in a sober moment.

'You don't regret keeping pigs though, do you?' I asked.

He thought for a moment. 'No, I don't. It's had its moments but on the whole I've enjoyed it.'

In his typically understated way, he had matched my thoughts exactly. We didn't regret it. It was hard, relentless work, but pigs were characters, and farming them and making beautiful food from their pork had been the adventure of a lifetime.

For the Love of Pigs

Despite the destruction they will wreak on a plot of land, and despite their capacity to eat you out of house and home, pigs are very lovable, and have many qualities that command deep respect from those who come to know them.

It's true that they are intelligent, although their intelligence revolves mostly around the procuring of food and survival. Even if you train a pig up to eat from a fork and smile at guests while sitting beside you at a table, it is still thinking mostly about the food.

Pigs are also companionable creatures. In commercial farming operations, they are often kept separately and fed a specific, carefully-calculated quantity of feed according to their weight and growth rate. This controls the speed at which they grow and separation from others prevents them from fighting over their food, and getting insufficient or not enough.

Our pigs were always kept in groups with their siblings. We used long feed troughs, which Oliver made from old steel gas containers cut in half lengthwise. While our pigs occasionally biffed each other out of the way to get to a more plentiful pile in the trough, they never actually fought each other. The small nature of our operation and those long troughs ensured there was a spot at the trough for everyone, and nobody got hurt.

It's when I consider sows that I feel the most sorrow, for the way we use pigs so singularly for consumption. When a lactating sow gets up and leaves her stall to come to the trough, her udders swinging and a gathering of warm piglets asleep in the dust behind her, it's saddening to know that one day all that magnificent capacity for mothering will be ended. When a sow feeds young piglets, she rolls over onto her side obligingly, sometimes lifting her legs out of the way as piglets scramble for her udders. As they get older, she will feed standing up, waiting patiently as the now larger piglets nudge and pump her udders vigorously for milk. If she thinks they've had enough and are just being greedy, she'll lie down on her belly so that her udders are inaccessible.

But in the commercial production of pork, those mothering instincts ultimately mean nothing and cannot save her. On a farm such as ours, when a sow's productive years decline, she could not be kept on for sentimental reasons, no matter how fond we were.

It remains a particular horror to me that a sow can be slaughtered and processed in the same way as a younger pig bred for consumption. A sow is larger than a seven-month old pig which has never been bred from. A sow has udders, that noble and beautiful mark of her parenthood. Yet her carcass will be suspended and emptied of fluids and offal like any other, her bones sent for anonymous use in the manufacture of food products, and her flesh used by makers of pies and sausage rolls. It seems a savage fate for a magnificent creature who has done no harm, but cared for her offspring with the same instincts as a human mother.

We have to reconcile ourselves to the matter of slaughter if we are going to eat meat and the industrialisation of the process is frankly hard to bear.

I think with envy of the long-standing traditions in French and Spanish villages, of rearing a pig for a year and slaughtering it for the benefits of multiple families. Traditional foods like cured meats, sausages, and the recipes and means of making them are all preserved in these traditions, enshrined in the culture of those places. But you need time and a slower pace of life for such a culture.

In Tasmania and Australia the culture is not as old and established as in Europe, despite the influx of Europeans over the past two centuries. Those traditions might still be carried out by family and cultural groups in some places but they are not prevalent. Occasionally old methods are adopted by new enthusiasts, kindled by initiatives like farmers' markets.

The beauty of such traditions is that they bring communities together and create a sense of belonging. They also pay due respect to the animal. It's altogether a more mindful and sentient process, making meat products from a carcass and thinking as you do so of the animal that it was.

Vegetarians and vegans would say that sparing the animal's life is the only means of offering proper respect and one can see their point. But as the old argument goes, if we were all vegetarian or vegan in order to spare the world's livestock their untimely death, there would be no requirement for those livestock in the first place. It would be a quieter, less inhabited world. A single pig makes for a great pet as it consumes household waste, but few could meet the feed demands of multiple pigs. Ironically, it's only in creating a demand for their meat that we ensure a breed will continue to exist in significant numbers.

Industrial processing of meat means most people have lost touch with our livestock, the farmers who raise it and the land it lives on. Moreover, we have allowed meat to become a commodity whose price is kept low to keep it 'affordable'. We eat it more often than we need to and in greater quantity than is good for us. We've lost sight of the capacity of livestock to contribute to families and communities in the more meaningful way they used to.

Rosie and Bella and all the pigs on our farm kept our family fed and housed, and added to our lives in many other ways. They kept us connected to the outdoors and the land around us, to the other foodstuffs on our table which also grew on our farm. Mostly they gave us a humility and gratitude for what we eat, and an awareness of its cost.

Pigs, endlessly deserving of our admiration and respect

When we were down to the last few pigs on the farm, Oliver arranged for two to be slaughtered and butchered into cuts and mince, from which he made sausages and bacon. This filled our freezers for months to come. We savoured those last meaty sausages, their softness in a casserole, their exceptional flavour and the absence of that briny, artificial tang which is the signature of most sausages. We exclaimed again over the succulence of a pulled pork shoulder served with pickled cabbage and roast potatoes, the crunchy, well-roasted morsels on the outside of the joint, caramelised and intensely savoury.

There was much about the farm that we did not miss. Oliver did not miss the relentless fortnightly cycle of production: of mincing and mixing his sausage recipe, of smoking joints for bacon, slicing legs and shoulders, portioning and packing the product, standing in the production room for hours on end to weigh and label it. The relentless graft of the business, constantly thinking about it, endless discussions and decision-making, constant worry about the weather on market days, and worry about feed prices, drought, mud, rain, swine flu and other biosecurity threats yet to come: those we did not miss for a second.

Yet what we gained from our farming adventure was immense. We discovered a whole new way of thinking about food and how it is produced. We were brought up close to the realities of farming, which are essentially birth, life and death, and hard decisions concerning them all. We learned to choose our meat carefully, and to understand that when we made compromises and purchased cheaper, somewhere up the supply chain a cost was being paid by both farmer and animal, in margins or welfare.

For Daisy, our farming years slowly converted her to a largely vegetarian diet. She could not reconcile the presence of pigs on our farm and pork on our table, or the presence of other meat on her plate however it was produced. It was not a concern for the welfare of farm animals that motivated her, but a dislike for the idea and mouth-feel of meat, knowing that it was essentially something's flesh. Even after a lifetime of eating meat and liking it, I can understand that reticence.

You can't really call industrial production of meat 'farming'. Industrial production is done indoors and produces a tasteless meat which has less value nutritionally and a rock-bottom price-tag. It's a morally bereft endpoint of our position at the top of the food chain. No wonder vegetarians and vegans opt out.

The word 'farming' suggests how it should be done: a more bucolic enterprise conducted outdoors where animals have good lives while they are alive, which produces a foodstuff which realises its full potential in flavour and nutritional value. That's an honourable trade.

In Tasmania, we do have industrial-model farming, but it's also common to see cattle and sheep and even pigs in the paddocks outdoors, and we are phenomenally lucky in this.

Kit has never had any qualms about eating meat, but the years of the business and seeing Oliver and me work in it had another effect. As he grew into his teenage years and became interested in scooters, mountain bikes and motorbikes, he began to see the difference between his friends' parents, some of whom had jobs in mining and heavy industry with money to spend on brand new motorbikes, and his own parents, well-educated but impoverished. Seeing us working hard for comparatively little gain gave both our children an awareness of the graft it takes to make a business happen. It became our fervent hope that they would choose a pathway other than self-employment as they entered the workforce. As teenagers, the conversations they now have with us suggest that this will be the case, and we're thankful. Farming and self-employment are both bloody hard. Combining the two seems foolhardy in the extreme.

So why do people do it? For some it's something they're born into and for many in Australia it's in their blood. Once you have lived with the seasons and the land, it's hard to want to live any other way.

For Oliver and me, there was the additional element of adventure.

I chose as a partner a man who was fun to be with, a risk taker and a dreamer. I have struggled to find my niche in life and it's only now, in my middle to late years that I'm doing so. I've made my fair share of unusual, non-traditional choices.

Risk-taking and adventurousness are great qualities to have and to find in someone in your younger days. By the time you're married with kids, you have to step things up a bit, find a sense of affluence in the way you live, not necessarily from financial income but from the situational and emotional richness that comes from choices made and values held.

You can carry on dreaming, as it would be disappointing and unadventurous not to. But you've got to get real as well.

Oliver and I dreamed of having a tiny pig farm and doing something different with our lives and by crikey, we did it, at least for a while. And it was fun. We learned a great deal, about pigs, small-scale farming and each other. Somehow, we're still together.

Market Day

Oliver is still a dreamer and so am I. But nowadays we're clearer about what we want from life. We've got proper jobs. Mine is part time so that I can still write, and continue turning this particular dream into a reality.

Without our dreaming, we wouldn't have had our farm, and I wouldn't have written those books. So we're glad for those dreams. But we're also glad it's over.

If we had been smart business people, we wouldn't have created a business in which we were present at every part of the supply chain. We wouldn't have chosen to raise slow-growing *(slow-growing!)* rare-breed pigs, make our own pork products from them, take them to market and sell it ourselves. We would have been sensible and got someone to do at least some of those things for us. We definitely should have thought twice about labouring so hard at that stage of our lives and our children's upbringing. We could have done with cracking on with proper jobs and topping up our superannuation, working in comfy offices out of the elements.

But we might have found that ever so slightly stultifying, as well as sensible and rewarding. We would have sacrificed things we didn't want to: living at home in a place of peace and serenity, and being there when our children left for school and when they returned home again. I waited a long time to have children, and I wanted to be present as a parent. I don't regret that for a minute, and the farm helped me do it.

We achieved direct control over our working lives. As Kit and Daisy grew, I came to believe that running a comfortable home where young people thrived was an important job. Raising the next generation and spending time with our families and in our communities is the real stuff of life, not working for the man. There is no doubt that our years running a farm and a market stall taught our children a great deal, and not just in mental arithmetic for giving customers their change, or how to restock a chiller cabinet. They learned how to make friends with other kids who happened to be present, and to occupy themselves, deriving hours of fun from filling our disposable gloves with water and creating rude shapes from them. Kit learned road rules and gained street wisdom, bringing his scooter with him to the market and taking off to ride the paths of City Park, one block and a pedestrian crossing away. Later he graduated to the skate park proper, and learned his way around more of Launceston. Daisy was the first of our children to stay at home on her own, a big step at thirteen, and this was the first thing she missed about the business when we closed it.

'One day a fortnight I was guaranteed a day when there was nobody else at home,' she said. As the family introvert, market days had been an unexpected blessing for her, once she was allowed to skip them.

Despite the novelty of keeping pigs wearing off, and even of watching them being born, she confessed to missing piglets. 'It's a little bit sad not having piglets,' she told me shortly after the last ones had gone. 'I don't miss sitting in the sheds for, like, four hours watching them being born. But seeing them walk out of the shed for the first time, and when they get the zoomies.'

Kit had a more calculated observation to make about market days. 'That's like sixty-five dollars' worth of work for me on a Saturday,' he said. As soon as he was old enough, he had got himself a weekend job at the local hardware store and was relishing the influx of cash into his bank account, far greater than the pocket money and allowance for sausage roles we had paid him. Both of our kids aspire to roles in essential services, child-care and building work, for employers who will pay them a salary and superannuation contributions, and both have entered their chosen fields early with work experience and part-time jobs. I can't help wondering whether it's a result of watching their parents slaving away in self-employment for hard-won gains.

Despite not being lucrative in most people's terms, for a moment there we were proud of our farming enterprise. We created a well-known and respected brand, one that we believed in. We were part of the small-scale gourmet farming sector that Tasmania has become famous for. And despite all the hard work, we enjoyed ourselves, met tremendous people and were part of a wonderful community.

Our farming adventure re-appraised our understanding of how meat is produced and changed our purchasing habits. Nowadays I look for the unusual cuts, the beef skirt as well as the steak, the chicken thighs as well as the breast, or better still a whole chicken. We eat vegetarian meals as well as meat-based. We don't need to eat meat every day to remain healthy; our planet cannot sustain the amount of meat we are farming. We are a greedy species and the world of livestock pays the ultimate price at a bewildering scale. In the western world, we have over-catered for ourselves to a ridiculous degree. I now attempt to buy meat for our family conscientiously, bearing in mind that it is not some anonymous product but the flesh of an animal that was born, raised and died at our behest.

We will never forget Rosie and Bella and Co-Pilot Bob. Despite using them as product, when I think of them it's with a level of respect I might ordinarily reserve for a person.

When I'm in my dotage I might look back occasionally with interest at my jobs in the corporate world, but I'll look back with pleasure and pride on the years we kept pigs, how much we learned about them, and the sheer bizarre unexpectedness of how we came to farm them. We look back on having created a business that made delicious foods which fed people well and occasionally delighted them, which connected with long-standing food traditions and tapped into the new appreciation of farm-made food in Tasmania. Most of all, we look back with joy on having kept two sows called Rosie and Bella and a boar named Co-Pilot Bob and multiple other nameless weaners and slips, on having known them and kept them, learned from them and admired them, those most beautiful, comical, humble and magnificent of creatures - pigs.

End

Small Farm Dream

Farming, small-scale or broad-acre, crop or livestock, is hard work. Oliver and I realised in time that we needed to wind up our enterprise. We found an exit route and took it with our family, our sanity and our marriage intact, and those last two things were by no means a given.

Others are not so fortunate. The man to whom this book is dedicated ran a similar farming operation: a pasture-fed poultry farm, small-scale production of a gourmet foodstuff. Just as I was finishing the writing of this book, he took his own life.

In the aftermath, one of Tasmania's farmers' markets placed a tribute on their website, speaking up, rightly, about how it is important to talk about rural suicide openly, because it is a problem that remains hidden and stigmatised by silence. They also admitted that when they put pen to paper, it became clear they knew little about him.

I can't claim to know everything that was going through my friend's mind when he did what he did. But when I heard of it, I knew instantly the kind of dark corner he might have found himself painted into. Most people in farming, broad-scale and small-scale, are familiar with those dark corners.

Farming is relentless. It's seven days a week. The livestock always needs feeding, the cows always need milking, the crops always need spraying, the hay always needs cutting and baling.

As I write, it's the week between Christmas and New Year, and when we went for our walk on Christmas Day, two tractors drove past us with hay baling equipment attached, one driven by a man, the other by his teenage daughter. Farmers rarely stop working.

When farmers go on holiday, all the preparations they do for a family holiday include finding someone to farm-sit and run things while they're away. We had to find people who would cope with electric fences, feeding regimes and boisterous pigs, and occasionally births and deaths.

In the weeks after my friend's death, a number of people asked why nobody anticipated what he was about to do. This seemed like an odd question. People who are about to take their own life can be secretive. When I saw him at the market in the weeks before his death, I noticed he had lost weight and was looking drawn. I noticed it, but I didn't remark on it, and I didn't think enough of it. It is not necessarily natural or automatic in us to expect the worst.

My friend's partner told me he would not have wanted anybody to feel guilty or to be blamed for what he did. I found that immensely comforting, and it rang distinctly true. Knowing him as I did, as a kind, accomplished, perceptive, deeply thoughtful, intelligent, reflective and compassionate man, I believe it utterly, and it helps me remember him with love.

The signs that farmers live on a knife edge are permanently there for us all to see, and we should all be paying attention.

Every time we buy a cheap chicken from a supermarket, it's a sign that a farming company is operating on very tight margins. My friend managed an industrial poultry farm in his early career and was eloquent on the subject of how little value there was in it for both chicken and consumer and everyone involved. He calculated that each chicken received about thirteen seconds of his time during its life. It was the reason he eventually left intensive farm management and set up his own business to run poultry on pasture, free range, and try to do things with the welfare of the animal at the centre.

Every time we buy a bottle of supermarket milk, a farmer has been paid a price set by the corporate that they are contracted to. It's the companies who set the 'milk price', which is governed not by fairness or acknowledgment of the hard work of dairy farming, but by the international commodity markets, because some of that milk product is sold overseas. Every so often there is a year when the 'milk price' that the farmer is paid drops so low it's barely worth the farmer milking the cows.

Every time the price of wheat and grain goes up, it's a sign that somewhere a farmer's costs are increasing, that it is costing them more to feed their livestock, whether it's pigs or cattle or ducks. This was the first thing that Oliver remarked upon when I told him my friend had taken his own life, and we were discussing what might have made him feel so desperate.

Small scale farmers whose costs are spiralling are already on tight margins and are then forced to consider whether they can put their retail price up and attempt to pass on some of their costs to their customers, and whether their customers will bear the increase, or whether they'll simply give up eating ethically produced, expensive meat, and go back to the supermarket, or choose another form of protein. It's a tight squeeze, having to make those decisions when your livelihood depends on it, and when you're out in the elements seven days a week facing those pigs or those ducks, thinking about how much they eat and whether you can cut it back.

Every time there's a flood, it's a sign that a farmer somewhere has had some livestock washed away or lost a crop. Every time there's a wet, humid spring, it's a sign that a farmer has probably lost some of that year's root crop or fruit crop to disease. Every time there's a tropical storm, a farmer somewhere has probably lost infrastructure, cropping trees, or sheds. A freak hailstorm passed through the small community of Hagley a few years ago and farming friends there had their hothouses ripped to shreds and that year's tomato crop decimated in the space of half an hour.

Farmers are on the front line. Every day they see the signs that farming is a tight squeeze, they face down the effects of weather events, climate change and wars. They see those effects close up on their land and in their balance sheets.

Those are all signs that we can all see every day.

What can we do about this, those of us who don't live on the land and those of us who do? How can we be expected to help?

Well, it's simple. Be good to farmers, especially those running a small family-run business or cooperative. Visit your local farmers' market, buy their products, pay more for them, buy in bigger quantity and freeze some. Go back and buy again. You will be buying a product that is higher in nutritional value than what you'd get in a supermarket. In some cases it might be more expensive, and in some cases it might be cheaper; vegetables from our farmers' market are a case in point. You'll be putting cash directly into a farmer's pocket, where it is of greater value to the individual than when you buy from a corporate or a supermarket.

Never be in any doubt that the people you see behind the stalls at farmers' markets are working hard. They're working very hard indeed, every day of the week.

Matt and his Strelleyfield Ducks

Rural Alive and Well (RAW) *is the charity organisation in Tasmania which aims to build healthy and resilient rural communities, to reduce the prevalence of suicide across Tasmania.*

RAW provides a confidential, no-cost psychological social support service for anyone experiencing life's more challenging seasons. If you have resonated with any of the situational stressors in this book, and you live in Tasmania, please reach out to RAW on 1800 729 827 or www.rawtas.com.au.

If you live in another part of Australia or the world, please seek out the people who offer similar support there. If you know someone you suspect needs assistance or support, please help them find it.

Acknowledgements

Many people help in the writing of books in ways they wouldn't necessarily know.

Thanks and a special mention goes to the members of Tresca Book Club. We share our love of books and many laughs, and those evenings are a highlight of my month.

Thank you to Rhonda and Keith McCoy for sharing their beautiful home and dog Rueban with me, and for providing me with a writing space overlooking kanamaluka / River Tamar. Thank you to Rhonda, for all the writerly talk and texts, and for your wisdom and friendship.

Thank you to my editor Susan Scott, also a farmer, for helping to make the text pristine (we hope!), and for that deep understanding of rural life which was needed for the task.

Our local library at Exeter, a tiny brick building, has been run by Sallie Scott and Helen Tait since I moved to Tasmania. Both have enthusiastically loaned out my first book and provided me with a welcoming space to write.

Thanks to anyone who has helped me with letters for grant applications, and to the Alliance of Independent Authors for knowhow on getting this book to market.

Every writer needs a cafe to write in and mine are The Cabin in Exeter and Clove Cafe in Launceston, highly recommended for great coffee, food and writing ambience.

Last but not least, thank you to Emily and Sam for coming

with us to markets and events and for enjoying pigs and goats and whatever else is thrown your way.

Thank you to Oliver for being such a constant, unquestioning supporter of my desire to write.

Sources and Further Reading

Andy Case, *Beautiful Pigs - Portraits of Fine Breeds*, Murdoch Books, 2010

Australian Pork, www.australianpork.com.au

Celia Lewis, *The Illustrated Guide to Pigs - how to choose them, how to keep them*, Skyhorse, 2011

Department of Primary Industries, New South Wales Government, *Pig Breeds in Australia fact sheet*

John Seymour, *The New Complete Book of Self-Sufficiency*, Dorling Kindersley, 2019

Matthew Evans, *On Eating Meat: the truth about its production and the ethics of eating it*, Murdoch Books, 2019

Slow Food Australia, *Ark of Taste*, https://slowfoodaustralia.com.au/2020/12/ark-of-taste/

Slow Food Foundation for Biodiversity, *Ark of Taste*, https://www.fondazioneslowfood.com/en/what-we-do/the-ark-of-taste/

Temple Grandin and Catherine Johnson, *Animals in Transla-

tion: Using the Mysteries of Autism to Decode Animal Behaviour, Bloomsbury Publishing, 2005

UVM Food Feed – Sustainable Food Systems and the University of Vermont, *Why Vermont Farms are Exploring Pigs and Whey,* https://learn.uvm.edu/foodsystemsblog/2016/06/14/pigs-and-whey/

About the Author

Fiona Stocker is an English writer now living and working in Tasmania, Australia. After gaining a degree in Theatre Studies at Warwick University, she worked in the arts, advertising and education in London. After travelling to Australia, she put down roots first in Brisbane and then in Tasmania. She and her husband Oliver have lived in the West Tamar Valley for sixteen years, with their two children. In 2022, she received a Graduate Certificate in Writing and Literature from Deakin University.

For news of further books by Fiona Stocker, visit the website and/or subscribe.

You can connect with me on:
- https://fionastockerwriter.com
- http://instagram.com/fionastockerbooks
- http://facebook.com/fionastockerwriter

Also by Fiona Stocker

Apple Island Wife - Slow Living in Tasmania

In search of a good life and a slower pace, the Stocker family upped sticks and moved to five acres in Tasmania, a land of promise, wilderness, and homes of uncertain build quality. It was the lifestyle change that many dream of and most are too sensible to attempt.

The first in the 'Wife' trilogy set in idyllic Tasmania.

"*Apple Island Wife* is both heart-warming and hilarious. Filled with raw, honest real-life accounts of trying to attain the good life fuelled with a pioneering spirit and a positive attitude. Compulsive reading for anyone who has ever thought they are not living the life they should!" STEVEN LAMB, RIVER COTTAGE

Sissinghurst Day - a short story

A volunteer gardener secretly visits the gardens of Sissinghurst Castle created by Vita Sackville-West and Harold Nicolson. Slipping in by stealth, he works alone there every Sunday during lockdown.

Written during lockdown, *Sissinghurst Day* is a story for our times, of love, nature and finding sanctuary in the world's most famous garden.

A short story, it is accompanied by an account by the author of writing it.

"A lovely, romantic and hugely atmospheric story, which captures the spirit of the place beautifully." **Juliet Nicolson.**

www.ingramcontent.com/pod-product-compliance
Lightning Source LLC
Chambersburg PA
CBHW070247010526
44107CB00056B/2372